Refugee Law in India

Shuvro Prosun Sarker

Refugee Law in India

The Road from Ambiguity to Protection

palgrave
macmillan

Shuvro Prosun Sarker
West Bengal National University
of Juridical Sciences
Kolkata, India

ISBN 978-981-10-4806-7 ISBN 978-981-10-4807-4 (eBook)
DOI 10.1007/978-981-10-4807-4

Library of Congress Control Number: 2017943472

Printed on acid-free paper

This Palgrave Macmillan imprint is published by Springer Nature
The registered company is Springer Nature Singapore Pte Ltd.
The registered company address is: 152 Beach Road, #21-01/04 Gateway East, Singapore 189721, Singapore

This book is dedicated to my parents:
Nepal Chandra Sarker, Administrative Service Officer (1981–2012), Bangladesh, Information Commissioner (2014–2019), Bangladesh and Shibani Sarker

List of International and Municipal Legal Materials

International Legal Materials

1. Cartagena Declaration on Refugees, Adopted by the Colloquium on the International Protection of Refugees in Central America, Mexico and Panama, November 22, 1984
2. Convention on the Elimination of All Forms of Discrimination against Women (United Nations General Assembly Resolution 34/180 of December 18, 1979)
3. Convention on the Rights of the Child (United Nations General Assembly Resolution 44 (XXV) of November 20, 1989)
4. Convention Relating to the Status of Refugees (189 United Nations Treaty Series, 1951)Protocol Relating to the Status of Refugees (606 United Nations Treaty Series, 1967)
5. Council Directive on Minimum Standards for Giving Temporary Protection in the Event of a Mass Influx of Displaced Persons and on Measures Promoting a Balance of Efforts between Member States in Receiving such Persons and Bearing the Consequences Thereof—Temporary Protection Directive (2001/55/EC of the European Council, July 20, 2001)

6. Directive on Common Procedures for Granting and Withdrawing International Protection—Asylum Procedures Directive (2013/32/EU of the European Parliament and of the Council, June 26, 2013)
7. Directive on Laying Down Standards for the Reception of Applicants for International Protection—Reception Conditions Directives (2013/33/EU of the European Parliament and of the Council, June 26, 2013)
8. Directive on Standards for the Qualification of Third-country Nationals or Stateless Persons as Beneficiaries of International Protection, for a Uniform Status for Refugees or for Persons Eligible for Subsidiary Protection, and for the Content of the Protection Granted—Qualification Directive (2011/95/EU of the European Parliament and of the Council, December 13, 2011)
9. International Convention on the Elimination of All Forms of Racial Discrimination (United Nations General Assembly Resolution 2106 (XX) of December 21, 1965)
10. International Covenant on Civil and Political Rights (United Nations General Assembly Resolution 2200A (XXI) of December 16, 1966)
11. International Covenant on Economic, Social and Cultural Rights (United General Assembly Resolution 2200A (XXI) of December 16, 1966)
12. OAU Convention Governing the Specific Aspects of Refugee Problems in Africa (14691 United Nations Treaty Series, 1969)
13. Universal Declaration of Human Rights (United Nations General Assembly Resolution 217(III)A, 1948)

Municipal Legal Materials

1. Balanced Refugee Reform Act (S.C. 2010, c. 8, Canada)
2. Citizenship Act, 1955 (Act No. LVII of 1950, India)
3. Foreigners from Uganda Order, 1972 (The Gazette of India, Extraordinary, Part II, Section 3, Subsection I, No. 268, October 20, 1972)
4. Foreigners Order, 1948 (India)
5. Immigration Act, 2002 (No. 13 of 2002, South Africa)

6. Immigration and Refugee Protection Act, 2001 (SC 2001, c. 27, Canada)
7. Notification No. GSR 685(E), Ministry of Home Affairs (The Gazette of India, Extraordinary, Part II, Section 3, Subsection I, No. 553, September 7, 2015)
8. Order No. GSR 686(E), Ministry of Home Affairs (The Gazette of India, Extraordinary, Part II, Section 3, Subsection I, No. 553, September 7, 2015)
9. Passport (Entry into India) Act, 1920 (Act No. XXXIV of 1920, India)
10. Protecting Canada's Immigration System Act (S.C. 2012, c. 17, Canada)
11. Refugees Act, 1998 (No. 30 of 1998, South Africa)
12. The Brazilian Refugee Act, 1997 (Law 9474/97 of July 22, 1997, Brazil)
13. The Constitution of India, 1950
14. The Foreigners Act, 1946 (Act No. XXXI of 1946, India)
15. The Registration of Foreigners Act, 1939 (Act No. XVI of 1939, India)
16. The Registration of Foreigners Rules, 1939 (India)

Preface

India is not a party to the 1951 Convention Relating to the Status of Refugees 1951 (hereinafter 1951 Refugee Convention) or the 1967 Protocol on the Status of Refugees (hereinafter 1967 Protocol).[1] However, prior to the drafting of the 1951 Refugee Convention, during the time of partition, India faced a massive inflow of refugees. The newly formed Indian State provided relief and rehabilitation to these refugees in spite of its limited emergency response capacity.[2]

In 1959, only a decade after gaining independence, India again faced an influx of refugees, this time from Tibet.[3] These refugees came with their religious leader, the Dalai Lama, for political and religious reasons as China began to wield its influence in Tibet. While it is true that these refugees came to India with the hope of returning to Tibet as soon as conditions there were normalized, at the time of writing it had been nearly fifty-seven years since their arrival in India. There was another steep rise in the number of refugees in 1965, this time from East Pakistan, as a result of the Indo-Pakistani War. People from minority communities fled East Pakistan for India due to fear of persecution by the Pakistani Army. In the period from 1964 to 1968 a large number of Chakmas migrated to India due to the ethnic disturbances in the Chittagong Hill Tracts area.[4] The largest wave of refugees, however, was admitted in 1971 when the Liberation War in Bangladesh began. Another wave of refugees arrived from the Chittagong Hill Tracts in Tripura, Bangladesh in 1986, when the Government of Tripura arranged for rehabilitation packages for these people.[5] Minority populations in

Bangladesh continue to cross the international border to escape religious persecution, and the Government of India has taken several steps to regularize the entry, stay and citizenship process for these persecuted minorities.[6]

India has attempted to regulate the status and protection of refugees by administrative means, but some doubt remains with regard to the effectiveness of such measures. In the absence of a legislative framework, the possibility of bias and discriminatory treatment of refugees cannot be ignored. Owing to the absence of specific legislation, the laws relating to the regulation of foreigners are applied to refugees in India with no difference made between foreigners and refugees as a separate class. The primary Indian law relevant to foreigners is the Foreigners Act, 1946 which empowers the Central Government to regulate the entry, presence and departure of foreigners in India. The administrative policies under the Act relating to aliens "are very skeleton and leave very wide discretion to the executive."[7] Owing to such broad governmental plenary power, bias is sure to creep in. That disturbs the basic tenet of the rule of law. There is no doubt that the "skeleton legislation with wide delegation of rule making power as well as conferment of very discretion on the administrative authorities are violation of the rule of law and can be challenged respectively on the grounds of unconstitutional delegation of legislative functions and the violation of right to equality."[8] As a result, refugees who have fled persecution are subject to the same rules and regulations as other foreigners entering India for any other purpose, and thus no legislative framework has been developed for identifying and determining refugee status.

Though India is not a signatory to the 1951 Refugee Convention, it has entered into various international human rights law agreements which put some constraints on unequal treatment of non-citizens and refugees. There is a significant body of international law that has elaborated the principle of non-discrimination as a non-derogable norm prohibiting discrimination on the basis of race, ethnicity or other related criteria. India's accession to the International Covenant on Civil and Political Rights (ICCPR),[9] the International Covenant on Economic, Social and Cultural Rights (ICESCR)[10] and the Convention on the Rights of the Child (CRC),[11] and ratification of the International Convention on the Elimination of All Forms of Racial Discrimination (ICERD)[12] and the Convention on the Elimination of All Forms of Discrimination against Women (CEDAW),[13] have excelled the quantum of protection from the idea of compassion to rights. This development of a body of international law that prohibits discrimination based on nationality has been further encouraged by the advocacy efforts of international organizations, non-governmental actors and so forth. At the same time, it is true that these international human rights law instruments do not address the rights of refugees or asylum seekers directly. However, the rights emphasized under these conventions are not limited only to the nationals of state parties, nor is their operation limited to citizens of one state in another state. Rather, they guarantee non-discrimination for all individuals within the state's territory and subject to its jurisdiction without distinction of any kind, such as race, color, sex, language, religion, political or other opinion, national or social origin, property, birth or other status.[14]

The way the Supreme Court of India has interpreted the Constitution in its decisions to highlight the duty of the state to accord refugee protection is phenomenal. In its two major decisions on the issue, the Supreme Court employed Article 14 of the Universal Declaration of Human Rights and Article 13 of the International Covenant on Civil and Political Rights to uphold the obligation of refugee protection.[15] The first instance was the case of *Khudiram Chakma v. State of Arunachal Pradesh*,[16] where the Supreme Court of India referred to the Universal Declaration of Human Rights in the context of refugees in India.[17] The pro refugee protection approach was further reflected in the case of *National Human Rights Commission v. Sate of Arunachal Pradesh*.[18] The Supreme Court of India held that Chakma refugees who had come from Bangladesh to escape persecution cannot be forcibly sent back to Bangladesh, as they might be killed, tortured or discriminated against, and as a result they would be deprived of their right to life under Article 21 of the Constitution of India.[19] The Supreme Court in the same case made a number of observations relating to the protection of Chakma refugees in India:

> We are a country governed by Rule of Law. Our Constitution confers certain rights on every human being and certain other rights on citizens. Every person is entitled to equality before the law and equal protection of the laws. So also, no person can be deprived of his life or personal liberty except according to the procedure established by law. Thus the State is bound to protect the life and personal liberty of every human being, be he a citizen or otherwise, and it cannot permit anybody or group of persons

> … to threaten the chakmas to leave the State, failing which they would be forced to do so … the State government must act impartially and carry out its legal obligations to safeguard the life, health and well being of chakmas residing in the state without being inhibited by local politics. Besides, by refusing to forward their applications, the chakmas are denied rights, constitutional and statutory, to be considered for being registered citizens of India.[20]

A subtle derivation from the above trend could claim that the obligation to protect refugees is paramount. The importance of Article 21 of the Constitution can be clearly inferred from the decisions rendered by the Supreme Court. Article 21 is a non-derogable right. It would therefore not be incorrect to claim that refugee protection is mandated by Article 21 of the Constitution of India. However, in reality, only those people who are able to go before the High Court or the Supreme Court to argue for their rights as refugees actually benefit. Thus it can be said that the protection of refugees through Article 21 is case-specific and lacks widespread respect among the administration. If we look through the various orders of the lower courts in this regard, we find that the lower courts have usually prosecuted those persons as illegal immigrants, at which point the High Court or the Supreme Court entered the scene. In several cases, the person sentenced by the lower judiciary was then ordered temporarily released by the High Court or the Supreme Court to be allowed to apply for refugee status from the United Nations High Commissioner for Refugees (UNHCR). Therefore trial court decisions generally do not seem to apply a standard practice of law of asylum or refuge. Thus it is clear that the Indian position, be it administrative or judicial, towards refugees' protection varies. Previously there has been no effort to discover why this is the case in a country like India which is governed by the rule of law. The reasons behind not acceding to the Refugee Convention have been discussed in Parliament, but there is hardly any study emphasizing the lack of government policy to frame a consistent protection standard. At the same time, four draft laws on refugee protection in the Lok Sabha, namely the Model National Law for the Refugees drafted by the Eminent Persons Group; the Asylum Bill, 2015 by Dr. Sashi Tharoor, MP; the National Asylum Bill, 2015 by Feroze Varun Gandhi, MP; and the Protection of Refugees and Asylum Seekers Bill, 2015 by Rabindra Kumar Jena, MP, have not yet received any recognition. Thus this book.

Kolkata, India — Shuvro Prosun Sarker

Notes

1. Convention Relating to the Status of Refugees (adopted July 28, 1951, entered into force April 22, 1954) 189 United Nations Treaty Series 137 (1951 Convention); Protocol Relating to the Status of Refugees (entered into force October 4, 1967) 606 United Nations Treaty Series 267 (1967 Protocol).
2. Prafulla K. Chakraborty, *The Marginal Men* (Naya Udyog, Calcutta, 1999) 1, Hiranmay Banerjee, *Utvastu* (In Bengali, Sishu Shahitya Samsad, Calcutta, 1970) 195.
3. Eileen Kaufman, 'Shelter from the Storm: An Analysis of U.S. Refugee Law as Applied to Tibetans Formerly Residing in India' [2008–2009] 23 Georgetown Immigration Law Journal 497, 530.
4. An indigenous tribal community generally resides at the Chittagong Hill Tracts of Bangladesh.
5. Malabika Das Gupta, 'Refugee Influx' [1986] 2(38/39) Economic and Political Weekly 1665.
6. The Gazette of India, Extraordinary, Part II, Section 3, Subsection I, No. 553, September 7, 2015. See also Shuvro Prosun Sarker, 'How Humanitarian is this?' *The Statesman* (October 8, 2015) 18; Shuvro Prosun Sarker, 'Bangladeshi Undocumented Migrants (Refugees) in India: A Humanitarian Problem Requiring A Humanitarian Solution' [2014] 26 Journal of Immigration, Asylum and Nationality Law 165, 174.
7. M.P. Singh, 'Positions of Aliens in India' (Legal Position of Aliens in National and International Law, Heidelberg Colloquium, 1985).
8. J.N. Saxena, 'Proposal for a Refugee Legislation in India' [1997] 2(2A) Bulletin on IHL & Refugee Law 391, 393.
9. International Covenant on Civil and Political Rights (adopted and opened for signature, ratification and accession by General Assembly Resolution 2200A (XXI) of December 16, 1966, entry into force March 23, 1976, in accordance with Article 49). India acceded to the Convention on April 10, 1979.
10. International Covenant on Economic, Social and Cultural Rights (adopted and opened for signature, ratification and accession by General Assembly Resolution 2200A (XXI) of December

16, 1966, entry into force January 3, 1976, in accordance with Article 27). India acceded to the convention on April 10, 1979.

11. Convention on the Rights of the Child (adopted and opened for signature, ratification and accession by General Assembly Resolution 44 (XXV) of November 20, 1989, entry into force September 2, 1990, in accordance with Article 49). India acceded the convention on December 11, 1992.
12. International Convention on the Elimination of All Forms of Racial Discrimination (adopted and opened for signature and ratification by General Assembly resolution 2106 (XX) of December 21, 1965.
13. entry into force January 4, 1969, in accordance with Article 19). India signed the convention on March 2, 1967 and ratified the convention on December 3, 1968.
14. Convention on the Elimination of All Forms of Discrimination against Women (adopted and opened for signature, ratification and accession by General Assembly Resolution 34/180 of December 18, 1979, entry into force September 3, 1981, in accordance with Article 27(1)). India signed the convention on July 30, 1980 and ratified it on July 9, 1993 with reservations.
15. See International Covenant on Civil and Political Rights, 1966, Article 2(1); International Covenant on Economic, Social and Cultural Rights, 1966, Article 2(1); Convention on the Rights of the Child, 1989, Article 2(1); Convention on the Elimination of All Forms of Discrimination Against Women, 1979, Article 2; International Convention on the Elimination of All Forms of Racial Discrimination, 1965, Article 2.
16. Article 14(1) of the Universal Declaration of Human Rights, 1948, Article 14(1): "Everyone has the right to seek and to enjoy in other countries asylum from persecution." International Covenant on Civil and Political Rights, 1966, Article 13: "An alien lawfully in the territory of a State party to the present Covenant may be expelled there from only in pursuance of a decision reached in accordance with law and shall, except where compelling reasons of national security otherwise require, be allowed to submit the reasons against his expulsion and to have his case reviewed by, and be represented for the purpose before, the competent authority or a person or persons especially designated by the competent authority." The Supreme Court of India used

these international mechanisms to hold that it is the duty of the state to protect refugees.

17. *Khudiram Chakma v. State of Arunachal Pradesh*, (1994) Supp (1) SCC 615.
18. Ibid. 665
19. *National Human Rights Commission v. State of Arunachal Pradesh*, (1996) 1 SCC 742.
20. Constitution of India, 1950, Article 21: "No person shall be deprived of his life and personal liberty except according to the procedure established by law."
21. National Human Rights Commission (n 18) 756.

Contents

List of Figures

List of Tables

List of Cases

Supreme Court

High Court

Trial Court

CHAPTER 1

Philosophy of Refugee Protection and Legal Condition of Refugees in India

1.1 Sovereignty and Cosmopolitanism: The Paradox

In the current world order, democratic states, most of which have affirmed various international law instruments such as covenants, conventions, declarations, resolutions and so on, have responsibility towards refugees. Further, states that include the principle of universal human rights as part of their municipal legal framework have responsibility towards refugees. Obviously, many states fit in both categories. However, problems arise with an increase in the magnitude of refugee movement, when a large number of refugees enter a state's territory and ask for their entitlements as per international law instruments or municipal laws or both. In this kind of situation the state may apply its sovereign right over its territory and close its border, but, on the other hand, the state is bound by responsibilities arising from the norms of universal human rights.[1] The question, then, is whether democratic states have any obligation to protect refugees, and if so, what are those obligations? I will attempt to find the answers to these questions from the perspectives of legal and political philosophy.

[1] Seyla Benhabib, 'Borders, Boundaries, and Citizenship' [2005] 38(4) Political Science & Politics 673, 674.

S.P. Sarker, *Refugee Law in India*,
DOI 10.1007/978-981-10-4807-4_1

Jean Bodin defined sovereignty as the "absolute and perpetual power of the commonwealth."[2] He envisaged sovereignty as single, absolute and unlimited power entrusted to the ruler; however, the ruler should be bound by legal and moral rules.[3] Other than these two limitations, Bodin says there must not be any limitation on the sovereign's power, which may lead to tyranny; however, it is the will of the sovereign to find reasons for limited power.[4] There is little difference between Bodin's ideas on the sovereign and those of Hobbes.

However, Hobbes's sovereign authority is created by a contract in which the people transfer their consent to the ruler in exchange for protection. The concept of sovereignty as supreme authority developed by Bodin and Hobbes is still relevant in today's world, even if there is limited government and human rights ensured by laws.[5] The states, by the use of its sovereign right, can control its borders with other states and decide who is welcome in its territory, and by what conditions, through laws. It is now an established practice for states to argue for and enact closed border regimes in the name of sovereignty.[6] Seyla Benhabib described this form of closed regime or legal order as a product of *sovereigntiste territorialism*, and quoted its characteristics in Harold Koh's words: "by commitments to territoriality, national politics, deference to executive power, and resistance to comity or international law as meaningful constraints on national prerogative."[7] She further divided this into two types—nationalist and democratic—on the basis of normative objections raised by the *sovereigntistes* towards global legal development.[8] In the nationalist type, legitimacy of law depends on the "self-determination of a discrete, clearly bounded people, considered to be a homogeneous entity—an ethnos—whose law expresses and binds its collective

[2] Jean Bodin, *On Sovereignty Four Chapters from the Six Books of the Commonwealth* (Julian H. Franklin ed. & trans., Cambridge University Press 1992) 1.

[3] F.H. Hinsley, *Sovereignty* (Cambridge University Press, 1986) 121.

[4] Ibid. 122.

[5] See also Dan Philpott, 'Sovereignty', [2014] *The Stanford Encyclopedia of Philosophy* http://plato.stanford.edu/archives/sum2014/entries/sovereignty/ accessed August 10, 2016.

[6] Ibid.

[7] Seyla Benhabib, 'Claiming Rights Across Borders: International Human Rights and Democratic Sovereignty' [2009] 103(4) American Political Science Review 691, 692.

[8] Ibid. 693.

will alone."[9] In this type it is important that the law expresses the will of a nation and is legitimized by the state as a self-determining entity.

The democratic type professes that the law is legitimate only when self-determining people are both author and subject of the law, and when there is a formal procedure for law-making.[10] It is the democratic *sovereigntistes* who are of the opinion that "recent trends towards a global legal system are dangerous and undesirable."[11] While several reasons are put forward by the democratic *sovereigntistes* in support of this claim, the most important are the following: culture and heritage, national interest and political self-determination.[12] From this point, a simple argument can be made following the terms of the *sovereigntistes* that a democratic state has no obligation to ensure the well-being of non-nationals, or rather refugees who come from different states and cultures. States can then make stricter border control laws and expel refugees from their territory without conforming to the standards of international law. This is one side of the paradox.

Democritus said, "to the wise man every country is a dwelling place, for the whole world is the fatherland of a good soul."[13] Cosmopolitanism is an ideology by which every person is seen as a citizen of the world. This ideology has its roots among the ancient Greeks, who believed that every person belongs to one global society by divine reason.[14] However, there were different positions with regard to the idea of citizenship and rights among the ancient Greeks. On the one hand, cosmopolitans literally believed in world citizens having no formal relation with any nation-state. On the other hand, they also believed that world citizenship involved some form of moral obligation towards others for divine reasons, and thus the idea of political membership was rooted in the idea of cosmopolitanism along with world citizenship. There are two different types of ideas associated with cosmopolitanism: moral and

[9] Ibid.

[10] Ibid.

[11] Ibid. See also Thomas Nagel, 'The Problem of Global Justice' [2005] 33(2) Philosophy & Public Affairs 113, 121.

[12] See generally Michael Walzer, *Spheres of Justice: A Defense of Pluralism and Equality* (Basic Books, New York 2005) 7; Quentin Skinner, *Liberty Before Liberalism* (Cambridge University Press 2012) 23.

[13] Hugh Harris, 'The Greek Origins of the Idea of Cosmopolitanism' [1927] 38(1) International Journal of Ethics 1, 7.

[14] Ibid.

political.[15] Ultimately, however, it is political cosmopolitanism that actually encompasses both these types and dictates that individuals, rather than states, have primacy in the cosmopolitan world.[16]

Arguments for absolute cosmopolitanism can be founded on the principle that "all individuals are free and equal" and should be guided by one world government with no affiliation with any other political platform, or that there should not be any other platform in the case of a world government. In the case of an absolute cosmopolitan world, words such as alien and foreigner would not exist, and therefore neither would the term refugee. The question arises, however, whether there is any validity to this absolute cosmopolitanism in the present-day modern world. I would argue that there cannot be a world with absolute cosmopolitanism, where there is no imaginary or actual contract between individuals and the government, which shapes the relationship between power (government) and care (citizens). However, Harris, quoting Frederick Pollock, argues that the cosmopolitan principles of reason and morality have significant importance in the formation of modern international law.[17] It can be argued, then, that interaction between a state and a non-citizen as a human being is one of the important concerns of cosmopolitan law. From this point of view, reconciliation is necessary since neither absolute sovereignty nor absolute cosmopolitanism can bring resolution to the refugee crisis in the present-day modern world. With this in mind, I now look to the cosmopolitan ideology of Immanuel Kant to find a possible theoretical framework within which the rights of refugees can be ensured.

1.1.1 *Cosmopolitan Ideology of Immanuel Kant: The Way*

Kant, in his essay titled "Perpetual Peace," develops a theory about the basis on which a peaceful world could be created. Peace will be attainable in the world, Kant says, when the following conditions are fulfilled[18]:

---

[15] Fred Dallmayr, 'Cosmopolitanism: Moral and Political' [2003] 31(3) Political Theory 421, 430.

[16] Thomas W. Pogge, 'Cosmopolitanism and Sovereignty' [1992] 103(1) Ethics 48, 49.

[17] Harris (n 13) 8.

[18] Pauline Kleingeld, 'Kant's Cosmopolitan Law: World Citizenship for a Global Order' [1998] 2 Kantian Review 72, 74.

1. There will be states with a republican model of governance. Such states must have a constitution.
2. There will be a federation of states. Rights of states should be realized through a mutual agreement by this federation of states.
3. There will be a right to hospitality for the individuals, limited to the extent that a state can refuse the visitor unless there is a threat to life and liberty upon such refusal.

On the basis of the conditions mentioned above, Kant formulated three different categories of rights, namely: constitutional, international and cosmopolitan.[19] The third category is the most important among the three for the protection of refugees, as the right to hospitality is the core of the cosmopolitan right. However, it is important to look into the first condition for a peaceful world. Kant's first condition for a peaceful world has two components: state and constitution.[20] A state in this case should be a republican state.[21] Thus, state formation and the model for the realization of its powers need to be seen according to Kantian philosophy. In this category, a republican state must have three different authorities, such as legislator, executive and judicial, for proper functioning.[22] Kant's republican state is governed by a civil constitution where the powers and functions of every authority are defined and separated.[23] In such a situation, the equality and freedom of individuals can be protected. In this way Kant argued for constitutional rights for the individuals in a republican order.

Kant's second condition for the attainment of peace is the formation of a federation of states.[24] In this kind of federation of states, Kant says, the right that will follow has to be realized between states, that is, the

[19] Ibid. See also Daniele Archibugi, 'Immanuel Kant, Cosmopolitan Law and Peace' [1995] 1(4) European Journal of International Relations 429, 432.

[20] Sean Hutchman, 'An Historical Examination of Kant's Cosmopolitanism' [2000] 1 Glendon Journal of International Studies 50, 52; See also Louis P. Pojman, 'Kant's Perpetual Peace and Cosmopolitanism' [2005] 36(1) Journal of Social Philosophy 62, 64.

[21] Archibugi (n 19) 444.

[22] Pojman (n 20) 64–65

[23] Hutchman (n 20) 50; Kleingeld (n 18) 81; See also Georg Cavallar, 'Cosmopolitanism in Kant's Philosophy' [2012] 5(2) Ethics and Global Politics 95, 107.

[24] Pojman (n 20) 66-67; Kleingeld (n 18) 72; Archibugi (n 19) 446. Benhabib (n 1) 674.

international right. By "federation of states" Kant means a collective body formed by states based on mutual understanding, but not the cosmopolitan state mentioned in the first section of this chapter. It will be the duty of the federation of states to form this international right by creating a platform on which the states can interact with each other on a similar footing.[25] Kant argues that with this federation of states there will be less war and more peace. However, there is a question about securing the rights of individuals in this federation of states. Kant limited the realization of this international right only to the states and not to the individuals.[26] This is probably due to his inclination towards a more logical resolution of the right to hospitality. In this case it can be assumed that when the first condition is fulfilled and the federation of states has been formed through the free will of all the states, then every state must see whether its right as a state and the rights of its citizens are secured everywhere. From this point, there will be discussions to uphold the natural rights or the principles of reason as rights guaranteed under a mutual agreement or treaty.[27]

The third condition for attaining peace, according to Kant, refers to one very specific right. It is called cosmopolitan right, and the core of this right is the right to hospitality.[28] It is important to see that the development of the modern international law and rights regime is already a factor in the interaction between states and citizens (whether national or non-national). Critics of Kant's third category of right argue that this third category of cosmopolitan right or the right to hospitality is already subsumed under the second category.[29] It is noteworthy that this cosmopolitan right or right to hospitality is available to the individual as a human being, and that the realization of this right is possible

[25] Pojman (n 20) 69; Cavallar (n 23) 98; Kleingeld (n 18) 78.

[26] Archibugi (n 19) 447; Pojman (n 20) 66.

[27] Pojman (n 20) 70; Kleingeld (n 18) 71; See also Seyla Benhabib, 'Carl Schmitt's Critique of Kant: Sovereignty and International Law' [2012] 40(6) Political Theory 688, 697.

[28] Kleingeld (n 18) 72; Hutchman (n 20) 50; See also James Bohman, 'Living without Freedom: Cosmopolitanism at Home and the Rule of Law' [2009] 37(4) Political Theory 539, 550.

[29] Kleingeld (n 18) 73; Cavallar (n 23) 98; See also Seyla Benhabib, 'Another Universalism: On the Unity and Diversity of Human Rights' [2007] 81(2) Proceedings and Addresses of The American Philosophical Association 7, 14.

in any other state where that particular individual is a non-national or foreigner.[30] Kant puts some limitations on the state's right to refuse the individual entry to its territory, such that no violent force should be used to uproot the individual and entry cannot be restricted if the individual's life or liberty is endangered by such refusal.[31] Kant justified this third category of right in two ways. Firstly, he talks about the original right of every human being to the earth. This refers to a time before the earth was divided into nation-states and before the concept of ownership of private property came into the picture; it is the original community of land that was shared by everyone.[32] Secondly, he talks about the inner right to freedom, which could mean the chance to interact with others, to try to form a community with others, to exchange thoughts and situational beliefs with others, and so forth.[33]

From this point I would like to point to several developments in the refugee protection regime which specifically support Kant's third condition of perpetual peace and third category of right, that is, the right to hospitality. *Non-refoulement* is a well-regarded principle of the refugee protection regime which is exclusively covered under Kant's third category of right.[34] Again, entry of refugees cannot be refused if their life and liberty would be put in danger by that refusal. The institutionalization of the cosmopolitan rights regime can be seen in the establishment of international organizations and several other treaties in connection with the rights of non-nationals in a foreign land.[35] Finally, it can be said that Kant's cosmopolitan ideology, established through the model of republican states, a federation of states and finally recognition of the right to hospitality, has shown the most important, feasible theoretical model on which basis the rights of refugees can be established and be protected. It is now necessary to look at possible ways to accommodate this right to hospitality within the political and legal spheres. In the next section I analyze John Rawls's theory of the "law of peoples" and Benhabib's theory of democracy and multiculturalism.

---

30 Kleingeld (n 18) 74; Cavallar (n 23) 108.

31 Kleingeld (n 18) 76; Archibugi (n 19) 446–448.

32 Kleingeld (n 18) 77; Benhabib (n 7) 695–699; Bohman (n 28) 544.

33 Kleingeld (n 18) 79; Benhabib (n 7) 695–699; Bohman (n 28) 545.

34 Benhabib (n 7) 697; Bohman (n 28) 540.

35 See generally Seyla Benhabib, 'The Law of Peoples, Distributive Justice, and Migrations' [2004] 72(5) Fordham Law Review 1761, 1779.

1.2 Global Justice and Refugees: The Way Forward

Rawls's "A Theory of Justice,"[36] in which he tries to extend the meaning of justice to a global justice, taking as an analogy Kant's second category of international right, is seen to be influential. In dealing with global justice, he tries to formulate the principles by which domestic and global political institutions should abide. He further indicates that human rights are part of the reasonable law of peoples, even in a non-liberal society that has met several reasonable conditions of domestic justice. However, Rawls was silent about the institutionalization of this theory in the modern world. Benhabib, on the other hand, taking as an analogy Kant's cosmopolitanism, argues for a model of global justice in which republican states will form a federation and the laws of that federation will be based on cosmopolitan norms and ethics. Benhabib's theory is also appealing as it is grounded in the ideas of a post-Westphalian sovereignty of states, the development of an international human rights law regime and the inception of the idea of political membership from the cosmopolitan theory of Kant. Benhabib's most important contribution can be seen in the case of refugee protection, where she emphasizes the political membership of all persons in the federation of republican states.

1.2.1 The Law of Peoples: John Rawls

Rawls refers to the common features of law applied to all people by the term "law of peoples." He further clarifies that there are several norms and principles of international law and practice that are grounded in the idea of rights and justice developed within the domestic political sphere.[37] He argues that global justice is possible only when there is absolute domestic justice, and the possibility of extending the ingredients of domestic justice to the international sphere was the focus of the law

---

[36] 'A Theory of Justice' yielded two principles. The first principle provided that each person has an "equal right to the most extensive system of equal basic liberties compatible with a similar system of liberty for all," and the second principle provided that social and economic inequalities are to be arranged for the "greatest benefit of the least advantaged. … and attached to offices and positions open to all under conditions of fair equality of opportunity." See John Rawls, *A Theory of Justice* (Harvard University Press, Cambridge 1971).

[37] John Rawls, 'The Law of Peoples' [1993] 20(1) Critical Inquiry 36, 43.

of peoples.[38] Rawls describes three features of the political conception of justice, originally included in his work on political liberalism[39]:

1. It applies to basic political, economic and social institutions; or to the law and practices of the society of political peoples.
2. It is independent of the influence of any religious, philosophical or moral doctrine.
3. It is substantially articulated by several fundamental thoughts that are already in practice in a liberal society.

Rawls also makes a distinction between the political conception of justice and justice as fairness.[40] While doing so, Rawls argues that justice as fairness is applicable at the domestic level or in a closed society governed by democracy and to the citizens of that society. But the political conception of justice is applicable to the interrelations between different societies or to the political relations between peoples. By this distinction Rawls tries to elaborate the idea that in the political conception of justice, the representatives of the peoples are the key actors in the relationship between peoples, and thus it lacks several ideas of justice as fairness.[41] Again, it is very important to note that Rawls makes a distinction between the law of peoples and the law of nations.[42] By the term law of peoples, Rawls refers to a family of political concepts that are interconnected with the principles of right, justice and common good and that apply to international relations between states. The law of nations is marked by Rawls as an incomplete but positive legal order which lacks sanctions. In this point it is important to note that Rawls's law of peoples is a broad term, or one with a broader ambit than the law of nations, which is also the case for Kant's cosmopolitan right and international

---

[38] However, it has been argued that the theory is obsolete and misleading as it is grounded on a closed society. See Seyla Benhabib, 'Citizens, Residents, and Aliens in a Changing World: Political Membership in the Global Era' [1999] 66(3) Social Research 709, 727.

[39] Rawls (n 37) 37.

[40] Rawls (n 37) 41.

[41] Those are: the fair value of political liberties, fair equality of opportunity and the difference principle.

[42] Rawls (n 37) 43.

right.[43] However, Rawls is silent about any term or concept more closely reflecting the right to hospitality.[44] While extending the liberal ideas of justice to the law of peoples, Rawls points out three important features[45]:

1. list of basic rights, liberties and opportunities;
2. high priority of fundamental freedoms;
3. measures assuring the greatest possible use of those freedoms by citizens.

Rawls also finds two more theories important in the extension of the law of peoples in liberal and hierarchical societies, and the list of basic principles for the law of peoples: ideal theory and non-ideal theory. In the ideal theory, Rawls looks to liberal and hierarchical societies for the basic requirements for the law of peoples to be fully respected and honored by the people.[46] The non-ideal theory talks of societies that refuse to comply, and those with unfavorable conditions for complying, with the reasonable law of peoples.[47] The basic principles of justice between free democratic people and in their relations mentioned by Rawls include:

1. Peoples are free and independent.
2. Peoples are equal and parties to their agreements.
3. Peoples have the right of self-defense but no right to war.
4. Peoples are to observe the duty of non-intervention.
5. People are to observe treaties and undertakings.
6. Peoples are to observe certain specified restrictions on the conduct of war.
7. Peoples are to honor human rights.

---

[43] Patrick Hayden, 'From the Law of Peoples to Perpetual Peace' [2000] 17(2) International Journal of World Peace 47, 51.

[44] Ibid.

[45] Rawls (n 37) 43.

[46] Rawls (n 37) 44.

[47] Ibid.

[48] Rawls (n 37) 46; For a detailed critique on these principles, see Burleigh T. Wilkins, 'Principles for the Law of Peoples' [2007] 11(2) The Journal of Ethics 161, 168.

8. Peoples have a duty to assist other peoples living under unfavorable conditions that prevent their having a just or decent political and social regime.[48]

Rawls's law of peoples provides a very sound theoretical basis for a global justice system.[49] However, several issues should be discussed here before taking this as a philosophical model for refugee protection or more broadly as a matter of global justice.[50] Matters of global justice require an inclusive approach, which is probably lacking in Rawls's law of peoples, as refugees and stateless persons have little to gain from the formulated principles.[5151] It must be understood that there is no conceptual dialogue on the institutional development which is highly regarded in cases of ensuring global justice.[52] Rawls begins formulating this theory on the basis of the original position, which is first discussed in his theory of justice. He further formulates the eight principles from the platform of the original position.

Rawls at the same time concentrates mainly on war and peace, which he regarded as the most important obstacles to ensuring global justice, rather than economic justice or political participation.[53] In the case of refugees or stateless people, it is important that they have some political participation in the society where they are living or planning to live. The law of peoples does not provide for any such principles of justice in the relationship between peoples. Benhabib argues that Rawls does not see political membership as an important factor in the law of peoples.[54] Rawls's principle no. viii, which talks about assisting people who are living under unfavorable conditions, makes the case against migration. If

---

[49] See generally Charles R. Beitz, 'Rawls's Law of Peoples' [2002] 110(4) Ethics 669, 689.

[50] See generally Thomas W. Pogge, 'Review: Rawls on International Justice' [2001] 51(203) The Philosophical Quarterly 246, 249; Brian J. Shaw, 'Doctrine of Right, Rawls, Kant's and Global Distributive Justice' [2005] 67(1) The Journal of Politics 220, 226.

[51] See generally Michael W. Doyle, 'One World, Many Peoples: International Justice in John Rawls's the Law of Peoples' [2006] 4(1) Perspectives on Politics 109, 112.

[52] Hayden (n 43).

[53] Doyle (n 51) 113; Shaw (n 50) 222.

[54] Benhabib (n 35) 1762.

[55] Benhabib (n 35) 1776; See generally Matthew J. Gibney, 'Liberal Democratic States and Responsibilities to Refugees' [1999] 93(1) The American Political Science Review 169, 178.

the peoples are to abide by this principle, then there will be no refugees, migrants or stateless persons. Unlike Kant, Rawls never speaks of any right to hospitality, which makes the case for refugees more problematic in a liberal democratic state or in a republic.[55]

1.2.2 Universalism and Political Membership: Seyla Benhabib

Benhabib tries to develop a universal normative framework for cases of migratory movement. In doing so she puts forward the idea of political membership. She is in favor of the right to membership of peoples within the framework of human rights, which should be incorporated into states' constitutions through citizenship and naturalization provisions.[56] She further defines political membership as the principles and practices of including refugees and immigrants within the political landscape of the state system.[57] Benhabib grounds her cross-border justice model heavily in Kant's right to hospitality.

It is important that unlike Rawls, Kant saw people as individual single entities in the cross-border relationship and characterized the right to hospitality not as philanthropy but as a positive moral right. Benhabib points to several important characteristics of Kant's hospitality principle[58]:

1. It is not kindness shown by one person to another because of his/her painful circumstances.
2. It is a right that belongs to everyone as a citizen of the world.
3. It regulates interactions between individuals belonging to different states.
4. It begins to function from the boundaries of one state for the people of other states.
5. It has spaced between human rights and civil rights.

Benhabib finally argues that Kantian cosmopolitanism is seen to be the way forward in the case of refugee and migratory movement, as Kant

---

[56] Benhabib (n 35) 1761.
[57] Ibid. 1762.
[58] Ibid. 1783.
[59] Ibid. 1786.

distinguishes between the terms Westphalian sovereignty and liberal international sovereignty. In supporting liberal international sovereignty, Benhabib argues that in this form, the relationship between nations depends on the observance of human rights, the rule of law and respect for democratic self-determination.[59] Kant, through the right to hospitality, considers first admittance or refuge as essential, but not political membership. However, Benhabib's contribution to the extension of the right to hospitality is that she talks about the right to hospitality as a matter with moral as well as legal consequences. In doing so, Benhabib extends her theory of just membership.[60] Benhabib presents the elements of the theory of just membership as[61]:

1. The right to first entry for refugees and asylum seekers should be recognized, and an open border policy should be developed by decriminalizing entry without certain documentation.
2. There should be a law against denationalization, as human beings should have the right to belong to a community.
3. An international legal personality is created through this right to have rights, entitling aliens to apply for citizenship in a new state.
4. The laws of citizenship should be non-discriminatory and justiciable.
5. The doctrine of state sovereignty should not be used as a reason to bar citizenship laws and process of citizenship and scrutiny by constitutional courts.

It should be noted that the new politico-philosophical discussion of a proper protection regime for refugees and asylum seekers started with Benhabib's theory of just membership and the extension of Kant's cosmopolitanism. Kant in 1795 drew up the three definitive conditions for perpetual peace while living in a monarchy, but it is true that the Kantian philosophy developed at that time inspired Benhabib in extending this right of hospitality towards a political membership format in this democratic world. Benhabib did not believe in eliminating borders, as democracies require borders to identify their representatives and accountability,

---

[60] Ibid. 1787.

[61] Ibid. 1787; see also Gibney (n 55) 177 for a discussion on humanitarianism and refugee rights.

but rather in putting greater moral obligations on states to recognize the entry of refugees and the principles of non-discrimination and non-refoulement.

The discussions in the previous sections of the chapter and the findings thereof will appear in subsequent chapters as philosophical guidance. Importantly, the next section of this chapter discusses the legal condition of refugees in India from the point of view of international obligations and national laws, along with an analysis with respect to the philosophical discussions made above.

1.3 Legal Condition of Refugees in India

The influx of refugees to India is not only a recent phenomenon. Refugees started flowing into India during the partition in 1947.[62] Though India is not a party to the 1951 Convention Relating to the Status of Refugees (hereinafter 1951 Refugee Convention) and its 1967 Protocol, in the past the Indian Government has always tried to provide prompt relief and rehabilitation to refugees entering India.[63] The relief and rehabilitation process for refugees during the partition of India was based on a very holistic approach and was organized at the highest levels of the Indian Government. Thereafter, refugees started coming to independent India from various neighboring countries as well as the Middle East and Africa. However, the assistance that was provided to refugees during partition, and the protection and rehabilitation extended to the first refugee group in India after independence (namely Tibetans), was not available to the refugees who came later, including those arriving today. It was expected that a country influenced by a rich religious and cultural tradition of hospitality (*Atithi Devo Bhava*), and governed by the rule of law, would be more proactive in ensuring the rights and protection of refugees in this evolving world of international human rights and protection of vulnerable people.

---

[62] B.S. Chimni (ed), *International Refugee Law: A Reader* (SAGE, New Delhi 2000) 462.

[63] Ibid. 463; see generally Kanti B Pakrasi, *The Uprooted: A Sociological Study of the Refugees of West Bengal, India* (Indian Statistical Institute, Calcutta 1971) 1.

[64] See UNHCR Subregional Operations Profile—South Asia (2015) http://www.unhcr.org/pages/49e4876d6.html accessed March 7, 2015.

The United Nations High Commissioner for Refugees (UNHCR) estimates the number of refugees currently present in India at around 205,764, of whom only 30,000 are registered with the UNHCR in New Delhi.[64] India chooses to deal with refugee protection through discriminative administrative measures coupled with strict laws dealing with the expulsion of foreigners. At the same time, there are several constitutional provisions which affirm the rights of non-citizens in the country, along with India's obligation to uphold international law through various conventions, protocols, resolutions, declarations and so forth. The following sections of this chapter reflect upon the constitutional provisions, national laws and administrative measures, and international obligations pertaining to refugees in India.

1.3.1 Constitutional Provisions Dealing with Rights of Non-Citizens

The Constitution of India, under various Articles, expresses the basic values held by the people of India. The inclusion of the fundamental rights chapter in the Constitution is in accordance with the trends of modern democratic thought. The objective is to ensure the inviolability of certain rights against interference by the state.

In the fundamental rights chapter of the Indian Constitution, there are listed several rights available to all persons on Indian soil irrespective of nationality. For the purpose of this present research, it is important to focus only on those Articles that accord rights to all persons present in India or that are available to non-nationals as well as Indian citizens. These rights are: equality before the law (Article 14), protection in respect of conviction for offences (Article 20), protection of life and personal liberty (Article 21), the right to education (Article 21A), protection against arrest and detention in certain cases (Article 22), prohibition of traffic in human beings and forced labor (Article 23), prohibition of employment of children in factories (24), freedom of religious practice and so on (Articles 25–28). It is important to note that only Article 14[65]

[65] Equality before law: The State shall not deny to any person equality before the law or the equal protection of the laws within the territory of India.

[66] Protection of life and personal liberty: No person shall be deprived of his life or personal liberty except according to procedure established by law.

[67] In a later chapter there will be discussion on the cases decided by the Supreme Court of India and various High Courts upholding refugee rights.

and Article 21[66] from the above list have been emphasized in the protection of the rights of refugees in India by the Supreme Court of India in various cases.[67]

In the matter of refugee rights, "it can be argued that Article 21 encompasses the principle of non-refoulement which requires that a State shall not expel or return a refugee in any manner whatsoever to the frontiers of territories where his life or freedom would be threatened on account of his race, religion, nationality, membership of a particular social group or political opinion."[68]

1.3.2 The Laws Dealing with Foreigners

There are several pieces of legislation dealing with entry, stay and exit (or removal) of foreigners in India. As there is no specific legislation that defines the term refugee or establishes provisions for dealing with refugee protection, India relies on laws dealing with foreigners to deal with refugees.

The first piece of legislation that should be mentioned is the Passport (Entry into India) Act, 1920.[69] This Act mandates that every individual entering India by water, land or air shall be in possession of a valid passport.[70] In case of contravention of the rules made under this Act, there will be punishment of imprisonment—which may extend to three months—a fine or both.[71] Under this Act, any police officer not below the rank of sub-inspector or any customs officer empowered with the general or specific order of the Central Government can arrest without warrant any person who has violated the rules or orders made, or of whom a reasonable suspicion exists.[72] The Central Government also has exclusive power to make special or general orders to remove any person

---

[68] B.S. Chimni, 'The Legal Condition of Refugees in India' [SAGE, 1994] 7 Journal of Refugee Studies 378, 380.

[69] Act No. XXXIV of 1920 (India).

[70] Ibid. Section 3(1).

[71] Ibid. Section 3(3)

[72] Ibid. Section 4.

[73] Ibid. Section 5.

[74] Passport (Entry into India) Rules, 1950, Rule 5.

[75] Act No. XVI of 1939 (India).

from the territory of India in case of violation of the rules.[73] To deal with the provisions of this Act, the government also enacted the Passport (Entry into India) Rules, 1950, which extend to the whole of India, requiring a proper visa in addition to a valid passport to enter India.[74]

The Registration of Foreigners Act, 1939 was enacted to provide for the registration of foreigners entering, staying in and departing from India.[75] In this Act, for the first time a foreigner is defined as a person who is not a citizen of India.[76] To operationalize the provisions of the Act, the government further enacted the Registration of Foreigners Rules, 1939 and further restructured it in 1992. In general, this Act and the Rules require every foreigner who enters and stays in India for more than 180 days to register as per the prescribed format and in time with the Foreigners Registration Officer (FRO) of that jurisdiction, and each time they change address or leave India, they must receive authorization from the FRO. In case of contravention or attempts to contravene, or failure to comply with the provisions and rules of this Act, there shall be punishment in the form of imprisonment for a term of up to one year, a fine of up to one thousand rupees or both.[77]

Another piece of legislation widely used in dealing with foreigners is the Foreigners Act, 1946.[78] Under this Act, the Central Government is vested with the power to make rules and order the prohibition, regulation or restriction of the entry, stay and departure of any foreigner or class of foreigner in India.[79] With the power granted under Section 3 of this Act, the Central Government enacted the Foreigners Order, 1948. In this Act, for the second time, a foreigner was defined as any person who is not a citizen of India.[80] The most important provisions affecting the life and liberty of any refugee or stateless person under this Act are those related to the determination of nationality. Under this Act, if any question arises about the nationality of a foreigner, the determination of nationality depends on the decision of the concerned authority as to which country the

[76] Ibid. Section 2(a).

[77] Section 5.

[78] Act No. XXXI of 1946 (India).

[79] Ibid. Section 3.

[80] Ibid. Section 3(a).

[81] Ibid. Section 8.

[82] Ibid. Section 14.

foreigner is connected with, and that decision cannot be challenged in any court of law.[81] The penal provision of this Act is much stricter than that of the other two Acts mentioned above, as any contravention of the provisions, rules or order made under this Act is punishable by imprisonment of up to five years.[82] Another provision that makes this Act central to the regime of entry, stay and departure (or removal) of any foreigner in India is that the provisions of this Act or the rules made under this Act shall be in operation along with the provisions of the Passport (Entry into India) Act, 1920 and the Registration of Foreigners Act, 1939.[83]

It is important to mention that the wide range of powers granted to the Central Government under the Foreigners Act, 1946 was significant in the drafting of the Foreigners Order, 1948. The Foreigners Order, 1948 is an amalgamation of many of the provisions of the Passport (Entry into India) Act, 1920 and the Registration of Foreigners Act, 1939 and the rules made thereunder. The Foreigners Order, 1948 restricts entry into India by a foreigner without a valid passport and visa and may impose restrictions on entry in the public interest.[84] Other important provisions include restrictions on sojourning in India,[85] restrictions on visiting prohibited places,[86] restrictions on visiting protected areas,[87] restrictions on employment,[88] restrictions on movement and so forth.[89]

Considering the inner meaning of the restrictive provisions of the laws dealing with foreigners in India mentioned above, it is clear that the legal provisions that apply to every foreign national should not apply to a person who is entering India as a refugee or asylum seeker, as these laws at the first instance treat that person as a violator of the laws and rules discussed above. As a consequence, the refugee or asylum seeker is detained and prosecuted prima facie without the chance to put forward his or her claim to refugee status.

[83] Ibid. Section 12.

[84] The Foreigners Order, 1948: Cl. 3(2)(a); Cl. 4(a) and Cl.5.

[85] Ibid. Cl. 7.

[86] Ibid. Cl. 8.

[87] Ibid. Cl. 9.

[88] Ibid. Cl. 10.

[89] Ibid. Cl. 11.

However, there are instances where the provisions and rules made under these Acts have been modified, specifically to provide refuge to persons from Uganda and minorities from Pakistan and Bangladesh in India. At the same time, it is true that Tibetan and Sri Lankan refugees hold residence permits similar to those issued to other foreigners in India, though any official notification or document is inaccessible to determine under which law they have been provided with those residence permits. In addition, those persons granted refugee status by the UNHCR in New Delhi receive similar residence permits from the governmental authority along with the long-term visa (LTV) annexed therein.[90] The next section will shed some light on those instances where the operation of the above-mentioned laws has been relaxed for persons from Uganda and for minorities from Pakistan and Bangladesh in India.

1.3.3 Administrative Measures: Notifications and Circulars

The Foreigners from Uganda Order, 1972 was designed to safeguard individuals of Indian origin resident in Uganda, who were persecuted by the regime of Idi Amin.[91] Under this Order, any Ugandan citizen coming to India must register their name, place of residence and intended duration of stay in India with the registration office. Persons from Uganda are exempted from the provisions of other laws applicable to foreigners by this Order.

In early 2010 the Government of India issued a notification by which certain powers to determine visa issues were delegated to the state governments/union territories concerned (now amended version available up to September 16, 2014).[92] This regulation, in paragraphs 48–50, described the terms, conditions and eligibility of Pakistani and Bangladeshi nationals for the LTV in India to acquire Indian citizenship. Four categories of persons are eligible for the LTV, of which three are based on marriage. However, it is interesting to take note of the fourth

[90]This matter will be discussed in detail under administrative measures in a later section in this chapter.

[91]The Gazette of India, Extraordinary, Part II, Section 3, Subsection I, No. 268, October 20, 1972.

[92]Delegation of powers to State Governments/UT Administrations/FRROs/FROs in Visa Matters (Ministry of Home Affairs, 16 September 2014) http://mha1.nic.in/foreigDiv/PwrDlgtFRRO.html accessed November 18, 2015.

category, that is, "cases involving extreme compassion." No definition of the term is given in the notification or in any other texts issued by the Government of India. It can be presumed that the category "cases involving extreme compassion" must include the refugees from these countries who fled because of persecution. There is another notification from the Government of India that allows Pakistani and Bangladeshi nationals who are staying in India on LTVs to take on employment of a purely private nature, excluding government, semi-government and cooperative jobs, which would enable them to earn their livelihood in India.[93]

In early 2013, the Election Commission of India declared that children of Tibetan refugees who were born in India between January 26, 1950 and July 1, 1987 can register to vote in India. This was based on a judicial decision by the Delhi High Court in 2010.[94] However, the same reasoning has not been applied to the children of any other refugee groups.

At the same time, it is important to note the recent decision and subsequent notification in the Gazette to exempt minorities from Pakistan and Bangladesh from the various provisions of the rules that deal with other foreigners. The notification says that Pakistani and Bangladeshi nationals belonging to minority communities who entered India on or before December 31, 2014 are exempted from the several provisions, rules and orders made under the Passport (Entry into India) Act, 1920 and the Foreigners Act, 1946.[95] These exemptions may apply in two scenarios: firstly, in the case of any person or group belonging to a minority community from Pakistan or Bangladesh who entered India with a valid passport and visa but, after a fixed time period, both or one of these documents expired, at which point they did not attempt to renew these documents and stayed in India. In this situation, that person or group can now stay in India if the date of entry into Indian territory was on or before December 31, 2014. The second scenario involves a person or group who entered into Indian territory without the necessary travel

[93]F. No. 14051/37/2010-F.VI, Ministry of Home Affairs, Govt. of India, 11 November, 2010 (On file).

[94]Namgyal Dolkar vs. Govt. of India, Ministry of External Affairs, W.P.(C) 12179/2009, Decided on: December 22, 2010, Delhi High Court.

[95]The Gazette of India, Extraordinary, Part II, Section 3, Subsection I, No. 553, September 7, 2015.

documents, such as a passport or visa. These persons also have the legal right to stay in India if they entered on or before December 31, 2014. The Government of India has adopted this policy on the grounds of humanitarian consideration, as declared, which should earn praise from the perspective of the protection of refugees from neighboring countries.

However, exempting someone, or specifically the minorities of Pakistan and Bangladesh, from punitive legal provisions can also be seen as simply an indemnity. Therefore the question before us is to what degree the Government of India has become humanitarian after taking up this policy, and what the future implications will be.[96]

The instances discussed above, along with some administrative measures to provide residence permits to refugees from Tibet and Sri Lanka and to those registered by the UNHCR in New Delhi, make the point clear that different measures were adopted for different refugee groups in India.

It is also clear that taking such differential measures is the result of a domestic refugee policy that is based neither on equality of treatment nor on legal principle, but on the shifting exigencies of domestic political opinion and foreign policy.[97] However, a country governed by rule of law and a written constitution, and having international obligations, should have one consistent and continuous policy for the protection of refugees. In the next section emphasis will be put on India's international obligations to protect refugees, though it has no direct obligation to refugees as a non-signatory of the 1951 Convention Relating to the Status of Refugees and its 1967 Protocol.

[96]See Shuvro Prosun Sarker, 'How Humanitarian is this?' *The Statesman* (October 8, 2015).

[97]H. Knox Thames, 'India's Failure to Adequately Protect Refugees, [1999] 7(1) Human Rights Brief 20, 21; See also Mike Sanderson, 'The Role of International Law in Defining the Protection of Refugees in India' [2015] 33 Wisconsin International Law Journal 46, 69.

[98]Emphasis could be laid down on the policy towards Tibetans, Sri Lankans (before the assassination of Prime Minister Rajiv Gandhi), Bangladeshis during the 1971 war and the present policy towards the minorities of Pakistan and Bangladesh.

1.3.4 *International Obligations*

The protection of refugees in India is at times very generous and based on compassion, but ultimately it is discriminatory on the basis of refugees' country of origin, date of admission, place of entry and so forth.[98] Though India is not a signatory to the 1951 Refugee Convention, it has entered into various international human rights law agreements that put some constraints on unequal treatment of non-citizens and refugees. There is a significant body of international law that has elaborated the principle of non-discrimination as a non-derogable norm that prohibits discrimination on the basis of race, ethnicity and other related criteria. India's accession to the International Covenant on Civil and Political Rights (ICCPR),[99] the International Covenant on Economic, Social and Cultural Rights (ICESCR)[100] and the Convention on the Rights of the Child (CRC),[101] and its ratification of the International Convention on the Elimination of All Forms of Racial Discrimination (ICERD)[102] and the Convention on the Elimination of All Forms of Discrimination against Women (CEDAW),[103] have excelled the quantum of protection from the idea of compassion to rights.

---

[99] International Covenant on Civil and Political Rights (adopted and opened for signature, ratification and accession by General Assembly Resolution 2200A (XXI) of December 16, 1966, entry into force March 23, 1976, in accordance with Article 49). India acceded to the Convention on April 10, 1979.

[100] International Covenant on Economic, Social and Cultural Rights (adopted and opened for signature, ratification and accession by General Assembly Resolution 2200A (XXI) of December 16, 1966 entry into force January 3, 1976, in accordance with Article 27). India acceded to the convention on April 10, 1979.

[101] Convention on the Rights of the Child (adopted and opened for signature, ratification and accession by General Assembly Resolution 44 (XXV) of November 20, 1989 entry into force September 2, 1990, in accordance with Article 49). India acceded to the convention on December 11, 1992.

[102] International Convention on the Elimination of All Forms of Racial Discrimination (adopted and opened for signature and ratification by General Assembly Resolution 2106 (XX) of December 21, 1965 entry into force January 4, 1969, in accordance with Article 19). India signed the convention on March 2, 1967 and ratified the convention on December 3, 1968.

[103] Convention on the Elimination of All Forms of Discrimination against Women (adopted and opened for signature, ratification and accession by General Assembly Resolution 34/180 of December 18, 1979 entry into force September 3, 1981, in accordance with Article 27(1)). India signed the convention on July 30, 1980 and ratified it on July 9, 1993 with reservations.

This development of a body of international law that prohibits discrimination based on nationality discrimination has been further encouraged by the advocacy efforts of international organizations, non-governmental actors and so forth. At the same time, it is true that these international human rights law instruments do not address the rights of refugees or asylum seekers directly.

However, the rights emphasized under these conventions are not limited only to the nationals of state parties, nor is their operation limited to citizens of one state in another state. Rather, they guarantee non-discrimination for all individuals within the state's territory and subject to its jurisdiction without distinction of any kind, such as race, color, sex, language, religion, political or other opinion, national or social origin, property, birth or other status.[104]

From this point, it is important to look at the text of the Universal Declaration of Human Rights (UDHR), which was adopted on December 10, 1948 in the United Nations General Assembly and which India voted in favor of adopting. The UDHR expressly mentions that "everyone has the right to seek and to enjoy in other countries asylum from persecution."[105] It does not grant individuals an absolute right to asylum, but it does obligate the state where asylum is sought to scrutinize the application for asylum. This obligation of the states is clearly mentioned in the ICCPR, as a decision must be reached according to law before expelling an alien from a state's territory.[106] Though this Article mentions persons who have entered a state territory lawfully, "if a State party deports a person within its territory and subject to its jurisdiction in such circumstances that as a result, there is a real risk that his

[104]See International Covenant on Civil and Political Rights, 1966, Article 2(1); International Covenant on Economic, Social and Cultural Rights, 1966, Article 2(1); Convention on the Rights of the Child, 1989, Article 2(1); Convention on the Elimination of All Forms of Discrimination Against Women, 1979, Article 2; International Convention on the Elimination of All Forms of Racial Discrimination, 1965, Article 2.

[105]Universal Declaration of Human Rights (General Assembly Resolution 217(III)A), 1948 : Art. 14(1)

[106]ICCPR (n 99) Art. 13.

[107]See A. R. J. vs. Australia, Communication No. 692/1996, 28 July 1997, Human Rights Committee, UN Doc. CCPR/C/60/D/692/1996.

[108]Sanderson (n 97) 76.

or her rights under the Covenant will be violated in another jurisdiction, that State party itself may be in violation of the Covenant."[107] Apart from that, there are several provisions in the ICCPR, ICESCR, ICERD, CEDAW and CRC upholding the principle of non-refoulement either expressly or as interpreted.[108]

In customary international law, non-refoulement is the principle with regard to refugees which is non-derogable in nature. A principle of law can qualify as a principle of customary international law only if there is consistent state practice and *opinion juris* means that the practice at issue is obligatory due to the existence of a rule requiring it.[109] In many cases it can be found that a country, though not a signatory to the 1951 Refugee Convention, has accepted a large number of refugees and assisted in their relief and rehabilitation, for example India, Bangladesh and Pakistan in the South Asian region. Again, in several instances these non-signatory countries have worked with the assistance of UNHCR representations on *refoulement* of refugees from its territory and given its reasons for doing do. So these activities by the non-signatory states give the impression that the two elements of customary international law are fulfilled in case of the principle of non-refoulement.

However, the question arises whether India is bound by this customary principle of non-refoulement, which conflicts with the national laws of India dealing with foreigners. The argument here would be that refugee and foreigner are two different categories of aliens having different objectives for entering Indian territory. Therefore, in this matter of non-refoulement, India should observe this principle.

1.4 Conclusion

The philosophical discussions in the first two sections of this chapter regarding the position of refugees vis-à-vis the nation-state brought to light several important elements which established the responsibility of democratic states towards refugees. Kantian cosmopolitanism, through the right to hospitality, has been seen to be the most important

[109] See International Court of Justice, *North Sea Continental Shelf, Judgment,* 1969 ICJ Reports 3, para. 74; see also International Court of Justice, *Nicaragua v. United States of America,* Jurisdiction and Admissibility, 1984 ICJ Reports 392, para. 77.

theoretical innovation in the history of the rights of non-nationals or refugees for the purpose of this present research.

Rawls should have been looking for some space for refugees or non-nationals within his theoretical framework of the law of peoples, but his theory is limited only to the peoples within the original position, which cannot accommodate refugees or asylum seekers within the boundary of the original position of realistic utopia.

However, Benhabib's theory is far more advanced, and with inspiration from the Kantian right to hospitality, she extends its meaning to a more rights-based regime of just membership for every refugee or asylum seeker through decriminalization of entry without travel documents, the right to non-refoulement, and the right to apply for and receive nationality in the receiving state.

In the later two sections of this chapter, I discussed the condition of refugees in India through a study of its treatment of refugees using national laws and administrative measures, along with provisions of the Indian Constitution and instruments of international law that bind India to non-discriminative treatment towards refugees. However, the findings of this study of laws and administrative measures reveal that there is discriminative practice on the basis of country of origin of refugees, and this discrimination affects their entitlement to resources and legal avenues to attain Indian citizenship or rights on a par with Indian nationals.

Examining the philosophical guidelines of refugee protection and the condition of refugees in India from the point of view of law, I am of the opinion that Indian policy towards refugees is not at all cosmopolitan, in terms of a right to hospitality, or just as per Benhabib's theory of universal cosmopolitanism. I would suggest that hospitality is culture itself and not simply one right or ethical principle. However, Indian policy towards refugees is inclined towards the politics of care and power, which allows policy-makers to have policy "A" for Tibetans, policy "B" for Pakistani and Bangladeshi minorities … and policy "Z" for others.[110] However, it is important to note that these policies are formulated under the aegis of the laws of the land using the administrative rule-making power.

Arguing from the international human rights law instruments and constitutional perspective of India, it may be said that there should not

[110]See Ranabir Samaddar, 'Introduction' in Ranabir Samaddar (ed), *Refugees and the State: Practices of Asylum and Care in India, 1947–2000* (SAGE, New Delhi 2003) 21, 24.

be any differential treatment towards refugees on the basis of their country of origin, rather simply all refugee groups should be treated alike with regard to their entitlements starting from qualification, asylum procedure, reception condition and so forth. There should also be a legal difference between a refugee who enters India due to persecution or fear of persecution, and a foreigner who enters India for any purpose other than to escape persecution. Finally, I would argue that Kantian cosmopolitanism can be the first step towards this goal, along with Benhabib's just membership principles, and point the way towards creating a legal framework for refugees in India.

CHAPTER 2

Response of Judiciary Towards Refugees in India

2.1 Trend of Justice in the Trial Courts

The discussion in the previous chapter on the legal conditions of refugees in India shows clearly that when a foreigner enters India without the required travel documents, he/she will be prosecuted under the relevant laws unless an exception is made by the rule-making power of the government.[1] The same is true for foreigners who have entered India to escape persecution or fear of persecution.[2] In this section of the chapter, I focus on some unreported cases decided by the Indian Trial Courts in matters related to refugees and the violation of the rules and orders under relevant laws.

In the case of *State v. Farid Ali Khan*,[3] the accused was arrested under the Foreigners Act, 1946 for not being able to show a valid refugee certificate issued by the United Nations High Commissioner for Refugees (UNHCR) and residence certificate issued by the government. However, the accused has all the valid documents but was unable to show them at the time of arrest, and the law allows the accused up to 24 h to produce

[1] See Veerabhadran Vijayakumar, 'Judicial Response to Refugee Protection in India' [2000] 12 International Journal of Refugee Law 235; B.S. Chimni, 'Legal Condition of Refugees in India' [1994] 7 Journal of Refugee Studies 378, 380.

[2] Ibid.

[3] Court of Metropolitan Magistrate, New Delhi, Decided on: November 1, 1995 http://www.refworld.org/docid/3f4b8f2e4.html accessed December 25, 2015.

S.P. Sarker, *Refugee Law in India*,
DOI 10.1007/978-981-10-4807-4_2

the documents. No time was given to the accused for this purpose, and on this finding the trial court discharged the accused. However, in *State v. Montasir M. Gubara*,[4] the accused is a refugee who is staying in India with refugee status. At the time of his arrest he was not able to produce his refugee certificate granted by UNHCR, which was placed before the court when trial started. Nevertheless, the court sentenced him to rigorous imprisonment for 6 weeks along with a fine. The case of *State v. Huson Vilvaraj* was registered under Section 14 of the Foreigners Act, 1946 against the accused, a Sri Lankan refugee.[5] The accused was arrested by the Delhi police as he was living in Delhi without travel documents. The court convicted the accused and sentenced him to simple imprisonment for 6 months and a fine. The trial court also observed that refugee status does not entitle a person to move about freely in another country, and that the person is always subject to the laws of the country which has accorded him the refugee status.

The case of *State v. Eva Massar Musa Ahmed* was registered under Section 14 of the Foreigners Act, 1946.[6] The accused is a Sudanese citizen who entered India with an expired Sudanese passport and no travel authorization from the Indian Government. The accused was held in custody for 10 days. She submitted before the court that she had been gang raped in Sudan for converting from Islam to Christianity and subsequently granted refugee status by UNHCR. The trial court, considering the situation of the accused, sentenced her to imprisonment for the days already spent in custody and a small fine.

In the case of *State v. Thang Cin*,[7] the accused is a citizen of Myanmar who entered India and applied for refugee status from UNHCR in New Delhi. He was arrested before receiving refugee status and was held in

---

[4]Criminal Case No. 427/P/1994, Court of Additional Chief Metropolitan Magistrate, Mumbai, Decided on: September 3, 1996 http://www.refworld.org/type,CASELAW,IND_MMM,IND,3f4b8fe14,0.html accessed December 25, 2015.

[5]Case No. 443/3 of 1997, Court Metropolitan Magistrate, New Delhi, Decided on: May 6, 1998 http://www.refworld.org/type,CASELAW,IND_MMM,IND,3f4b8f702,0.html accessed December 25, 2015.

[6]FIR No. 278/95, Court of Metropolitan Magistrate, New Delhi, Decided on: October 26, 1995 http://www.refworld.org/type,CASELAW,IND_MMM,IND,3f4b8c084,0.html accessed December 25, 2015.

[7]FIR No. 330/01, Court of Metropolitan Magistrate, New Delhi, Decided on June 3, 2002 http://www.refworld.org/type,CASELAW,IND_MMM,,3f4b90bd4,0.html accessed December 25, 2015.

judicial custody for about 9 months. Afterwards, the accused received refugee status from UNHCR in New Delhi and the court took a lenient view on convicting him under the Foreigners Act, 1946. The court sentenced him to the term already spent in prison and set him free.

In *State v. Mohd Ehsan*,[8] the petitioner was a refugee against whom an order of deportation was passed by the trial court. However, after submission of the refugee certificate issued by UNHCR before the court, the order of deportation was cancelled. However, he was sentenced to a fine and in case of default sentenced to 6 months of simple imprisonment. In the case of *State v. Benjamin Zang Nang*,[9] the accused served his sentence of imprisonment under the Foreigners Act. He was ordered deported from India after the completion of his sentence in prison. However, the accused pleaded for the court to send him under the custody of UNHCR to apply for refugee status. This plea was rejected by the court as the court has no jurisdiction to hand him over to UNHCR.

In *State v. Mohd Riza Ali*,[10] the accused was charged under various sections of the Indian Penal Code for holding forged travel documents, as well as under the Foreigners Act. The accused submitted a refugee certificate granted by UNHCR before the court and thus the court released him from the charges under the Foreigners Act, but the trial continues for the offences under the Penal Code. In the case of *State v. Kishan Chand and Habib Iranpur*,[11] the second accused pleaded guilty under the Foreigners Act, 1946. The second accused submitted that he is a refugee mandated by UNHCR in New Delhi and that he left Iran because he had suffered persecution. The court sentenced the second accused to 1 month of rigorous imprisonment

[8] FIR No. 435/1993, Court of Metropolitan Magistrate, New Delhi, Decided on March 17, 1994 http://www.refworld.org/type,CASELAW,IND_MMM,IND,3f4b8fa74,0.html accessed December 25, 2015.

[9] GR Case No. 1235/1994, Court of Assistant Chief Judicial Magistrate, Sealdah, 1996 http://www.refworld.org/type,CASELAW,IND_MMM,,3f3223584,0.html accessed December 25, 2015.

[10] FIR No. 414/93, Court of the Assistant Chief Metropolitan Magistrate, New Delhi, Decided July 7, 1995 http://www.refworld.org/type,CASELAW,IND_MMM,IND,3f4b8fc24,0.html accessed December 25, 2015.

[11] Criminal Case No. 66/96, Court of Metropolitan Magistrate, New Delhi, Decided on: May 31, 1996 http://www.refworld.org/type,CASELAW,IND_MMM,IND,3f4b8f8b4,0.html accessed December 25, 2015.

and a fine. In the case of *State v. Mohd. Yaashin*,[12] the accused was charged under the Indian Penal Code for procuring a false passport and travel document to enter India, and was also charged under the Foreigners Act. On the basis of the refugee certificate granted by UNHCR, he was released from the charges under the Foreigners Act. However, the court fined him and in case of default he was sentenced for a period of 30 days. The case of *State v. Chandra Kumar & Others* has received extensive media coverage,[13] as the trial court in this case not only quashed the order of deportation but also ordered the Government of India to table the Refugee and Asylum Seekers (Protection) Bill, 2006 before the Parliament. The accused was arrested for procuring false documents to leave India and travel to Italy. The prosecution wanted to deport him after he had served his sentence. However, the court decided that to send the refugee-accused back to the refugee camp in Tamil Nadu.

Thus, by and large, the trial courts have been unable to develop any standard practice in cases against refugees. There are many variations, which are primarily a result of reliance on colonial laws which do not deal with the situation of refugees. In some cases the court took a lenient approach to sentencing when a refugee certificate was issued by UNHCR, but finally convicted the refugee. However, there have been decisions by the High Court in which they ordered the withdrawal of the case under the Foreigners Act, 1946 when refugee status was granted to the accused.[14] It is important to note that the trial court can do very little in the case of a refugee situation when the laws of the country make no clear-cut distinction between a refugee and a foreigner. In the next section, I look into the judgments of various High Courts which deal with refugees to extend the ambit of the query of the present chapter.

[12] Case No. 528/2, Court of Metropolitan Magistrate, New Delhi, Decided on: June 4, 1997.

[13] FIR No. 78/10, Court of Metropolitan Magistrate (Dwarka), New Delhi, Decided on: September 20, 2011.

[14] See (n 20) and (n 21).

2.2 Decisions of High Courts and the Development of Precedence

There are over one thousand cases initiated by refugees or related to refugees present in India that have come in front of various High Courts of India. It is important to note that with the exception of some sixty cases, all were against decisions of state or other parties under the Acts which were enacted for rehabilitation of displaced persons during the partition of India.[15] There are very few cases concerning refugees that have come to various High Courts of India under the Acts which were enacted under Entries 14, 17, 18 and 19 of List One of Schedule 7.[16] The matters covered under these cases include rights of refugees against deportation and detention, resettlement, repatriation, right of compensation, right to livelihood, acquisition of citizenship and so forth. After careful analysis of the judgments of these cases, some are discussed in the following paragraphs under different categories. These cases reflect the protection of refugees in India and show the extent of protection under humanitarian considerations and international developments by defining the government's power to deal with foreigners exclusively under various central laws.[17] After careful discussion of these cases, an attempt is made to show the trend toward protection of refugees by the High Courts. However, in many of these cases the High Courts were not convinced that refugees constituted a different class distinguishable from other foreigners based on having entered India to escape persecution.

2.2.1 *Settlement/Compensation*

In the case of *Khudiram Chakma v. Union Territory of Arunachal Pradesh and Ors*,[18] the petitioner explained that he along with fifty-six

---

[15]Constitution of India, 1950, Concurrent List, Entry 27: Relief and rehabilitation of persons displaced from their original place of residence by reason of the setting up of the Dominions of India and Pakistan.

[16]Constitution of India, 1950, Union List, Entry 14: Entering into treaties and agreements with foreign countries and implementing of treaties, agreements and conventions with foreign countries; Entry 17: Citizenship, naturalization and aliens; Entry 18: Extradition, Entry 19: Admission into, and emigration and expulsion and passports and visas.

[17]Vijayakumar (n 1) 236.

[18]High Court of Gauhati, AIR 1992 Gau 105, Decided on: April 30, 1992.

Chakma families migrated from East Pakistan (presently Bangladesh) on March 30, 1964 due to ethnic disturbances. They were first given shelter in a government camp in Assam, thereafter taken to Bettiah of Bihar and finally taken to Abhayapur Block, Tirap District, Arunachal Pradesh in 1966. These families were able to negotiate with the local Raja about their situation, and the Raja gave them some land to cultivate. In 1984 the Chakmas received an order from the state government to move from Joypur village to the vacant lands of two other villages.

On the first issue of this case, the court, after analyzing the provisions of the Constitution of India and the Citizenship Act, 1955, came to the conclusion that the Chakmas are not citizens of India, so they are foreigners.[19] The second issue, of the state government directing the Chakmas to move to another place, was also upheld by the court in connection with the Foreigners Act, 1946 and the Foreigners Order, 1948. In this regard the court also relied on Regulation 5 of 1873, Scheduled District Act 1974, that no person other than a native has any right to acquire land or the product of land within the inner line.[20] On the third issue, the Court decided that the decision taken by the government was in conformity with the provisions of the Constitution of India and other laws dealing with foreigners.[21] However, on humanitarian grounds the court ordered the state government to compensate the Chakmas for the land they had prepared for cultivation. The government also ordered that all arrangements be made for the construction of housing and a water facility before shifting the Chakmas to the new place.[22] However, this decision was challenged in the Supreme Court of India, which generated additional litigation and finally resulted in the landmark judgment on refugee protection by the Supreme Court of India.

2.2.2 *Opportunity to Seek Asylum*

The petitioner in the case of *Ms. Zothansangpuii v. The State of Manipur* is a citizen of Myanmar who entered India in order to escape

[19] Ibid. Para.16–18.

[20] Ibid. Para.19–22.

[21] Ibid. Para.23–31.

[22] Ibid. Para.32–34

a terrorizing situation created by the Myanmar Army.[23] She was prosecuted by the Chief Judicial Magistrate under various Sections of the Foreigners Act, 1948 and is presently serving her sentence in prison. She submitted a petition to the High Court to rule that she should not be deported back to Myanmar after serving her sentence, and that she be given an opportunity to visit UNHCR to seek asylum in India. The Court ruled in her favor and ordered the state not to deport her for a period of 1 month after the completion of her sentence to enable her to seek asylum in India.

In the case of *Khy-Htoon and Ors v. The State of Manipur*,[24] the petitioners are citizens of Myanmar who were on trial for offences under the Foreigners Act, 1946. The petitioners asked for interim bail to allow them to appear before UNHCR in New Delhi to apply for refugee status. The court granted interim bail for 2 months on personal bond, and ordered them to seek refugee status.

In the case of *Mr. Bogyi v. Union of India*,[25] the petitioner is a citizen of Myanmar who entered India to escape persecution. He is also an under-trail prisoner charged under various Sections of the Foreigners Act, 1948. He submitted a petition requesting interim bail to enable him to visit New Delhi to seek asylum. The court ordered in favor of the petitioner with the direction that if the petitioner was successful in obtaining refugee status, he would not serve any sentence in prison in the present case leveled against him.

In the case of *U. Myat Kyaw v. State of Manipur*,[26] the petitioner entered India with travel documents to flee the political disturbance in Myanmar and approached the authorities after arriving in India. A criminal case was registered under Section 14 of the Foreigners Act, 1948 and the petitioner was placed in judicial custody. The petitioner approached the High Court to request the opportunity to seek refugee status from UNHCR in New Delhi. The court allowed the petition and ordered interim bail for 2 months to allow him to seek refugee status from

[23] High Court of Gauhati (Imphal Bench), Civil Rule No. 981 of 1989, Decided on: September 20, 1989.

[24] High Court of Gauhati, Civil Rule No. 515 of 1990, Decided on: September 11, 1990.

[25] High Court of Gauhati, Civil Rule No. 1847/89, Decided on: September 17, 1989.

[26] High Court of Gauhati (Imphal Bench), Civil Rule No. 516 of 1991, Decided on: November 26, 1991.

UNHCR. The court further ordered that because the petitioner might not be able to provide local surety, he would be released on personal bond.

2.2.3 Deportation

The case of *Seyed Ata Mohamamdi v. Union of India and Ors* involved a petition to the court not to deport the petitioner to his native country of Iran.[27] During the hearing the petitioner was granted refugee status by UNHCR. On the basis of the refugee certificate, the Government of India made a statement that there was no question of deportation of the petitioner to Iran and that he could travel to any country he wished under the resettlement program. As a result of this statement, the court disposed of the petition. In the case of *Mohammad Sediq v. Union of India and Ors*,[28] the petitioner was a refugee of Afghan origin who received a refugee certificate from UNHCR in New Delhi in 1987. This refugee certificate was extended on an annual basis until 1999.[29] In 1998 the petitioner received the impugned order from the government under Section 3(2)(c) of the Foreigners Act, 1948 to leave India on or before May 15, 1998 and not to re-enter India thereafter.[30] The petitioner contended that he had not been given any opportunity for a hearing before the order was issued, and that due to the disturbances in Afghanistan he was not able to return there as he feared he would suffer harm if he did so. The petitioner asked that the order be quashed as a violation of the principles of natural justice, that he be allowed to reside in India as a refugee, and that a direction be issued to exempt the petitioner and other such refugees, as a class or description of foreigners, from the application of the Foreigners Act, 1946.[31] The court observed that when any refugee is asked to leave the country, he/she must be allowed an opportunity for a hearing; however, the extent of the opportunity will depend on the

[27] High Court of Bombay, A.D. 1458 of 1994.
[28] High Court of Delhi, 1998 (47) DRJ 74, Decided on: August 21, 1998.
[29] Ibid. Para.3.
[30] Ibid. Para.1.
[31] Ibid.

facts and circumstances of each case.[32] Further, the court held that the order passed by the Foreigners Registration Officer, New Delhi is a valid order on account of the activities of the petitioner, which is prejudicial to the security of India and a reasonable opportunity of hearing has to be given to him.[33]

In *Ktaer Abbas Habib Al Qutaifi and Anr v. Union of India and Ors*,[34] the petitioners are Iraqi refugees who entered India in 1996 and were subsequently granted refugee status by UNHCR in New Delhi.[35] The petitioners asked to be handed over to UNHCR instead of being deported to Iraq. The court in this case reflected intently upon international law principles of refugee protection and India's obligations under various human rights instruments.[36] Finally, on the basis of the principle of non-refoulement and humanity, the court ordered in favor of the petitioners that they not be deported from India until December 31, 1998 and ordered the respondents to consider the petition as per the law laid down in the judgment.[37] In the case of *Dongh Lian Kham and Ors v. Union of India and Ors*,[38] both petitioners are citizens of Myanmar belonging to the ethnic Chin community. They entered India in 2009 and 2011 respectively along with their families and were issued refugee certificates by UNHCR in New Delhi valid until 2017.[39] On the basis of the refugee certificate issued by UNHCR, the Ministry of Home Affairs (MHA) issued them with long-term visas (LTVs). The petitioners were convicted under the Narcotic Drugs & Psychotropic Substances Act, 1985 by a competent court and served prison terms. After their release from prison, the MHA detained them in a camp and started procedures for deportation. The petitioners contended that if they were to be deported to Myanmar, they would face persecution and their lives would be threatened. The MHA contended that given the conviction of the petitioners, they represented a threat to the security of the nation, and that their involvement in drugs also posed a threat to the social fabric,

---

32 Ibid. Para.16.

33 Ibid. Para.22 and Para.23.

34 High Court of Gujarat, 1999 Cri.L.J 919, Decided on: October 12, 1998.

35 Ibid. Para.1.

36 Ibid. Para.6–9, 18 and 19.

37 Ibid. Para.21.

38 High Court of Delhi, 226 (2016) DLT 208, Decided on: 21 December 2015.

39 Ibid. Para.3–6.

so the decision was taken by the MHA to deport them.[40] The petitioners asked that the MHA order be quashed because they are refugees with rights under Article 21 and Article 14 of the Constitution of India, and based on the principle of non-refoulement of customary international law.[41] The court observed that the government has the power to expel any foreigner from the territory of India and there is no law or provision of the Constitution that can affect this power of the government. However, the prohibition of deportation of refugees to a country where they will face persecution can be regarded as a guarantee under Article 21 of the Constitution of India, as non-refoulement protects the life and liberty of a human being, irrespective of his/her nationality.[42] Finally, the court, in consideration of the good conduct of the petitioners in social life and their family status, ruled that the MHA, in consultation with UNHCR, should find an opportunity to deport the petitioners to a third country other than Myanmar and that the petitioners shall not be deported from India until a decision is made on this issue.[43]

2.2.4 *Repatriation and Resettlement*

A petition to direct the government to stop the involuntary repatriation of Sri Lankan refugees to their native place came before the court in the case of *Gurunathan and Others v. The Government of India and Others.*[44] The Government of India came up with a plan to the effect that Sri Lankan refugees would not be sent back to their native place against their will and that there would be no force used in the process. Considering that as a guarantee, the court disposed of the petition. The issue of involuntary repatriation again came before the Madras High Court in *P. Nedumaran and Dr. S. Ramadoss v. Union of India and Another,*[45] in which case the court disposed of the petition with a decision similar to that in the previous case.

[40] Ibid. Para.20.

[41] Ibid. Para.13–15.

[42] Ibid. Para.26 and 30.

[43] Ibid. Para.32 and 33.

[44] High Court of Madras, W.P. Nos. 6708 and 7916 of 1992.

[45] High Court of Madras, W.P. No. 12298 and 12343 of 1992, Decided on: August 27, 1992.

In the case of *Aung Thant Min v. Union of India*,[46] the petitioner had previously been granted interim bail by order of the High Court of Gauhati to seek refugee status from UNHCR. The petitioner duly received the status and the refugee certificate. The present petition came before the court to direct the government to issue him an exit visa to travel to Canada under the UNHCR resettlement program. The Government of India had no objection to this petition, and the Government of Manipur is in the process of withdrawing the case against the petitioner under the Foreigners Act, 1946. On the basis of the above, the court ordered the government to issue an exit visa to the petitioner. The case of *Saifullah Bajwa v. Union of India* came to the court with a request to withdraw a writ petition against the Government of India as the petitioners had been granted resettlement by UNHCR.[47] This case first came before another bench of the High Court in 2008 with a request to direct the government to provide asylum to the petitioners as they had been persecuted in Pakistan and to release them into the custody of UNHCR in New Delhi.[48] In that case, it was revealed that the Government of India was not inclined to grant asylum, and put the petitioners in Tihar Jail. The court ordered that UNHCR be allowed to intervene and directed the government not to deport the petitioners to their country of origin. Finally, the petitioners were given the opportunity to resettle in another country by UNHCR, and the petition was withdrawn.

2.2.5 Detention

The case of *Ramsingh v. State of Rajasthan* is a revision petition before the Court.[49] The petitioner is a Pakistani citizen who came to India during the 1971 war and stayed at a refugee camp. It is alleged by the state that the petitioner crossed the border back into Pakistan in 1972 and then re-entered Indian territory in 1973, and thus he was charged under Section 14 of the Foreigners Act, 1946 and Rule 3 of the Passports (Entry into India) Rules, 1950. The petitioner was convicted and sentenced to rigorous imprisonment by the

[46] High Court of Delhi, W.P. (CRL) 110 of 1998, Decided on: March 4, 1998.

[47] High Court of Delhi, W.P. (CRL) 465/2011, Decided on: December 9, 2011.

[48] High Court of Delhi, W.P. (CRL) 1470/2008, Decided on: December 2, 2010.

[49] High Court of Rajasthan, 1978 WLN (UC) 90, Decided on: March 15, 1978.

Chief Judicial Magistrate, which decision was further affirmed by the Sessions Judge in 1977. In this case the court, after careful examination of the records of the lower court, found no evidence to prove the petitioner had left India in 1972. Finally the court held that the petitioner was entitled to the benefit of the doubt and acquitted him of the charges.[50]

In the case of *Kalavathy v. State of Tamil Nadu*,[51] the division bench of Madras High Court dealt with the contention of the petitioners that the detention order under Section 3(2)(e) of the Foreigners Act, 1946 is in violation of Articles 14, 21 and 22 of the Constitution of India.[52] The state of Tamil Nadu was accused of ordering refugees of Sri Lankan origin to reside in special camps. The state contended that only a small proportion of the Sri Lankan refugees who might have association with militant organizations in Sri Lanka were ordered to stay in special camps.[53] The court, considering the rival contentions, held that classifying refugees and ordering them to stay in special camps does not violate the provisions of the Constitution, and thus the state has the power under the Foreigners Act, 1948 to do so, and further that it is not a total restriction of the movement of the foreigner.[54]

In the case of *Yogeswari v. The State of Tamil Nadu*,[55] the son of the petitioner was detained under Section 3(2)(e) of the Foreigners Act, 1946. The detainee is a Sri Lankan refugee who was granted bail by the court of competent jurisdiction for charges against him under various Sections of the Indian Penal Code. However, before his release from prison the detainee received a detention order under the Foreigners Act. The court in this case held that detention under the Foreigners Act has to be in compliance with Article 21 and Article 22(4) of the Constitution of India and that as a pre-constitutional Act it does not contain safeguards, and thus the division bench of the court quashed the detention order under the Foreigners Act.[56]

---

[50] Ibid. Para.5 and 6.

[51] High Court of Madras, 1995-2-LW(Crl)690, Decided on: April 28, 1992.

[52] Ibid. Para.1–8.

[53] Ibid. Para.9.

[54] Ibid. Para.18–26.

[55] High Court of Madras, Habeas Corpus Petition No. 971 of 2001, Decided on: April 10, 2003.

[56] Ibid. Para.20 and 24.

In *Premavathy v. State of Tamil Nadu*,[57] it was decided by the division bench of Madras High Court, where similar contentions were raised by the petitioners, that the state was detaining them under Section 3(2)(e) of the Foreigners Act, 1948 in violation of their rights contained under Articles 14, 21 and 22 of the Constitution of India. The two previous contradicting judgments of the division bench of Madras High Court, one in Kalavathy and another in Yogeswari, set the stage for this case. However, in this case the division bench sided with the Kalavathy case and held that restricting the movement of the foreigners by the order of the state under Section 3(2)(e) of the Foreigners Act cannot be termed preventive detention and does not violate the provisions of the Constitution of India.[58] However, the court finally directed the state to review those detention decisions every 2 years and to provide more facilities to the special camps.[59]

In the case of *Selvakulendran v. State of Tamil Nadu*,[60] the petitioner is a Sri Lankan refugee who entered India in 1989 and stayed in India with his family in Tiruchirappalli, Tamil Nadu.[61] It is very important to note that the petitioner and his family members were given ration cards by the Civil Supplies Department and their names were included in the voter list. The petitioner was arrested by the police under various Sections of the Indian Penal Code, and after spending some time in prison the petitioner was granted bail. However, he was not released from the prison and an order was passed by the government under Section 3(2)(e) of the Foreigners Act, 1948 requiring the petitioner to reside in the special camp for Sri Lankan immigrants and prohibiting him from leaving the boundaries of the special camp without permission from the District Collector.[62] The court held that the right to move throughout the territory of India is not available to a foreigner, and that

[57] High Court of Madras, 2004 Cri.L.J 1475, Decided on: November 14, 2003.

[58] Ibid. Para.27–38.

[59] Ibid. Para.39–42.

[60] High Court of Madras, Habeas Corpus Petition No. 1249 of 2005, Decided on: March 15, 2006.

[61] Ibid. Para.2.

[62] Ibid. Para.10.

particularly in this case it was reasonable to impose this restriction on the petitioner because of his criminal conduct.[63] In the case of *Maheswaran v. State of Tamil Nadu*,[64] the petitioner, a Sri Lankan refugee, was arrested by the police as a suspect in the bomb blast at Madras Airport in 1984. He was tried and finally acquitted of the charges by the trial court in 2004. In the meantime, while he was awaiting trial, the state government issued an order under Section 3(2)(e) of the Foreigners Act, 1948 to confine the petitioner to a special camp for Sri Lankan refugees.[65] The petitioner challenged this order through this writ petition. The court held that under the Foreigners Act the government is empowered to restrict the movement of foreigners in consideration of the security of the state.[66] The court also observed that there was no absolute restriction of the petitioner's movement by this order of the government, and dismissed the petition.[67]

In the case of *Premanand v. State of Kerala*,[68] the petitioner was charged under Section 13 and 14 of the Foreigners Act, 1948 and Section 3 of the Passports (Entry into India) Act, 1920.[69] The petitioner in this case is a Sri Lankan refugee who was residing in a refugee camp in Chennai. He along with some other Sri Lankan refugees came to Alwaye, Kerala at the instruction of Mr. Ramesh, who would arrange to send them to Australia for a better life. The Kerala police apprehended the refugees and brought a case under the Sections mentioned above. The present petition was for bail, which the High Court of Kerala granted on condition of a bail bond of 10,000 rupees and the refugee-petitioner returning to the refugee camp in Chennai.[70] The Refugee Rehabilitation Commissioner was ordered to keep watch over the petitioner and make him available before the trial court as and when

---

[63] Ibid. Para.13.

[64] High Court of Madras, Habeas Corpus Petition No. 1208 of 2005, Decided on: March 21, 2006.

[65] Ibid. Para.2.

[66] Ibid. Para.8.

[67] Ibid. Para.9.

[68] High Court of Kerala, 2013 (3) KLJ 543, Decided on: July 12, 2013.

[69] Ibid. Para.1.

[70] Ibid. Para.9.

required. In *B. Sivashankar v. State of Tamil Nadu*,[71] the petitioner is another Sri Lankan refugee. He is in judicial custody in a case under various Sections of the Indian Penal Code and the Foreigners Act, 1946. The petitioner received the impugned detention order under the National Security Act, 1980 from the state and filed this petition challenging that order.[72] Though, no bail application was pending before any court regarding the original criminal case of the petitioner, the state, anticipating his release on bail, made this impugned detention order. The court found the reason for the detention to be vicious in character as there was an absence of cogent materials for arriving at this subjective satisfaction.[73] The court also found a violation of Article 22(5) of the Constitution of India in this case, and finally quashed the detention order.[74] *T. Sathishkumar v. State of Tamil Nadu* was a related case on the same issues and was decided by the court similarly.[75]

2.2.6 Service Matter and Livelihood

The case of *Digvijay Mote v. Government of India and Anr* came before the court with a request to direct the government to provide food for the children of Sri Lankan refugees who are staying and studying in a residential school in Karnataka.[76] The Government of Karnataka arranged for the supply of food, and thus the court disposed of the petition without discussing its merit. In the case of *Satish Kumar Singh and Ors v. Union of India (UOI) and Ors*,[77] the petitioners requested a ruling that Tibetan nationals employed with the Central Tibetan Schools Administration (CTSA) ought not to be regularized or given permanent employment because CTSA is an organization governed by the Central

[71] High Court of Madras, Habeas Corpus Petition No. 2718 of 2013, Decided on: June 25, 2014.

[72] Ibid. Para.1.

[73] Ibid. Para.11.

[74] Ibid. Para.12, 14, 17.

[75] High Court of Madras, Habeas Corpus Petition No. 2721 of 2013, Decided on: June 25, 2014.

[76] High Court of Karnataka at Bangalore, WAN No. 354 of 1994, Decided on: February 17, 1994.

[77] High Court of Delhi, W.P. (C) Nos. 1006/2003 and 6161-63/06, Decided on: April 20, 2006.

Civil Services Rules. The CTSA was established in 1961 for the education of the children of Tibetan refugees, and 236 Tibetan refugees were given employment with the CTSA.[78] During the proceedings, the Government of India issued a notification that a one-time exemption would be made to regularize the 236 Tibetan refugees then working with CTSA, and that no more Tibetan refugees would be appointed to regular posts under CTSA in future.[79] After this notification the court found that the issue had been resolved and dismissed the petition.

2.2.7 Acquisition of Indian Citizenship

In the case of *Smt. Shishuwala Pal and Anr v. Union of India and Ors*,[80] the petitioners—mother and son—were citizens of East Pakistan who came to India during the 1971 war as refugees. They were rehabilitated in a refugee camp, but later moved to their relative's residence in Madhya Pradesh. The second petitioner studied up to Bachelor's level in India and was elected in the Panchayat election in 1983 from Madhya Pradesh.[81] After the said election, the petitioners were arrested by the police for deportation to Bangladesh. The petitioners asked for a direction to restrain the respondents from treating them as foreign nationals and from taking them into custody for deportation outside India.[82] The court, after considering the provisions of the Citizenship Act, 1955, held that the petitioners were not citizens of India but were still foreigners.[83] It was the domain of the Government of India to decide whether they would be allowed to stay in India on humanitarian grounds, and the petitioners had statutory remedy under the Citizenship Act, 1955.[84] With these observations the court dismissed the petition.

In the case of *Namgyal Dolkar v. Govt of India, Ministry of External Affairs*,[85] the Delhi High Court clarified the position of the law that every child born in India between January 26, 1950 and July 1, 1987,

[79] Ibid. Para.11.

[78] Ibid. Para.2, 3, 9, 10.

[80] High Court of Madhya Pradesh, AIR 1989 MP 254, Decided on: October 31, 1988.

[81] Ibid. Para.2.

[82] Ibid. Para.1.

[83] Ibid. Para.11.

[84] Ibid.

[85] High Court of Delhi, W.P (C) 12179/2009, Decided on: December 22, 2010.

irrespective of the parents' nationality, is an Indian citizen by birth. This case was raised when Namgyal Dolkar, the child of Tibetan parents, was denied an Indian passport by the Regional Passport Officer (RPO), Delhi. When dealing with the petition the court noted that the petitioner was born within the cut-off dates mentioned in the Citizenship (Amendment) Act, 1986, and therefore there is no doubt that she is a citizen of India by birth. The court quashed the RPO's order dated March 24, 2009 on the grounds that the petitioner is a citizen of India and directed the RPO to reconsider the petitioner's application for an Indian passport within a period of 8 weeks. Finally, the petitioner was issued an Indian passport.[86]

In the case of *Sasikumar v. State of Tamil Nadu*,[87] the petitioner was born on March 10, 1987 in Trichy Government Hospital. The parents of the petitioner are refugees who came to India after the outbreak of war in Sri Lanka. The petitioner challenged the validity of the order of detention in a camp for Sri Lankan refugees passed on September 4, 2008 under Section 3(2)(e) of the Foreigners Act, 1946, as the petitioner is a citizen of India by birth under Section 3(1)(a) of the Citizenship Act, 1955.[88] The government contended that the petitioner is a Sri Lankan citizen and can be detained under the powers conferred on the government under the Foreigners Act, 1946. However, the court, after carefully considering the provisions of the Citizenship Act, 1955, held that the petitioner is a citizen of India by birth as he was born before the cut-off date of July 1, 1987.[89] The court quashed the order of detention by the state government.

The case of *Tenzin Choephag Ling Rinpoche v. Union of India* came before the Karnataka High Court for the same reason as was decided by the Delhi High Court in 2011 in the case of Namgyal Dolkar.[90] The petitioner in this case, Tenzin Rinpoche, was born November 18, 1985 in Dharamsala, Kangra District, Himachal Pradesh. The petitioner applied for an Indian passport and the application was denied by a letter

---

[86] Vandana Kalra, 'Citizen Nymgal' *Indian Express* (January 27, 2011).

[87] High Court of Madras (Madurai Bench), W.P. (MD) No. 10080 of 2008 and M.P. (MD) No. 2 of 2008, Decided on: August 25, 2011.

[88] Ibid. Para.1–6.

[89] Ibid. Para.14 & 15.

[90] High Court of Karnataka at Bangalore, W.P. No. 15437 of 2013, Decided on: August 7, 2013.

of the RPO dated February 19, 2013 after consulting with the MHA, whereby it was stated that children born to Tibetan parents could not automatically claim citizenship in India. The court finally relied on the judgment of the Delhi High Court and ruled that the petitioner is a citizen of India and entitled to receive an Indian passport.[91]

In the case of *Sri Gopal Das v. The Union of India and Ors*,[92] the petitioner was identified as a foreigner of Bangladeshi origin by the Foreigners Tribunal, Silchar in 2012. He brought this petition to quash the order of the tribunal, claiming that he was born in 1968 in India. It was also contended that even if the petitioner had come from Bangladesh, as a Hindu he was subject to persecution there and so should not be deported and should be granted Indian citizenship. The court held that this was a political issue and so was not a consideration in the forum of the court.[93] The court found no merit in the contention and held that the foreigner be detained and deported to his country of origin.[94]

The case of *Nityananda Malik and Ors v. State of Meghalaya and Ors* resolved an important question relating to citizenship of India for persons who came to India before March 24, 1971 from Bangladesh and their children.[95] The forty petitioners in this case are children of refugees from Bangladesh. Their forefathers entered India around 1961 and were rehabilitated in Meghalaya. The petitioners' citizenship certificates were seized by the Deputy Commissioner of the district on the grounds that they are not citizens of India. The affidavit filed by the Union of India made the case clear for the court to decide the matter, as it mentioned that as per the understanding between India and Bangladesh, persons who came to India on or before March 24, 1971 would not be sent back to Bangladesh.[96] The court held that the petitioners are citizens of India by birth and that their names have to be included in the electoral roll, and dismissed the petition.[97]

---

[91] Ibid. Para.11 & 12.

[92] High Court of Gauhati, WP(C) 2134 of 2013, Decided on: August 30, 2013.

[93] Ibid. Para.15.

[94] Ibid. Para.12.

[95] High Court of Meghalaya, WP(C) No. 235 of 2010, Decided on: May 15, 2014.

[96] Ibid. Para.6 & 7.

[97] Ibid. Para.9–11.

2.3 Ambit of Protection and the Jurisprudence Developed by Indian High Courts

Considering the decisions of cases in various High Courts, it can be pointed out that there is a compassionate regime of protection available to refugees in India in general, but only when the refugees reach the higher courts to appeal the decisions of the government or trial courts. In specific matters of compensation for resettlement, opportunity to seek refugee status, repatriation and the right to Indian citizenship, the High Courts have shown courage in deciding cases in favor of refugees, both on humanitarian grounds and based on law. It has been seen in various High Court judgments that India's international obligations to protect refugees were discussed along with the humanitarian traditions of Indian culture. However, there have been conflicting judgments in matters relating to detention and deportation, as discussed in the two previous sections of this chapter. It is noteworthy that the High Courts have based their decisions on the facts and circumstances of each case. For instance, in cases concerning deportation, some decisions have affirmed deportation instantly, while others have passed an interim order to restrict deportation for the time being. In all these cases, importantly, national and other security reasons have played a very important role in these decisions. In cases of detention, again, there has been much ambiguity in the decisions of the same High Court (High Court of Madras) when the division benches were given different judgments. Finally, the right of the state to restrict the movement of a refugee is recognized as a sole right that cannot be called detention. The following points are more clearly stated to clarify the stand taken by the various High Courts:

1. Article 21 is available to protect a non-citizen within the Indian territory and it implies by interpretation the principle of non-refoulement. However, this does not confer any right to reside or resettle in India, or to unrestricted movement in India.
2. The power of the government to expel foreigners is absolute if their stay is contrary to the security of the state.
3. In cases of repatriation of refugees, it should be voluntary in nature subject to the security of the state.
4. Children of refugees are entitled to the right to Indian citizenship if they were born between January 26, 1950 and July 1, 1987.

5. In matters involving respect for international legal principles, the court will apply these principles in a harmonious manner.
6. The relevant international conventions and treaties are not binding unless made law by the Parliament. However, the government has an obligation to respect them.
7. The government has an obligation to ensure the protection of refugees when they have been granted refugee status by UNHCR.

2.4 The Supreme Court in Refugee Protection

It is important to note that the flow of cases regarding matters of refugee protection in the High Courts, as discussed in the previous sections, is not great. There are several possible reasons for the small number of cases, but it is noteworthy that appeals of cases decided in the High Courts or fresh cases in the Supreme Court are also very few in number. The general trend of justice delivery could be described under these circumstances as: refugees are fined and sentenced under relevant laws dealing with foreigners; sometimes, if they are lucky, they have the chance to appeal that order before a higher court with the help of a compassionate lawyer or an NGO, and often the case is decided in the refugee's favor.[98] However, at the same time, judgments on refugee protection are limited to individual cases and do not apply to all persons in the same category or circumstance. Nevertheless, the way the Supreme Court of India has interpreted the Constitution in its decisions to highlight the duty of the state to accord refugee protection is phenomenal. In its several decisions, the Supreme Court has employed international human rights law provisions to uphold the obligation of refugee protection. In this section of the chapter, I analyze all the judgments of the Supreme Court of India on matters related to refugees and their protection.

First, however, it is important to clarify the point that many court decisions on refugee matters have taken as precedent two cases decided by the Supreme Court that restricted the rights of refugees. In the case of *Hans Muller of Nurenburg v. Superintendent, Presidency Jail, Calcutta and Others*,[99] the Supreme Court in 1955 declared that the Foreigners

[98] Ranabir Samaddar, 'Introduction' in Ranabir Samaddar (ed), *Refugee and the State: Practices of Asylum and Care in India 1947–2000* (SAGE, New Delhi 2003) 50.

[99] Supreme Court of India, 1955 AIR 367, Decided on: February 23, 1955.

Act confers on the central government the absolute and unfettered discretion to expel a foreigner from India, and that there is no provision to limit this discretion in the Constitution.[100] In the case of *Louis De Raedt v. Union of India and Others*,[101] the Supreme Court observed that the fundamental right of the foreigner is confined to Article 21 for life and liberty and does not include the right to reside and settle in India as mentioned in Article 19(1)(e), which is applicable only to citizens of India.[102] These two cases dealt exclusively with the factual circumstances of foreigners who entered India for a purpose other than to escape persecution. The court decisions to restrict the rights of refugees that were made on the basis of these two decisions failed to distinguish between two classes of persons—refugees and other foreigners. This was the judicial trend for a long time, mostly in the High Courts, but recent decisions by the Supreme Court have shown the way towards this distinction in the Chakma cases. It can also be argued that the observations made in the Chakma cases should become the standard of law in distinguishing between refugees and other foreigners as different categories.

2.4.1 Cases of Chakma Refugees

State of Arunachal Pradesh v. Khudiram Chakma came before the Supreme Court as a special leave petition against the decision of the Gauhati High Court discussed previously in this chapter.[103] In the case before the Gauhati High Court, the decisions were: the Chakmas are not citizens of India; the state government's order to move the Chakmas is lawful; the Chakmas do not have any right to acquire land or the products of the land within the inner line; and the state government should compensate the Chakmas on humanitarian grounds. Both parties in the case before the Gauhati High Court proffered separate special leave petitions against the order: the Chakmas appealed the first three directions, while the state government appealed the last direction regarding compensation to the Chakmas.

---

[100] Ibid. Para.35.

[101] Supreme Court of India, 1991 AIR 1886, Decided on: July 24, 1991.

[102] Ibid. Para.13.

[103] Supreme Court of India, AIR 1994 SC 1461, Decided on: April 27, 1993.

The Chakmas contended that they are citizens of India under Section 6-A of the Citizenship Act, 1955 as they came to Assam in 1964 from the specified territory, which is prior to the cut-off date of January 1, 1966.[104] The state government pointed out two important conditions which must be fulfilled to be a citizen of India under the Section 6-A: one must be a person of Indian origin who came to Assam before January 1, 1966 from the specified territory, and be an ordinary resident of Assam as it existed in 1985, that is, at the time of signing of the Assam Accord.[105] The Chakmas entered Assam in 1964, but they are not resident in Assam as in 1985 they moved to Arunachal Pradesh. The Supreme Court accepted the contentions of the state government in this regard and affirmed the decision of the Gauhati High Court that Chakmas are not citizens of India.[106] The state government further contended that as the Chakmas are not citizens of India, the government has the power under the Foreigners Act, 1946 to direct the Chakmas to live in a particular place or restrict their entry to any protected place.[107] The Supreme Court also affirmed this contention and relied on the order of the Gauhati High Court in this regard.[108] The state government contended that the donation of land to the Chakmas by the local Raja was not valid as per Bengal Eastern Frontier Regulation, 1873 and the Foreigners Order, 1948, and this was also accepted by the Supreme Court.[109] The last matter in this case remained to be decided, that is, the order of compensation by the Gauhati High Court in favor of the Chakmas on the event of being evicted. The Supreme Court in this specific matter considered the position of Chakmas as refugees and quoted Blackburn and Taylor thus:

> Article 14 of the Universal Declaration of Human Rights, which speaks of the right to enjoy asylum, has to be interpreted in the light of the instrument as a whole, and must be taken to mean something. It implies that although an asylum seeker has no right to be granted admission to a foreign State, equally a State which has granted him asylum must not later

---

[104] Ibid. Para.28–30.
[105] Ibid. Para.32–34.
[106] Ibid. Para.59–65.
[107] Ibid. Para.53–54.
[108] Ibid. Para.72.
[109] Ibid. Para.35, 42, 66.

> return him to the country whence he came. Moreover, the Article carries considerable moral authority and embodies legal prerequisite of regional declarations and instruments.[110]

However, the court, finally considering refugees and aliens in the same category, and as per the laws established by the Bengal Eastern Frontier Regulation, 1873 and the Foreigners Act, 1946, ruled that compensation in this case was not required.[111] After the final decision of the above case in the Supreme Court, the Chakmas experienced increased pressure from several political organizations within the state of Arunachal Pradesh. The Chakmas started contacting various organizations across the country to help them in the struggle for their rights in India. Finally, this matter came before the National Human Rights Commission (NHRC), resulting in a landmark case on refugee protection in India. This case dealt with rival contentions by the central and state government over the issue of citizenship of Chakmas, but finally a writ of mandamus was issued as requested by the NHRC.

The case of *National Human Rights Commission v. State of Arunachal Pradesh and Anr* came before the Supreme Court of India by virtue of Section 18 of the Protection of Human Rights Act, 1993.[112] The NHRC filed this petition to safeguard the life and liberty of the Chakmas within the state of Arunachal Pradesh. The issue of protection of life and liberty and the denial of Indian citizenship to the Chakmas came to the notice of the NHRC through a letter from the People's Union for Civil Liberties (PUCL) in 1994.[113] The NHRC, after receiving the letter from the PUCL, started functioning as per the mandate under the Protection of Human Rights Act, 1993. However, after a year of intervention by the NHRC there was little hope for the Chakmas, as political pressure was being put on them to leave Arunachal Pradesh and the state government was not taking action to safeguard the Chakmas. The NHRC was also doubtful about its own efforts to sustain the Chakmas in their own habitat, and decided to approach the Supreme Court to seek appropriate relief.[114]

---

[110] Ibid. Para.79.

[111] Ibid. Para.80–82.

[112] Supreme Court of India, (1996) 1 SCC 742, Decided on: January 9, 1996.

[113] Ibid. Para.5.

[114] Ibid. Para.8.

The request by the NHRC to the court was to process the application of the Chakmas for Indian citizenship under Section 5(1)(a) of the Citizenship Act by the state and central government and to safeguard the life and liberty of Chakmas in the face of the political pressure to leave Arunachal Pradesh. The state of Arunachal Pradesh contended that it had taken adequate security measures to safeguard the Chakma villages with the posting of Central Para Military Forces there and that there was no threat of infringement on the life and liberty of the Chakmas. The state government also contended that the Chakmas are not citizens of India as per the decision of the Supreme Court in the case of *State of Arunachal Pradesh v. Khudiram Chakma*, so the state of Arunachal Pradesh can ask the Chakmas to leave the state.[115] The second respondent in this case, Union of India, testified before the court about its willingness to grant citizenship to the Chakmas under Section 5(1)(a) of the Citizenship Act on the basis of the Joint Statement of the Prime Ministers of India and Bangladesh in 1972, and with regard to the children of these Chakma families who were born before July 1, 1987 having a legitimate claim to Indian citizenship by birth.[116] However, the Union of India further contended that the state of Arunachal Pradesh had not forwarded the application for granting Indian citizenship to the Chakmas to the MHA as required under the Citizenship Act, 1955 and the Citizenship Rules, 1956.[117]

The Supreme Court considered the contentions of all the parties and rejected the argument by the state of Arunachal Pradesh that the lives and personal liberty of the Chakmas were not in danger in the state of Arunachal Pradesh, concluding that they were in danger due to political pressure as well as economic blockades in the Chakma villages and that the Chakmas are entitled to protection under Article 21 of the Constitution of India.[118] Secondly, rejecting the contention of the state of Arunachal Pradesh on the issue of citizenship of Chakmas, they decided that the previous judgment of the Supreme Court was conclusive only with regard to Section 6-A of the Citizenship Act and has no relevance with regard to fresh applications by Chakmas under

[115] Ibid. Para.11–14.

[116] Ibid. Para.10.

[117] Ibid.

[118] Ibid. Para.15 and 16.

Section 5(1)(a) of the Citizenship Act.[119] The pro refugee stand of the Supreme Court in this case is well illustrated by the following observation:

> We are a country governed by Rule of Law. Our Constitution confers certain rights on every human being and certain other rights on citizens. Every person is entitled to equality before the law and equal protection of the laws. So also, no person can be deprived of his life or personal liberty except according to the procedure established by law. Thus the State is bound to protect the life and personal liberty of every human being, be he a citizen or otherwise, and it cannot permit anybody or group of persons ... to threaten the Chakmas to leave the State ... the State government must act impartially and carry out its legal obligations to safeguard the life, health and well being of Chakmas residing in the State without being inhibited by local politics. Besides, by refusing to forward their applications, the Chakmas are denied rights, constitutional and statutory, to be considered for being registered citizens of India.[120]

Finally, the Supreme Court issued the following directions to the state of Arunachal Pradesh and Union of India by way of writ of mandamus and disposed of the petition[121]:

1. The life and personal liberty of each and every Chakma residing within the state shall be protected, if necessary by the use of paramilitary forces.
2. Chakmas shall not be evicted from their homes except in accordance with law.
3. The quit notices and ultimatums should be dealt with by the first respondent in accordance with the law.
4. The applications made for registration as citizens of India by Chakmas under Section 5 of the Act shall be forwarded by the Collector to the central government.
5. While the Chakmas' applications for citizenship are pending, they shall not be evicted.

[119] Ibid. Para.17–19.

[120] Ibid Para.20.

[121] Ibid. Para.21.

The judgment in this case, the first of its kind for any of the refugee groups in India, made a remarkable contribution to the development of a framework for protecting refugees within Indian territory. A subtle derivation from the above trend would stand to claim that the obligation to protect refugees is paramount. The directions in this case were mostly implemented by the state, though the issue of granting citizenship remains in question.

In the case of *Committee for Citizenship Rights of the Chakmas of Arunachal Pradesh and Ors v. State of Arunachal Pradesh and Ors*,[122] which came before the Supreme Court in 2007, it was contended that the state of Arunachal Pradesh had not complied with the direction to forward the applications for citizenship by the Chakmas to the central government. The Union of India in its reply contended that it had taken the decision to grant citizenship to the Chakmas of Arunachal Pradesh, and that for the materialization of the granting of citizenship the applications had to be forwarded to the MHA by the local Collector in whose jurisdiction the Chakmas are residing. The MHA received the applications directly in their office and forwarded them to the Collector for his comments, as per the requirement of the Citizenship Rules, 1956. However, with the exception of some that received negative comments, most of the applications had not reached the MHA.[123] After hearing all the parties, the court ordered the respondents to confer citizenship rights on the Chakmas within 3 months of the date of the order.[124] The observation made by the court is very important as it clearly indicates the right of the Chakmas to Indian citizenship:

> We find merit in the contention of the petitioners. It stands acknowledged by this Court on the basis of stand of the Government of India that the Chakmas have right to be granted citizenship subject to the procedure being followed. It also stands recognized by judicial decisions that they cannot be required to obtain any Inner Line permit as they are settled in the State of Arunachal Pradesh.[125]

[122] Supreme Court of India, WP (Civil) No. 510 of 2007, Decided on: September 17, 2015.

[123] Ibid. Para.6, 10, 11.

[124] Ibid. Para.20.

[125] Ibid. Para.16.

Though the Chakmas' right to Indian citizenship has been recognized by the Supreme Court in two landmark cases, the process remains unfinished.

2.4.2 Cases Relating to Refugees of Other Nationalities

The Supreme Court of India has at times acted in conformity with the principle of non-refoulement and has stayed orders of deportation from India while the application for refugee status is pending. These decisions can be seen as evidence that the laws applicable to other foreigners are not applicable to refugees. In the case of *Dr. Malavika Karlekar v. Union of India and Anr,*[126] the Supreme Court ordered that twenty-one nationals of Myanmar who have applied for refugee status cannot be deported to Myanmar while the decision is pending with UNHCR. In *N. D. Pancholi v. State of Punjab and Others,*[127] as well as in *The Mailwand's Trust of Afghan Human Freedom v. State of Punjab & Ors,*[128] the Supreme Court ordered that the refugees shall not be deported from India without the notice of the court.

The pending litigation filed by Swajan, a non-governmental organization in Assam, in *Swajan and Anr v. Union of India and Anr* before the Supreme Court of India is deciding the question of granting refugee status to the minorities of Bangladesh who entered India after March 25, 1971 to escape persecution.[129] However, as discussed in the previous chapter, the Government of India already issued a Gazette Notification regarding this matter, to provide refuge to the minorities of Bangladesh as well as Pakistan, on September 7, 2015. The matter is still pending before the Supreme Court for final orders.

2.5 Conclusion

Throughout the chapter an effort has been made to list and analyze all the important judicial decisions that will contribute to the conceptualization of the general trend of justice delivery in matters relating to

[126] Supreme Court of India, WP (CRL) No 583 of 1992, Decided on: September 25, 1992.

[127] Supreme Court of India, WP (CRL) No 243 of 1988, Decided on: June 9, 1988.

[128] Supreme Court of India, WP (CRL) No 125 and 126 of 1986.

[129] Supreme Court of India, WP Civil No. 243 of 2012 (Pending).

refugees. It has been found that the inconsistency of decision-making by trial courts has given a space to refugees for further litigation in the High Courts, resulting in a binding but complex jurisprudence. The conflicting or narrow nationalist kind of decision-making by the High Courts (in the 1990s) at times has given refugee sympathizers (such as the NHRC, the PUCL and Swajan) and concerned refugee groups (such as the Chakmas) the courage to come before the Supreme Court of India seeking redress as per the standards laid down by the comity of nations. It is also important to note that in the historical case of the Chakmas, the Supreme Court made the humanitarian space for the Chakmas, while the Union of India was busy primarily accusing the state of Arunachal Pradesh and the state of Arunachal Pradesh was not acting to protect the lives and liberty of the Chakmas. Though in a realistic situation there might be a conflict between the humanitarian situation and political considerations, here the Supreme Court of India created the space based on real considerations of life and liberty. To conclude this discussion of the judicial decisions of the Supreme Court, I can argue that the following points can be taken as granted in a refugee situation:

1. India is bound by the principle of non-refoulement subject to the condition that the presence of the concerned refugee poses no danger or threat to the security of the country. The lives and liberty of refugees in India are protected by Article 21 of the Constitution of India. Refugees and other foreigners represent two different categories of persons.
2. The Constitution of India mandates that the state shall endeavor to foster respect for international law and treaty obligations in the dealings of organized people with one another. Thus the comity of nations requires that rules of international law may be accommodated in the municipal law even without express legislative sanction.
3. The provisions of the international law instruments which elucidate and effectuate the fundamental rights guaranteed by the Indian Constitution can be relied upon by the courts as facets of those fundamental rights, and thus can be enforced by national courts.

CHAPTER 3

Parliamentary Proceedings, Response of National Human Rights Commission and Institutions Towards Refugees in India

3.1 Proceedings in the Parliament Regarding the Refugee Situation

The issues of the presence of refugees in India and related matters of rehabilitation, relief, detention, eviction and so forth have stormed both houses of the Indian Parliament. On various occasions Members of Parliament (MPs) have asked specific questions about relief and rehabilitation, detention and deportation, the process for granting citizenship, voluntary repatriation, national law of refugees, security concerns and so on. There have been continuous discussions since the beginning of the parliamentary system in India. However, the data related to these discussions are presently available from 13th Lok Sabha and the 174th Session of the Rajya Sabha onwards. Earlier data are not currently available due to the digitalization process currently being undertaken to preserve the data in digital format. MPs have shown interest in the refugee situation in India and have asked the government to take measures to mitigate the crisis. It can be concluded in general from the discussions that the MPs consider refugees a vulnerable class and insist that the government conceive an effective plan to reduce the plight of refugees by granting citizenship, expediting the citizenship granting process, proposing a new bill and so on. For the purpose of this research it is also important, apart from analyzing the preset laws on foreigners in India and the judicial protection given to refugees by the higher courts, to analyze the parliamentary discussions in order to identify a direction that

S.P. Sarker, *Refugee Law in India*,
DOI 10.1007/978-981-10-4807-4_3

may lead to consensus on a framework for refugee protection and provide political space to refugees in the largest democracy in the world. At the same time, it is important to note that the questions asked by the MPs in relation to refugees have been answered mostly by the Ministry of Home Affairs (MHA) on the basis of their available records and policy decisions. Ironically, therefore, the answers provided by the MHA have became a part of the largest set of primary data available from the Government of India. The following sections address and analyze these parliamentary proceedings.

3.1.1 Discussions in Rajya Sabha and Lok Sabha

Matters related to refugees were discussed in the Rajya Sabha from December 6, 1995, as per presently available data, until May 11, 2016. During this 20-year period, from the 174th to the 239th Session of the Rajya Sabha, matters related to refugees were discussed 106 times.[1] The 13th Lok Sabha discussions began on October 20, 1999 and continued until February 5, 2004. During this time the issues of refugee protection and related matters were discussed 27 times by way of replying to starred and un-starred questions by various ministries of the Government of India. Discussions in the 14th Lok Sabha ran from June 2, 2004 until February 26, 2009 and refugee-related matters were discussed 21 times during this period. In the 15th Lok Sabha discussions were held from June 1, 2009 through February 21, 2014, during which refugees issues were discussed 28 times. In the current 16th Lok Sabha, discussions related to refugees began on June 4, 2014, and as of August 10, 2016 issues related to refugees had been discussed 15 times. Thus, over the course of approximately 16 years in the proceedings of Lok Sabha, refugee-related matters were discussed 91 times.[2] It can be said that the number of discussions is not all that great, but their significance lies in the content, where documentation of the ever-shifting nature of the ad hoc policy of the Government of India, along with the discriminatory measures based on country of origin of refugees, were recorded. In the following sections some of these important discussions are emphasized and analyzed.

[1] See List of Questions Related to Refugees in Rajya Sabha.

[2] See List of Questions Related to Refugees in Lok Sabha.

3.1.1.1 Absence of Specific Law for Refugee Protection

It is a matter of great importance for research on refugee law in India to discover the reasons why the Government of India did not sign the Refugee Convention, as well as for its policy not to have national legislation pertaining to refugees. This section focuses on these matters in discussions in both houses of the Indian Parliament.

Regarding its reasons for not signing the Refugee Convention, the government initially explained that India regards the Refugee Convention and its Protocol as a partial regime that does not take into account conditions of refugee flows in developing countries and does not address questions of mixed flows.[3] It is very important to note that the government's reasons for not signing the Refugee Convention or its Protocol were elaborated on in the 14th Lok Sabha, and at the same time the government rejected the recommendation from the National Human Rights Commission to enact a national law for refugees.[4] The reasons as presented by the Minister of Home Affairs are as follows:

1. The Convention is only a partial regime for refugee protection.
2. The Convention and Protocol are designed primarily to deal with individual cases and not with situations of mass influx.
3. They do not adequately address situations faced by the developing countries.
4. The situations of mixed flows have not been adequately addressed as in many cases refugees are, in fact, economic migrants.
5. There is no balance between rights and obligations of receiving and source states.
6. The concept of international burden-sharing has not been developed adequately in the Convention.
7. The Convention and the Protocol do not address the question of minimum responsibility of states not to create refugee flows.
8. Cooperation with other states in the resolution of refugee problems has not been addressed in the Convention and its Protocol.

In the matter of enacting a law for refugees, the Government of India mentioned in the Rajya Sabha that while there has been an increase in

---

[3] Lok Sabha, Un-starred Question No. 3693, Answered on 13.12.2000.

[4] Lok Sabha, Un-starred Question No. 277, Answered on 21.02.2006.

the number of refugees, there is no major difficulty in dealing with the refugees as the existing laws are considered, by and large, adequate by the government.[5] Further, the government said in the Lok Sabha that it is not facing any major difficulties in dealing with the refugees as the existing laws are adequate, and so the question of enacting a new law does not arise while answering a question about whether, in the absence of any law, the government is finding it difficult to deal with refugee issues.[6] Interestingly, however, in 2002 the Minister of Law, Justice and Company Affairs of the Government of India told the Lok Sabha that a separate law to deal with refugees was being considered by the government.[7] He also mentioned that the government had started the process of consulting various agencies for this purpose. Again in 2005 in the Lok Sabha the MHA affirmed that the government had received a proposal for framing a national law for refugees, but the source of the proposal was not disclosed.[8] The statement also mentioned that the government asked for comments from various concerned governmental agencies on this matter. Again on the national law for refugees the government said before the Lok Sabha that a draft model law titled Refugee and Asylum Seekers Protection Act, 2000 was prepared by Justice P.N. Bhagwati and that the government had initiated the process of taking a final stand on this matter, keeping in view the existing domestic laws and national security considerations.[9]

In 2010 the question was again asked in the 15th Lok Sabha about the government's plan with regard to enacting legislation for the protection of refugees.[10] The government responded that a proposal to enact legislation to provide for the establishment of an effective system to protect refugees and asylum seekers, both before and after the grant of asylum and matters connected, was under consideration by the government and that it had not yet taken a final view of the matter. Ironically, however, in 2014, in response to a question about the government's consideration of enacting a law for refugees in India, the government put

[5] Rajya Sabha, Starred Question No. 2533, Answered on 16.08.2000.

[6] Lok Sabha, Starred Question No. 406, Answered on 22.08.2000.

[7] Lok Sabha, Un-starred Question No. 5631, Answered on 02.05.2002.

[8] Lok Sabha, Un-starred Question No. 3952, Answered on 20.12.2005.

[9] Lok Sabha, Starred Question No. 224, Answered on 08.08.2006.

[10] Lok Sabha, Un-starred Question No. 3943, Answered on 20.04.2010.

no direct reply to the question, whereas it mentioned that the standard operating procedure had been issued in 2011 to deal with foreign nationals who claim to be refugees.[11]

3.1.1.2 Arrival of Refugees, Number and Related Problems

It is largely accepted by the Government of India that there is no centrally maintained database of information about the refugee population in the country. However, the government has often provided estimates about specific refugee groups. In the case of the newly arriving Chakmas in Tripura, the government estimated that since 1986 as many as 56,543 Chakma refugees from Bangladesh had taken shelter in Tripura, of whom 11,911 had already been repatriated to Bangladesh.[12] As of 1997, 44,632 Bangladeshi refugees were still in Tripura. In response to a question in 2000, the government noted that a total of 1943 newly arrived refugees of Sri Lankan origin had been registered with the Chief Immigration Officer in Chennai, and the government had no data or estimates on the number of unregistered refugees.[13]

Regarding the number of refugees and their nationality, the government said that 233,672 foreigners from different countries had asked for refuge in India as of December 31, 2000, and ironically noted that only Tibetans and Sri Lankans are treated as refugees by the government.[14] In response to a question in the 15th Lok Sabha about the arrival, number and repatriation process of refugees from Sri Lanka, the government replied that a small number of Sri Lankan refugees continue to arrive in Rameswaram.[15] The reply also mentioned that as of May 31, 2009, a total of 101,162 refugees of Sri Lankan origin (73,695 refugees in camps, 27,467 outside camps) were living in the country and the government was following a policy of voluntary repatriation with respect to these refugees.

The government in the Lok Sabha mentioned that the continued presence of large numbers of refugees from various countries has created additional problems, including placing a financial burden upon the

[11] Rajya Sabha, Un-starred Question No. 2999, Answered on 06.08.2014.

[12] Rajya Sabha, Starred Question No. 82, Answered on 20.11.1997.

[13] Lok Sabha, Un-starred Question No. 2952, Answered on 14.03.2000.

[14] Lok Sabha, Starred Question No. 338, Answered on 16.04.2002.

[15] Lok Sabha, Un-starred Question No. 4423, Answered on 04.08.2009.

government.[16] In response to a question about possible security issues, the government replied that in order to safeguard against possible threats from Sri Lankan refugees, complete verification of the antecedents is undertaken by local police as soon as they arrive.[17] Refugees are then sent to different camps, and suspect persons are sent to special camps where their movement is restricted to the camp. The government also noted that state governments have been instructed from time to time to strengthen coastal security, and that the entry of refugees is discouraged through various measures. As a result of these efforts, the inflow of refugees up to July 2001 was only 348 as against 4977 in 1999 and 1620 in 2000 from Sri Lanka. However, in the 14th Lok Sabha in 2004, in response to a question about the increased refugee population in India and its adverse affect on the security, development and economy of the country, the government said that no such problem exists.[18]

3.1.1.3 Rehabilitation, Relief and Other Assistance for Refugees

The matter of discrimination in relation to rehabilitation, relief and other assistance has been clearly discussed in Parliament. With regard to a question about the rehabilitation of Bengali refugees from the 1947 partition, the government answered in the year 2000 that few were left with rehabilitation in West Bengal.[19] However, it was revealed that the rehabilitation of refugees who arrived in India along with His Holiness the Dalai Lama in 1959 has been completed.[20] In response to a question about Afghan refugees, the government noted that in keeping with the traditional policy of friendship towards the people of Afghanistan, all Afghan nationals, including those of Indian origin, who come to India with valid travel documents/passports are allowed to stay unhindered and are granted six months visa extensions.[21] The government also said that it would provide temporary shelter to Afghan refugees who do not support the Taliban who request such shelter in India.

---

[16] Lok Sabha, Un-starred Question No. 7820, Answered on 16.05.2000.
[17] Lok Sabha, Un-starred Question No. 4256, Answered on 21.08.2001.
[18] Lok Sabha, Un-starred Question No. 5874, Answered on 24.08.2004.
[19] Lok Sabha, Un-starred Question No. 768, Answered on 29.02.2000.
[20] Lok Sabha, Un-starred Question No. 1030, Answered on 07.12.2004.
[21] Lok Sabha, Un-starred Question No. 5433, Answered on 29.08.2001.

On the issue of the rehabilitation of refugees from Sri Lanka and Tibet, the government said that foreigners seeking refuge in India are not to be rehabilitated in India permanently but are to be provided relief pending their repatriation to their homeland, as per the policy guidelines of the Government of India.[22] In the case of Tibetan refugees, the Government of India has been providing assistance in the form of temporary settlement and the majority of these refugees have been settled either through self-employment or with the government's assistance through agricultural and handicraft schemes in different states of India.[23] In the case of Sri Lankan refugees, certain essentials such as shelter in camps, cash assistance, clothing and subsidized rations are provided on humanitarian grounds pending their repatriation. Again, the government informed the Rajya Sabha that Sri Lankan refugees residing in camps are provided with accommodation, electricity, drinking water and so forth free of cost.[24] In addition, other facilities such as monthly cash assistance, free clothing materials, utensils, subsidized rations and so on are provided. Further, the state governments (Tamil Nadu and Odisha) are also extending various welfare schemes such as the Girl Child Protection Scheme, Social Security Scheme, Maternity Financial Assistance Scheme, Marriage Assistance Scheme and others to Sri Lankan Tamil refugees in the camps.[25]

Ironically in the case of Tibetan refugees, it was made clear before the Rajya Sabha that the Tibetan refugees have been issued ration cards by various state governments and have been provided rehabilitation assistance under various agricultural and handicraft schemes.[26] In response to a question about rehabilitation of Tibetan refugees, the government informed the 15th Lok Sabha that some state governments had allotted land to Tibetan refugees for resettlement on a lease basis without proprietary rights.[27] Again on the issue of rehabilitation and assistance for Tibetan refugees the government replied before the Rajya Sabha that

[22]Lok Sabha, Un-starred Question No. 5470, Answered on 30.04.2002.

[23]See Dawa Norbu, 'Refugees from Tibet: Structural Causes of Successful Settlements' 26(2) The Tibet Journal 3, 8.

[24]Rajya Sabha, Starred Question No. 75, Answered on 02.03.2016.

[25]Rajya Sabha, Un-starred Question No. 1175, Answered on 04.05.2016.

[26]Rajya Sabha, Un-starred Question No. 494, Answered on 26.02.1997.

[27]Lok Sabha, Un-starred Question No. 4511, Answered on 30.08.2011.

the Tibetan Rehabilitation Policy, 2014 had been issued by the MHA.[28] Details of the benefits to be extended by state governments under the current Tibetan Rehabilitation Policy, 2014 are as follows:

1. The concerned State Governments must necessarily sign a lease document for the land occupied by the Tibetan Refugees. Such lease documents should be signed for a period of 20 years or till it is revoked/cancelled.
2. Rent Tenancy Certificate must be issued by the concerned State Governments.
3. The land under the occupation by Tibetan Refugees should not be disturbed.
4. Extending the benefits of the respective State Government Schemes as well as the Centrally sponsored schemes such as Mahatma Gandhi National Rural Employment Guarantee Scheme (MNREGS), Targeted Public Distribution System (TPDS) and National Food Security Act (NFSA), Indira Awas Yojana (IAY), National Rural Livelihood Mission (NRLM), Rajiv Awas Yojna (RAY), National Rural Health Mission (NRHM), etc.
5. Extending the infrastructural facilities and basic amenities like roads, electrification, and drinking water schemes in or around the Tibetan Settlements.
6. Undertaking skill up-gradation and training programmes for the Tibetan Refugees.
7. Permitting the Tibetan Refugees to run Tibetan Bazars to trade in Tibetan Artifacts, handlooms and handicrafts.
8. Tibetan refugees should be entitled for flood/famine relief as is extended to the Indian Citizens.
9. Qualified professionals from amongst the Tibetan Refugees may be permitted to pursue/take jobs in private and non-Government Sectors in any field for which they are professionally qualified.
10. Allowing the Tibetans to undertake such economic activities as they may desire and to that extent trade licenses/permission be given.

[28] Rajya Sabha, Starred Question No. 69, Answered on 29.04.2015.

3.1.1.4 Repatriation, Detention and Other Issues Related to Refugees

From several discussions in the Parliament it is now evident that the Government of India wants to prevent refugee inflows into India. On the issue of the influx of refugees from Sri Lanka, in a reply in the year 2000, the government noted that the state government and the central agencies in Tamil Nadu had been advised to take all possible measures, including intensified coastal patrolling, collection and collation of advance intelligence, and strengthening of naval detachments in Tamil Nadu, to limit the inflow.[29] However, because of the ongoing disturbances in Sri Lanka, no organized repatriation was possible. This reply also noted that the government continuously made efforts to repatriate the refugees and to prevent others from entering India. In response to a question about the places of residence of Sri Lankan refugees and their repatriation process, the government replied that the refugees were staying in the states of Tamil Nadu and Odisha, primarily in camps and special camps.[30] This reply also mentioned that the Government of India was waiting for the consent of the Sri Lankan Government to repatriate these refugees back to Sri Lanka. The policy of strict measures to prevent fresh refugee influx from Sri Lanka was still in place in 2010, and the government affirmed that its approach is to discourage the entry of Sri Lankan refugees.[31] However, when Sri Lankan refugees do arrive, they are granted relief in the refugee camps and kept there with the ultimate object of repatriation back to Sri Lanka. This reply also referred to a proposal from the Chief Minister of Tamil Nadu suggesting the possible permanent settlement of Sri Lankan Tamil refugees in Tamil Nadu.

On the issue of detaining and deporting refugees from Myanmar, a question was asked about the notice issued by the National Human Rights Commission to the Government of India and the Government of Mizoram for the alleged detention and forcible deportation of Chin refugees to Myanmar.[32] The government replied that the National Human Rights Commission had issued notices to the central and state governments in response to an Amnesty International report alleging the forcible return of ethnic Chin asylum seekers from Myanmar. The

[29] Lok Sabha, Un-starred Question No. 270, Answered on 25.07.2000.

[30] Lok Sabha, Un-starred Question No. 3397, Answered on 20.03.2001.

[31] Rajya Sabha, Un-starred Question No. 1445, Answered on 10.03.2010.

[32] Lok Sabha, Un-starred Question No. 3575, Answered on 12.12.2000.

Government of Mizoram confirmed that a special drive had been carried out to detect and push back only those nationals of Myanmar who were indulging in illicit practices, and claimed that the state government is empowered to do so according to various laws for dealing with foreigners. In response to a question about demonstrations by Tibetans in India against China, the government replied that India recognizes the Tibet Autonomous Region as part of the territory of the People's Republic of China and does not allow Tibetans to engage in anti-China political activities in India.[33] However, the Tibetan refugee community in India had demonstrated peacefully in many parts of India, including Himachal Pradesh, Goa, Karnataka, Arunachal Pradesh, Jammu & Kashmir, Uttarakhand, Meghalaya, Assam, Union Territory of Chandigarh, Uttar Pradesh, Maharashtra, West Bengal, Orissa and Tamil Nadu.

3.1.1.5 Citizenship for Refugees

The government clarified its position regarding the Chakma refugees of Arunachal Pradesh when a question was asked in the 14th Lok Sabha about the steps already taken, or being taken, by the government to deport the Chakma and Hajong refugees temporarily settled in the state of Arunachal Pradesh.[34] In reply, the government said that as per the decision of the Supreme Court of India, Chakma refugees settled in Arunachal Pradesh would not be evicted on the grounds that they are not citizens of India until the Government of India had taken a decision on their applications for citizenship. In response to a question about Tibetan refugees and their right to citizenship, the government replied that approximately 150,000 Tibetan refugees were living in India and that the children of Tibetan refugees who were born between January 26, 1950 and July 1, 1987 are citizens of India by birth.[35]

On the matter of granting citizenship and other necessary support to Pakistani refugees from minority communities, the government said in the Rajya Sabha that persons who migrated from Pakistan to India are considered for citizenship under the Citizenship Act, 1955 and minorities from Pakistan are eligible for the long-term visa (LTV).[36] In

[33] Rajya Sabha, Starred Question No. 456, Answered on 24.04.2008.

[34] Lok Sabha, Un-starred Question No. 5875, Answered on 24.08.2004.

[35] Rajya Sabha, Un-starred Question No. 1483, Answered on 09.03.2011.

[36] Rajya Sabha, Un-starred Question No. 507, Answered on 13.08.2014.

addition, Pakistani minorities who have been granted an LTV can take up any employment in the private sector as per standard operating procedure.

3.1.1.6 Standard Operating Procedure and Exemption

In response to a question about the present policy on determination of refugee status and further protection, the government replied that a guideline was issued in 2011 to allow refugees to receive LTVs and take up employment in the private sector or undertake studies in any academic institution.[37] In the 16th Lok Sabha, in response to a question about the standard operating procedure, the government replied that under the standard operating procedure, a person claiming to be a refugee on the grounds of a well-founded fear of persecution on account of race, religion, sex, nationality, ethnic identity, membership of a particular social group or political opinion, can be recommended by the state government/union territory administration to the MHA for an LTV.[38] These persons are also eligible to apply for citizenship under the Citizenship Act. In response to a question about granting asylum to foreigners fleeing religious persecution, the government replied in the Rajya Sabha that it had circulated a standard operating procedure to all state governments/union territories on December 29, 2011 for dealing with foreign nationals who claim to be refugees.[39] However, in response to a question in the 16th Lok Sabha, the government said it had issued notification to regularize the entry and stay of persons belonging to minority communities in Bangladesh and Pakistan who were compelled to seek shelter in India due to religious persecution or fear of religious persecution and who entered India on or before December 31, 2014.[40]

3.1.1.7 Introduction of Bills in Lok Sabha

Three new bills have been introduced in the Lok Sabha, namely the Asylum Bill, 2015 by Dr. Sashi Tharoor, MP; the National Asylum Bill, 2015 by Feroze Varun Gandhi, MP; and the Protection of Refugees and

---

[37] Lok Sabha, Un-starred Question No. 7538, Answered on 22.05.2012.

[38] Lok Sabha, Un-starred Question No. 739, Answered on 15.07.2014.

[39] Rajya Sabha, Un-starred Question No. 2744, Answered on 17.12.2014.

[40] Lok Sabha, Un-starred Question No. 894, Answered on 01.03.2016.

Asylum Seekers Bill, 2015 by Rabindra Kumar Jena, MP The provisions of these bills are discussed in greater detail in Chap. 7.

3.1.2 Exposure of an Inconsistent and Discriminatory Policy

It important to note that discussion about a policy for refugees must address the following issues: a definition of the term refugee and its scope, the concept of non-refoulement and its scope, the administrative-judicial machinery to determine the status of asylum seekers, and the amount of assistance required by the refugee.[41] Within a policy of refugee protection the issues of safe arrival, relief, rehabilitation, other humane assistance, and political support from the government and the community are the key elements to be decided by the government. However, it has been shown that none of these matters have been considered in the government's policy of refugee protection in India. Ironically, the issue of refugee protection in India has in fact given the government enormous power to decide to whom to provide protection, deny such protection, or take a middle way and provide some while denying most.[42]

Discussions in the Parliament of India revealed very clearly that some refugee groups are well cared for and provided with relief, rehabilitation and other assistance, while at the same time others are refused, neglected or intentionally overlooked. This policy is actually a result of "calculated

[41] Ranabir Samaddar, 'Introduction' in Ranabir Samaddar (ed), *Refugees and the State: Practices of Asylum and Care in India, 1947–2000* (SAGE, New Delhi 2003) 21.

[42] See generally Annu Jalais, 'Dwelling on Morichjhanpi: When Tigers Became Citizens, Refugees Tiger-Food' [2005] 40(17) Economic & Political Weekly 1757–1762; K. Maudood Elahi, 'Refugees in Dandakaranya' [1981] 15 (1/2) The International Migration Review 219–225; Ross Mallick, 'Refugee Resettlement in Forest Reserves: West Bengal Policy Reversal and the Marichjhapi Massacre' [1999] 58(1) The Journal of Asian Studies 104–125; Victor Barnouw, 'The Sindhis, Mercantile Refugees in India: Problems of Their Assimilation' [1966] 27(1) Phylon40–49; Joya Chatterji, ''Dispersal' and the Failure of Rehabilitation: Refugee Camp-dwellers and Squatters in West Bengal' [2007] 41(5) Modern Asian Studies 995–1032.

[43] The "calculation" in the kindness refers to the admission of refugees into the United States of America from communist countries as a way of underlining a political message. The door was "half open" because almost no refugees from right-wing dictatorships have been admitted. For further discussion on calculated kindness based on America's history of providing asylum to refugees from communist countries, see Gil Loescher and John

kindness,"[43] or in other words a "strategic ambiguity"[44] that questions the ethics of care for refugees. Within the policy of refugee protection in India, it is noteworthy that national security considerations played a significant role in the case of refugees from Sri Lanka, while humanitarian considerations played a crucial role in the settlement of Tibetans and more recently minority groups from Pakistan and Bangladesh. For other refugees, it remains unclear who will protect them and how their well-being will be protected, and for what reasons, in India. Parliamentary discussions very clearly reveal the government's inconsistent and discriminatory policy, which is not properly based on the hospitality principle, national security concerns, or obligations of international law; rather, it remains a mystery based on policy-making by a postcolonial state that defines its care of refugees with an aim to wield power in geopolitical discourse.[45]

3.2 Role of National Human Rights Commission in Refugee Protection in India

The National Human Rights Commission (NHRC) was established under the Protection of Human Rights Act, 1993.[46] As per the functions of the NHRC, the following were operational at times to intervene on behalf of refugee groups in India: inquiry of petition presented to the NHRC by a victim or any person on his/her behalf into a complaint of

---

Footnote 43 (continued)
A. Scanlan, 'Calculated Kindness: Refugees and America's Half Open Door, 1945 to the Present' *The Free Press* (New York 1986) 209.

[44] See B. S. Chimni, 'Status of Refugees in India: Strategic Ambiguity' in Ranabir Samaddar (ed), ***Refugees and the State: Practices of Asylum and Care in India**, 1947–2000* (SAGE, New Delhi 2003) 443.

[45] See generally Omar Chaudhary, 'Turning Back: An Assessment of Non-Refoulement under Indian Law' [2004] 39(29) Economic & Political Weekly 3257–3264; Abhijit Dasgupta, 'Repatriation of Sri Lankan Refugees: Unfinished Tasks' [2003] 38(24) Economic & Political Weekly 2365–2367; Gautam Ghosh, 'God is a Refugee: Nationality, Morality and History in the 1947 Partition of India' [1998] 42(1) The International Journal of Social and Cultural Practice 33–62.

[46] Act No. 10 of 1994.

violation of human rights or acting *suo moto*;[47] review of the constitutional and legal safeguards provided for the protection of human rights and recommendation of measures for their effective implementation;[48] and study of treaties and other international instruments on human rights and recommendations for their effective implementation.[49] The interventions of the NHRC are discussed categorically in the following sections.

3.2.1 Response to Forcible Eviction of Chakma Refugees

The annual reports of the NHRC have documented its actions to protect refugees in India since 1994. The cases of Chakma and Hajong refugees settled in Arunachal Pradesh were first reflected in the NHRC's annual report of 1994–1995.[50] This report described the background of the problem and the actions taken by the NHRC in this regard. The report states that the NHRC received representations from the People's Union for Civil Liberties (PUCL) and Amnesty International regarding the plight of Chakma and Hajong refugees living in Arunachal Pradesh.[51] The representations stated that these groups, comprising respectively Buddhists and Hindus, had fled on grounds of religious persecution from the Chittagong Hill Tracts between the years 1964 and 1971. They were first settled in Assam and then shifted to present-day Arunachal Pradesh. The NHRC also received representation from members of the Chakma community about the process of evicting them from Arunachal Pradesh by use of political force, which was supported by the state government.[52]

The NHRC, in a communication to the state government of Arunachal Pradesh on September 29, 1994, stated that it was the obligation of that government to accord protection to the persons and property of the members of those communities and to ensure that

[47] Ibid. Section 12(a).

[48] Ibid. Section 12(d).

[49] Ibid. Section 12(f).

[50] Annual Report, National Human Rights Commission [1994–1995] 41–42.

[51] See generally Nirmala Chandrahasan, 'Access to Justice and Aliens: Some Insights into Refugee Groups in India' [1998] 16 Windsor Yearbook of Access to Justice 135, 142.

[52] See Chunnu Prasad, 'Students' Movements in Arunachal Pradesh and the Chakma-Hajong Refugee Problem' [2007] 42(15) Economic & Political Weekly 1373, 1375.

their human rights were not violated, and asked for a detailed report on the situation. It also urged the MHA to ensure prompt and necessary action by the state government. The state government in its reply stated that the lives and property of members of the two communities were not under threat and that an adequate police force had been deployed to protect them. The MHA reported that the state government of Arunachal Pradesh had been advised to ensure normalcy in the law and order situation and to provide essential commodities and medical facilities to the Chakma and Hajong refugees. As regards the granting of citizenship, the MHA reported that the matter was under consideration, in consultation with the state government. The NHRC Chairperson addressed another letter on December 7, 1994 to the Union Home Minister and also to the Chief Minister of Arunachal Pradesh, stressing the need to provide adequate protection to the members of these two communities with a view not only towards instilling in them a sense of safety and security, but also in order to ensure that their human rights were fully respected.

Thereafter, the NHRC's annual report of 1995–1996 laid out the background for its filing of the famous "Chakma Case" before the Supreme Court of India. The report stated that after receiving fresh complaints in this matter and recognizing the gravity of the situation, the NHRC issued a direction to the state government of Arunachal Pradesh on October 29–30, 1995.[53] The NHRC decided to approach the Supreme Court of India through a writ petition to enforce the constitutional right to life under Article 21 of the Constitution of India, as it was uncertain whether the efforts taken would be effective and sufficient to sustain the Chakmas in their own residential habitat.[54] The case was decided in favor of the Chakmas, as discussed in Chap. 2.[55]

---

[53] Annual Report, National Human Rights Commission [1995–1996] 61–62.

[54] The National Human Rights Commission took this step under Section 18(b) of the Protection of Human Rights Act, 1993 which reads: "Section 18. Steps during and after inquiry: The Commission may take any of the following steps during or upon the completion of an inquiry held under this Act, namely:- (b) approach the Supreme Court or the High Court concerned for such directions, orders or writs as that Court may deem necessary."

[55] *National Human Rights Commission v. State of Arunachal Pradesh and Anr,* (1996) 1 SCC 742. See also Chunnu Prasad, 'Migration and the Question of Citizenship: People of Chittagong Hill Tract in Arunachal Pradesh' [2006] 67(3) The Indian Journal of Political Science 471, 480.

3.2.2 *Steps Towards Signing the Refugee Convention*

After the successful conclusion of the Chakma refugee case in the Supreme Court of India, the activities of the NHRC then shifted towards a dialogic model with the Government of India to find a way to sign the 1951 Refugee Convention. This initiative was first mentioned in the NHRC's annual report of 1997–1998.[56] It was reported that on October 2, 1997, the NHRC initiated a dialogue with senior officers of the Ministry of External Affairs, Government of India requesting them to examine afresh the possibility of India becoming party to the 1951 United Nations Convention Relating to the Status of Refugees and the 1967 Protocol.[57] The Secretary of the Ministry of Foreign Affairs responded that the Ministry would look into the matter and send reports to the NHRC, which was appreciated by the NHRC.[58] Afterwards, the Ministry of External Affairs informed the NHRC that the matter was being re-examined in consultation with other concerned ministries and departments.[59] The NHRC noted this development with appreciation and recommended that the Ministry of External Affairs constitute a small group of experts to look into the matter expeditiously. However, there were no further developments on this initiative as there was a significant delay on the part of the government to devise a possible solution. Afterwards, the NHRC began to put more emphasis on formulating a national law for the protection of refugees.

3.2.3 *Steps Towards a National Refugee Law*

The NHRC's views regarding the necessity of India developing a national policy and possibly a national law, fully in line with the 1951 United Nations Convention Relating to the Status of Refugees and the 1967 Protocol, gained strength as the NHRC continued to receive complaints about human rights violations against refugees from various parts of India.[60] During this period, the NHRC continued to take *suo moto* cognizance of news items highlighting the plight of Sri Lankan

---

[56] Annual Report, National Human Rights Commission [1997–1998] 24.

[57] Ibid. Para.4.12.

[58] Ibid. Para.4.13.

[59] Ibid. Para.4.14.

[60] Annual Report, National Human Rights Commission [1999–2000] 45–46.

refugees in Tamil Nadu, Karnataka and elsewhere. It is mentioned in the report that the Government of India indicated that the possibility of enacting relevant legislation as well as the possibility of signing the 1951 Convention Relating to the Status of Refugees and the 1967 Protocol was under consideration. The annual report of 2000–2001 described further initiatives by the NHRC with regard to the matter of a national law,[61] and related several complaints it had received from non-governmental organizations alleging inconsistency and discrimination in refugee-related policy on the basis of country of origin, particularly in the matter of forced repatriation.[62] The Government of India reported to the NHRC that a legal framework to deal with refugee issues already exists in the relevant provisions of the Indian Constitution, and that India undertakes its obligations under various international human rights instruments, particularly the International Covenant on Civil and Political Rights (ICCPR), and a series of judicial pronouncements. In addition, refugee-specific legislation has been enacted whenever necessary, such as the legislation dealing with refugees from Pakistan in the period 1947–1950 and the Foreigners from Uganda Order, 1972. However, the NHRC found the reply of the Government of India unconvincing and opined that a comprehensive national law should be devised, keeping in view the decisions of the Supreme Court as well as international law instruments on the subject.[63] Following this, the annual report of 2002–2003 detailed the NHRC's activities in support of a national law for refugees[64] The NHRC stressed that comprehensive national legislation to deal with refugees in India should distinguish between bona fide refugees and economic migrants, illegal immigrants and other foreigners.[65] The NHRC criticized the government for holding membership in the Executive Committee of the office of the United Nations High Commissioner for Refugees (UNHCR) while remaining reluctant to enact a national law for refugees. The NHRC further opined that greater priority should be given to this matter by the Government of India as the existing laws, regulations and practices in respect of refugees

[61] Annual Report, National Human Rights Commission [2000–2001] 46–47.

[62] Ibid. Para.4.23.

[63] Ibid. Para.4.24.

[64] Annual Report, National Human Rights Commission [2002-2003] 75–76.

[65] Ibid. Para.5.20.

are inadequate for the present time and the possible challenges that are likely to arise in the future.[66]

Finally, in its annual report of 2003–2004 the NHRC noted that the MHA had sought the views and comments of the NHRC on the Model National Law on Refugees prepared by Justice P.N. Bhagwati.[67] The NHRC then formed an expert committee consisting of persons with knowledge in the field of refugee protection and laws to comment on this matter considering humanitarian considerations, security concerns and other related aspects.[68] However, after the constitution of this expert committee there were no further deliberations by the NHRC in this regard, and the annual reports of the NHRC from 2005 to the present day have been silent on efforts towards a national law for refugees, for reasons that are unclear.

3.3 UNHCR Operation in India

In the matter of refugee protection in India, the role of UNHCR is seen to be limited in terms of the number of refugees they assist. Though there exists a central database to provide an accurate number of the refugees present in India, the UNHCR website shows that in June 2015 the total number of refugees in India was 205,764.[69] Out of this population only 30,000 refugees were registered with UNHCR in New Delhi.[70] Thus, the main principle of UNHCR's operation in India is burden-sharing. As per the estimate given by the Government of India, the number of refugees under its mandate is about 211,911.[71] As a matter of policy of the Government of India, the mandate of UNHCR is limited to refugees from countries other than Sri Lanka, Tibet, Pakistan and Bangladesh.[72] Among the refugees registered with UNHCR in India, most are from Afghanistan and Myanmar, while others are from countries in Africa, Central Asia and Middle East. However, UNHCR has also

---

[66] Ibid. Para.5.21

[67] Annual Report, National Human Rights Commission [2003–2004] 55

[68] Ibid. Para.5.22.

[69] UNHCR Sub-regional Operations Profile- South Asia [2015] http://www.unhcr.org/pages/49e4876d6.html accessed November 19, 2015.

[70] Ibid.

[71] Lok Sabha, Un-starred Question No. 6307, Answered on: 05.05.2015.

[72] Chimni (n 44) 459.

assisted refugee groups who are under the mandate of the Government of India when such assistance has been requested.

At the request of the Government of India, UNHCR began to provide assistance to Tibetan refugees in India in 1964 through the League of Red Cross Societies.[73] In 1969 an agreement was signed with the Government of India to permit UNHCR to establish a branch office in New Delhi to coordinate a more substantial program of assistance to Tibetan refugees.[74] During the war of independence of Bangladesh in 1971, UNHCR acted as a focal point for assisting the refugees from what was then East Pakistan who had fled to India.[75] As most of the monetary assistance was disbursed through the Government of India, neither the government nor the UNHCR considered setting up a proper office. However, in 1975 UNHCR wrote to the Foreign Minister of India that it would be closing its New Delhi branch office and deploying its staff to Portuguese colonies in Africa, which were in a state of transition due to decolonization.[76] According to the Government of India, this decision was politically motivated, as Chinese diplomats at the United Nations had strongly criticized UNHCR's provision of assistance to Tibetan refugees in India. However, in 1980–1981 UNHCR restarted its operation under the auspices of the United Nations Development Programme.[77] Based on an agreement signed in 1992, UNHCR was allowed to open one field office in Chennai to assist Sri Lankan Tamil refugees in the matter of repatriation.[78] Thus the UNHCR operation is generally focused on determination of refugee status for those who have applied to its office in New Delhi, as well as

[73] Sarbani Sen, 'Paradoxes of the International Regime of Care: The Role of the UNHCR in India' in Ranabir Samaddar (ed), *Refugees and the State: Practices of Asylum and Care in India, 1947-2000* (SAGE, New Delhi 2003) 396, 399.

[74] Ibid.; see generally Franz Michael, 'Survival of a Culture: Tibetan Refugees in India' [1985] 25(7) Asian Survey 737, 739; Dorsh Marie de Voe, 'The Refugee Problem and Tibetan Refugees' [1981] 6(3) Tibet Journal 22, 25.

[75] Sen (n73) 400.

[76] Sen (n73) 401.

[77] Chimni (n 44) 458; see also Mike Sanderson, 'The Role of International Law in Defining the Protection of Refugees in India' [2015] 33 Wisconsin International Law Journal 55.

[78] Chimni (n 44) 459; sanderson (n 77) 56.

repatriation assistance for Sri Lankan refugees in Chennai.[79] Apart from these, other activities carried out by UNHCR include[80]

1. promoting Model Law and National Legislation;
2. partnerships with other international organizations such as the Asian-African Legal Consultative Organization (AALCO);
3. sensitization of politicians and parliamentarians;
4. building awareness among non-governmental organizations;
5. building awareness with media;
6. outreach to schools;
7. promoting refugee research and studies in India;
8. surveying existing laws and judicial decisions;
9. promoting refugee protection principles with bureaucrats and others.

The Executive Committee of the High Commissioner's Program (ExCom) was established in 1959 by a resolution of the Economic and Social Council of the United Nations.[81] ExCom plays a significant role in setting UNHCR policy vis-à-vis standards for international protection, and its mandate in the UNHCR statute to make policy directives, and the High Commissioner's obligation to follow such directives, leaves little room for doubt that the conclusions of ExCom are binding on the High Commissioner.[82] Ironically, India became a member of the ExCom in 1995. India's move in this regard was very careful, as ExCom membership is not considered de facto acceptance of the obligations of the 1951 Refugee Convention or 1967 Protocol.

---

[79] Sanderson (n 77) 56.

[80] Rose Varghese, 'Country Paper—India', *Presented at the Seventh Informal Regional Consultation on Refugees and Migratory Movements in South Asia* (December 15–16, 2002 New Delhi).

[81] See United Nations, G.A. Re s. 1166 (XII), 5, U.N. Doc. A/RES/I 166 (XII), Nov. 26, 1957; Economic and Social Council, Establishment of the Executive Committee of the Programme of the United Nations High Commissioner for Refugees, E.S.C. Res. 672 (XXV), 1(a), E/RES/672, April 30, 1958.

[82] Sanderson (n 77) 58; Jerry Sztucki, 'The Conclusions on the International Protection of Refugees Adopted by the Executive Committee of the UNHCR Programme' [1989] 1 International Journal of Refugee Law 298.

3.4 Role of Eminent Persons Group

The Eminent Persons Group (EPG) was established in 1994, primarily for three important reasons: to obtain the views and support of eminent personnel and former government officials of the South Asian region; to develop a South Asian perspective on the pathways that would lead to a lasting solution; and to find ways of reconciling the narrow power-political interests of states with their international humanitarian responsibilities.[83] It is noteworthy that the EPG has played a primary role in some regional initiatives for refugee protection in South Asia. The protection of refugees in this region is heavily dependent on inter-state policy, as none of the South Asian countries are party to the Refugee Convention. It is always assumed by defenders of refugee rights that refugee policy in this region is based on the belief that "when there is no law, everything becomes arbitrary," and this can be said to be true in most cases.[84] The attempt by the EPG to bring a uniform model of refugee protection to South Asia through systematic dialogue between governments and other organizations is admirable.[85] The most important step in this regard was taken in 1997 at Dhaka by the EPG under the Chairmanship of Justice P.N. Bhagwati to frame a Model National Law for Refugees (MNLR), to act as a guide for the governments of South Asian countries to frame their own national laws.[86] This consultation was so persuasive that the Law Minister of Bangladesh accepted a copy of the MNLR from the Chairperson to place before the Parliamentary Committee of Law and Justice.[87] However, since then no South Asian country has passed a law relating to the protection of refugees, and the EPG has failed to intervene with the governments. There were suggestions for discussions by the governments at the South Asian Association for Regional Cooperation (SAARC) level on the basis of the MNLR

[83] Pia Oberoi, 'Regional Initiatives on Refugee Protection in South Asia' [1999] 11 International Journal of Refugee Law 197, 198.

[84] See generally Markandey Katju, 'India's Perception of Refugee Law' [2001] 1 ISIL Yearbook of International Humanitarian and Refugee Law 251; V. Suryanarayan, 'Need for National Refugee Law' [2001] 11 ISIL Yearbook of International Humanitarian and Refugee Law 254, 254.

[85] See B. S. Chimni, 'Reforming the International Refugee Regime: The Dialogic Model' [2001] 14(2) Journal of Refugee Studies 151, 162.

[86] Oberoi (n 83) 198.

[87] Oberoi (n 83) 199.

and national-level dialogue among government agencies, human rights organizations and UNHCR to find a durable solution for refugee protection.[88] In this context, it is unclear why none of the South Asian countries pursued these consultations, especially India.

The decision by India and many other South Asian countries not to enact a national refugee law is largely the result of their political ignorance, historical mishaps, unstable democratic conditions and exaggerated concerns over security issues.[89] It is true that various decisions by the High Courts and Supreme Court of India provide a semblance of a refugee protection scheme which is not rights-based but rather humanitarian in nature.[90] In fact, these kinds of interim, person-based orders have very little effect on the development of refugee law jurisprudence. However, the judiciary now recognizes refugees as a class of persons, and refugee law in India has been introduced via the back door.[91] Finally, the MNLR prepared by the EPG during the Dhaka Summit, which keeps an eye on the definition of refugee, the system of status determination, incorporating rights and duties of both refugees and receiving states, and striking a balance between humanitarian considerations and security concerns after 9/11, is seen to be phenomenal.[92] At the same time, the geopolitics of the South Asian region may not allow any country to compromise itself by incorporating the MNLR in its national legislative system, as every country has security and economic stability concerns.[93] However, the text of the MNLR will be a valuable resource for countries in forming their own national legislation for refugee protection.[94] It is

[88] Oberoi (n 83) 201.

[89] Probodh Saxena, 'Creating Legal Space for Refugees in India: the Milestones Crossed and the Roadmap for the Future' [2007] 19 International Journal of Refugee Law 246, 272.

[90] See T. Ananthachari, 'Refugees in India: Legal Framework, Law Enforcement and Security' [2001] 1ISIL Yearbook of International Humanitarian and Refugee Law 119.

[91] Ibid. 249.

[92] See generally Arun Sagar and Farrah Ahmed, 'The Model Law for Refugees: An Important Step Forward?' [2005] 17 Student Bar Review 74.

[93] See B.S. Chimni, 'The Geopolitics of Refugee Studies: A View from the South' [1998] 11(4) Journal of Refugee Studies 350, 352.

[94] See Fali S. Nariman, 'Refugee Protection' [2002] 2ISIL Yearbook of International Humanitarian and Refugee Law 07, 10; see generally Ranabir Samaddar, 'Institutional Requirement on Protection and Care of the Victims of Forced Migration in South Asia' [2002] 2 ISIL Yearbook of International Humanitarian and Refugee Law 74, 75.

important to note that the NHRC in India regarded the MNLR very positively and encouraged the Government of India to enact a national law for refugees, although without success.[95]

3.5 Conclusion

The descriptive study presented in this chapter suggests that there is a mixed situation in terms of arrival of refugees, such that the majority of the refugee population arrived as part of a mass influx (i.e. refugees from Tibet, Sri Lanka, Myanmar, Afghanistan and the former East Pakistan—presently Bangladesh), while a small number arrived individually (i.e. those from countries in Central Asia, Middle East and Africa). It has also been shown that after their arrival, refugees experience different conditions based on their nationality and the size of their population. For example, Tibetan refugees have received far more relief, rehabilitation and other assistance than any other refugee group in India. Though Sri Lankans also arrived in large numbers, they have received far fewer entitlements from the government than the Tibetan refugees have. It is also important to note that the Government of India has never given any reason for the discriminatory treatment of refugees on the basis of nationality. However, the current policy of standard operating procedure for refugees is seen to be an instrument that does not differentiate between nationalities in terms of earning a livelihood and educational opportunities.[96] At the same time, there is no available data from the government reviewing the implementation of the standard operating procedure in terms of its success or failure. The framing of the MNLR by the EPG, and the NHRC's taking it under consideration, had been viewed as a very positive step in the period from 1996 to 2000. At the same time, the Government of India's reluctance to establish a proper legislative framework is obvious in that it has taken almost 16 years to decide about the possibility of enacting such legislation for refugees.[97]

It is also evident that the "calculated kindness" shown towards the refugees in India has been questioned by parliamentarians, the NHRC and civil society organizations. In such a situation of "calculated

---

[95] See Section 3.2.3 for elaborate discussion.

[96] See Section 3.1.1.6 for elaborate discussion.

[97] See Section 3.1.1.1 and Section 3.2.3 for elaborate discussion.

kindness," only a human rights-based approach can bring balance to the protection mandate.[98] Meanwhile, the burdens faced by the Government of India and UNHCR in terms of caseload is massively unequal. From the side of the government, various central and state administrative agencies are involved in refugee-related matters. In order to equalize the practice of Tibetan resettlement, the government issued a standardized policy for all state governments. However, no such resettlement policy exists for the other refugee groups present in India. Therein lies the major challenge, from the perspective of human rights: to formulate an equal human rights-centric policy to extend uniform treatment across the different refugee groups.[99] In other words, there is a need to ensure the prevention of discrimination between refugee groups in relation to the kinds of assistance and opportunities provided to them.[100] Therefore, a new approach to the overall protection framework in situations of mass entry and in situations of individual entry should focus on all relevant factors, such as status determination, temporary protection, measures for the social security of refugees, planning for a durable solution and so forth. Parliamentarians and related organizations have set this as a goal for the future.[101]

---

[98] Samaddar (n 94) 86.

[99] B.S. Chimni, 'The Legal Condition of Refugees in India' [1994] 7 Journal of Refugee Studies 378, 400.

[100] Ibid.

[101] See generally Saurabh Bhattacharjee, 'India Needs a Refugee Law' [2008] 43(9) Economic & Political Weekly 71, 75.

CHAPTER 4

Field Study on Condition of Refugees in India

4.1 Approach of the Empirical Study

Methodology refers to the strategies used to collect information required for a particular research project. It is generally important to include reflection on the ideas and propositions that lie behind the techniques. Numerous approaches are used and available for the examination that fulfills the requirements of an investigation as methods of social research are closely tied to different visions of how social reality should be studied.[1] This section reviews of the exploration approach, plan, examining outline, information gathering and evaluation systems included in leading the study and the tools included to examine the planned research theory.

For the purpose of the present research, interpretivism is embraced as the paradigm. On the basis of the connection between theory and research, epistemological considerations and ontological considerations, there are two distinct forms of research strategy: quantitative and qualitative.[2] This study employs the qualitative approach as its investigative method.

[1] Alan Bryman, *Social Research Methods* (Oxford University Press, 2001) 05.
[2] Bryman (n 1) 20.

S.P. Sarker, *Refugee Law in India*,
DOI 10.1007/978-981-10-4807-4_4

Table 4.1 Number of Refugees Recognized from 2000 to 2014 (by Country) by UNHCR in India

Country Name	*Recognized Refugees*	*Country Name*	*Recognized Refugees*	*Country Name*	*Recognized Refugees*
Afghanistan	5696	Pakistan	66	Turkmenistan	01
Angola	01	Palestine	349	Uganda	01
Bangladesh	04	Romania	03	Uzbekistan	03
Cameroon	01	Russia	03	Yemen	06
China	09	Rwanda	11	Maldives	03
Ivory Coast	11	Saudi Arabia	01	Myanmar	17252
Congo	59	Sierra Leone	01	Iran	201
Cuba	01	Somalia	1218	Iraq	259
Egypt	01	Sudan	165	Israel	13
Eritrea	81	Syria	36	Liberia	01
Ethiopia	55	Togo	01	Libya	01

Source UNHCR Population Statistics, http://popstats.unhcr.org/en/overview

4.1.1 Data Collection Technique and Sampling Design

The primary materials have been collected through interviews using a structured, open-ended schedule.[3] In this case, the interviews were in the form of discussion between the refugee and the researcher.[4] In these discussions one character, the researcher, is seeking answers on different matters, for a particular purpose, from the other person, the refugee (Tables 4.1 and 4.2).

Considering the huge refugee population in India, it was essential to come up with a sample size and selection strategy for conducting the interviews. A sampling outline or plan is a strategy used to choose the target audience from the available open populace/sampling frame. There are two sorts of sampling methods: probability sampling and non-probability sampling. This investigation follows the convenience sampling method, which is a non-probability sampling method.[5] As the name suggests, the sample is distinguished essentially by the convenience of the researcher. The target population of the study is the refugees residing in India who can be easily found or contacted for interviews (Fig. 4.1).

[3] See Annexure II.

[4] M. Denscombe, *The Good Research Guide* (McGraw-Hill International USA 2007) 173.

Table 4.2 Refugees Registered by Govt. of India until 2014

Country Name	*Recognized Refugees*
Sri Lanka	101,896
Tibet	110,095

Source Parliamentary Question No. 6307, answered on May 5, 2015, Lok Sabha

Fig. 4.1 Summary Flow—Data Collection

4.2 Data Analysis and Interpretation

[6]The examination method utilized in this study for the evaluation of the collected data is text analysis. For the purpose of data analysis and interpretation the qualitative data interpretation software NVivo 11 has been used (Fig. 4.2).

4.2.1 Description of Interviewed Refugees

For the purpose of interviewing, a total of 114 refugees have been selected through a convenience sampling method. The interviews were conducted in New Delhi, Darjeeling and Chennai with the help of UNHCR India, the Bosco Refugee Assistance Program and the Tibetan Settlement Office in Darjeeling in April and May 2016. Refugee groups represented in the interviews were from Afghanistan (28 interviews), Iran (3 interviews), Iraq (2 interviews), Myanmar (29 interviews), Somalia (9 interviews), Sri Lanka (17 interviews), Sudan (4 interviews) and Tibet (22 interviews). Of the refugees interviewed, 36 were female and 78 were male. The

[5]Peter Reason, 'Choice and Quality in Action Research Practice' [2006] 15 Journal of Management Inquiry 187, 188.

[6]D.E. Polkinghorne, 'Narrative Configuration in Qualitative Analysis' [1995] 8(1) Qualitative Studies in Education 5, 11.

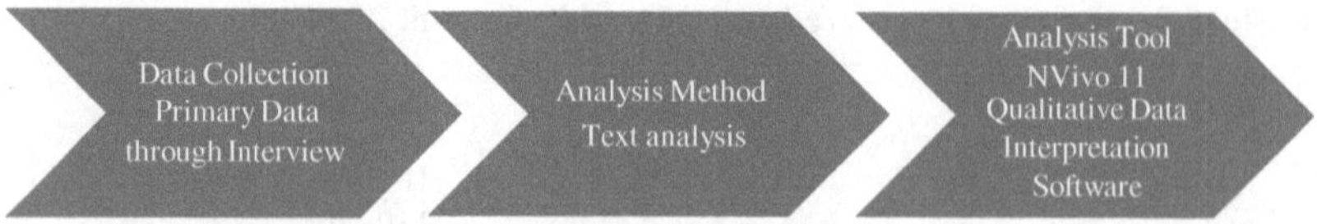

Fig. 4.2 Summary Flow—Data Analysis and Interpretation

interviewees are followers of Hinduism (25 refugees), Islam (49 refugees), Buddhism (22 refugees), Sikhism (4 refugees) and Christianity (14 refugees). Table 4.3 presents this data in a systematically tabular format.

4.2.2 *Arrival in India*

The first arrival of a refugee in any country involves several variables, such as companions upon arrival, means of travel and possession of travel documents. These factors are often significant at the time of application for refugee status. In a country like India where entry of foreign nationals without required travel documents (i.e. passport and visa) is punishable under the Foreigners Act, 1948, an enquiry into the details upon arrival of refugees may reveal important indications of the beginning of differential treatment.

Figure 4.3 demonstrates the results of an origin-based query to identify companions at the time of arrival in India. It reveals that most of the interviewed refugees entered India with their families, whereas relatively few entered alone or with other refugees. This trend suggests that maintaining family unity is one of the major concerns among refugees entering India. However, arrival in a group is evident only in cases of refugees from Myanmar, and the religion-based query in Fig. 4.4 demonstrates that it is the Rohingyas from Myanmar who have entered with other refugees.

Figure 4.5 reveals the results of a gender-based query, where it is evident that it is primarily males who have entered India alone and in a few cases with other refugees. From all the interviews, only one female refugee reported arriving without any family members but with other refugees.

Another important factor that was emphasized in the interviews was the means of arrival of refugees to India. Figure 4.6 demonstrates the results of an origin-based query, which found that refugees

Table 4.3 Details of Interviewed Refugees

Sl. No.	*Name (Original names have been changed to protect the privacy of the interviewed refugees)*	*Age*	*Country of Origin*	*Gender*	*Religion*
1.	AFG01	21	Afghanistan	Male	Islam
2.	AFG02	27	Afghanistan	Female	Islam
3.	AFG03	47	Afghanistan	Female	Islam
4.	AFG04	24	Afghanistan	Male	Islam
5.	AFG05	41	Afghanistan	Female	Islam
6.	AFG06	36	Afghanistan	Female	Islam
7.	AFG07	31	Afghanistan	Male	Islam
8.	AFG08	29	Afghanistan	Male	Islam
9.	AFG09	21	Afghanistan	Female	Islam
10.	AFG10	21	Afghanistan	Female	Islam
11.	AFG11	35	Afghanistan	Male	Islam
12.	AFG12	21	Afghanistan	Male	Islam
13.	AFG13	51	Afghanistan	Female	Islam
14.	AFG14	18	Afghanistan	Male	Islam
15.	AFG15	32	Afghanistan	Male	Hindu
16.	AFG16	20	Afghanistan	Male	Hindu
17.	AFG17	39	Afghanistan	Male	Sikh
18.	AFG18	35	Afghanistan	Male	Hindu
19.	AFG19	27	Afghanistan	Female	Hindu
20.	AFG20	27	Afghanistan	Male	Hindu
21.	AFG21	33	Afghanistan	Female	Sikh
22.	AFG22	18	Afghanistan	Female	Islam
23.	AFG23	28	Afghanistan	Male	Islam
24.	AFG24	37	Afghanistan	Male	Sikh
25.	AFG25	31	Afghanistan	Male	Hindu
26.	AFG26	28	Afghanistan	Male	Hindu
27.	AFG27	29	Afghanistan	Female	Sikh
28.	AFG28	23	Afghanistan	Male	Hindu
29.	IRN01	38	Iran	Male	Islam
30.	IRN02	44	Iran	Male	Islam
31.	IRN03	35	Iran	Male	Islam
32.	IRQ01	47	Iraq	Male	Islam
33.	IRQ02	28	Iraq	Male	Islam
34.	MMR01	21	Myanmar	Male	Islam
35.	MMR02	29	Myanmar	Male	Islam
36.	MMR03	18	Myanmar	Male	Islam
37.	MMR04	60	Myanmar	Male	Islam
38.	MMR05	30	Myanmar	Male	Islam
39.	MMR06	28	Myanmar	Male	Islam
40.	MMR07	30	Myanmar	Female	Islam

(continued)

Table 4.3 (continued)

Sl. No.	*Name (Original names have been changed to protect the privacy of the interviewed refugees)*	*Age*	*Country of Origin*	*Gender*	*Religion*
41.	MMR08	24	Myanmar	Male	Islam
42.	MMR09	20	Myanmar	Male	Islam
43.	MMR10	37	Myanmar	Male	Islam
44.	MMR11	45	Myanmar	Male	Islam
45.	MMR12	43	Myanmar	Female	Christian
46.	MMR13	23	Myanmar	Male	Christian
47.	MMR14	21	Myanmar	Female	Christian
48.	MMR15	40	Myanmar	Male	Christian
49.	MMR16	34	Myanmar	Male	Christian
50.	MMR17	24	Myanmar	Female	Christian
51.	MMR18	29	Myanmar	Male	Christian
52.	MMR19	35	Myanmar	Male	Christian
53.	MMR20	19	Myanmar	Male	Christian
54.	MMR21	29	Myanmar	Male	Christian
55.	MMR22	65	Myanmar	Female	Christian
56.	MMR23	27	Myanmar	Male	Christian
57.	MMR24	26	Myanmar	Male	Christian
58.	MMR25	55	Myanmar	Male	Christian
59.	MMR26	25	Myanmar	Male	Islam
60.	MMR27	22	Myanmar	Female	Islam
61.	MMR28	19	Myanmar	Male	Islam
62.	MMR29	21	Myanmar	Female	Islam
63.	SOM01	22	Somalia	Female	Islam
64.	SOM02	38	Somalia	Male	Islam
65.	SOM03	28	Somalia	Female	Islam
66.	SOM04	30	Somalia	Male	Islam
67.	SOM05	31	Somalia	Female	Islam
68.	SOM06	31	Somalia	Male	Islam
69.	SOM07	27	Somalia	Male	Islam
70.	SOM08	33	Somalia	Female	Islam
71.	SOM09	25	Somalia	Male	Islam
72.	SRL01	42	Sri Lanka	Male	Hindu
73.	SRL02	27	Sri Lanka	Male	Hindu
74.	SRL03	36	Sri Lanka	Male	Hindu
75.	SRL04	19	Sri Lanka	Male	Hindu
76.	SRL05	34	Sri Lanka	Male	Hindu
77.	SRL06	38	Sri Lanka	Male	Hindu
78.	SRL07	25	Sri Lanka	Male	Hindu
79.	SRL08	27	Sri Lanka	Male	Hindu
80.	SRL09	26	Sri Lanka	Female	Hindu

(continued)

Table 4.3 (continued)

Sl. No.	*Name (Original names have been changed to protect the privacy of the interviewed refugees)*	*Age*	*Country of Origin*	*Gender*	*Religion*
81.	SRL10	28	Sri Lanka	Female	Hindu
82.	SRL11	46	Sri Lanka	Female	Hindu
83.	SRL12	45	Sri Lanka	Male	Hindu
84.	SRL13	33	Sri Lanka	Female	Hindu
85.	SRL14	39	Sri Lanka	Female	Hindu
86.	SRL15	45	Sri Lanka	Male	Hindu
87.	SRL16	37	Sri Lanka	Male	Hindu
88.	SRL17	26	Sri Lanka	Male	Hindu
89.	SUD01	28	Sudan	Male	Islam
90.	SUD02	31	Sudan	Male	Islam
91.	SUD03	27	Sudan	Male	Islam
92.	SUD04	36	Sudan	Male	Islam
93.	TIB01	51	Tibet	Female	Buddhism
94.	TIB02	68	Tibet	Male	Buddhism
95.	TIB03	28	Tibet	Female	Buddhism
96.	TIB04	43	Tibet	Female	Buddhism
97.	TIB05	61	Tibet	Female	Buddhism
98.	TIB06	49	Tibet	Female	Buddhism
99.	TIB07	59	Tibet	Female	Buddhism
100.	TIB08	51	Tibet	Male	Buddhism
101.	TIB09	57	Tibet	Female	Buddhism
102.	TIB10	63	Tibet	Male	Buddhism
103.	TIB11	62	Tibet	Male	Buddhism
104.	TIB12	29	Tibet	Male	Buddhism
105.	TIB13	26	Tibet	Male	Buddhism
106.	TIB14	25	Tibet	Male	Buddhism
107.	TIB15	52	Tibet	Male	Buddhism
108.	TIB16	55	Tibet	Male	Buddhism
109.	TIB17	24	Tibet	Female	Buddhism
110.	TIB18	19	Tibet	Male	Buddhism
111.	TIB19	26	Tibet	Male	Buddhism
112.	TIB20	37	Tibet	Female	Buddhism
113.	TIB21	61	Tibet	Male	Buddhism
114.	TIB22	29	Tibet	Male	Buddhism

from Myanmar and Tibet entered Indian territory on foot, whereas Sri Lankan refugees arrived by boat. Refugees from Sudan, Somalia, Iraq, Iran and Afghanistan entered by air. This trend suggests that India's

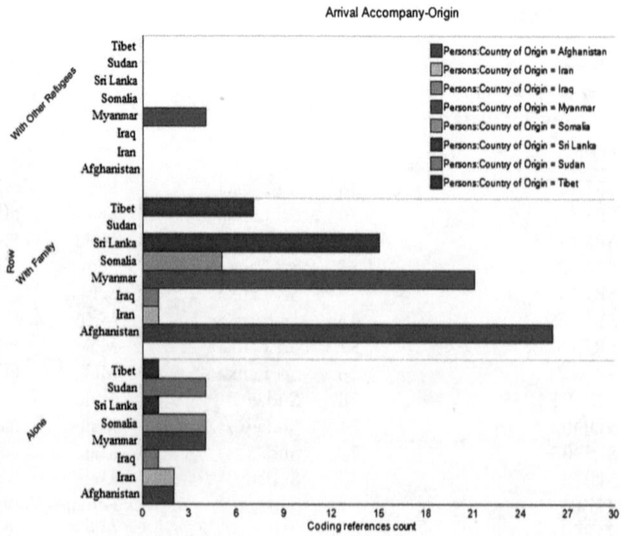

Fig. 4.3 Companions upon Arrival in India (origin-based query)

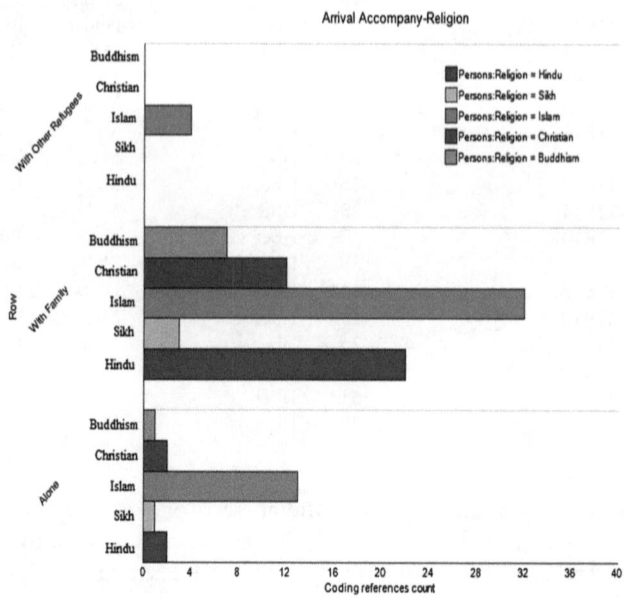

Fig. 4.4 Companions upon Arrival in India (religion-based query)

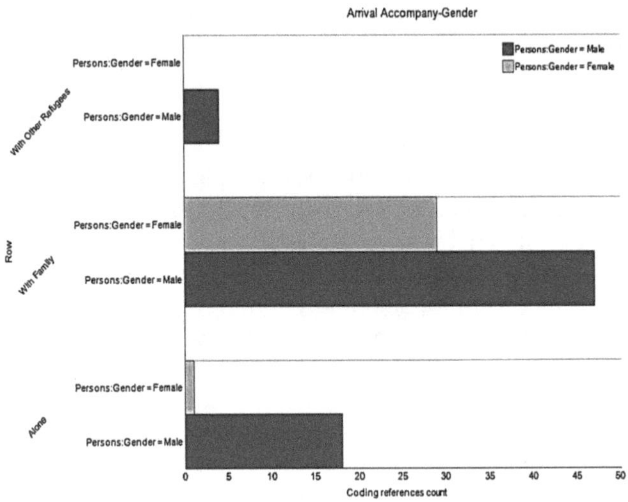

Fig. 4.5 Companions upon Arrival in India (gender-based query)

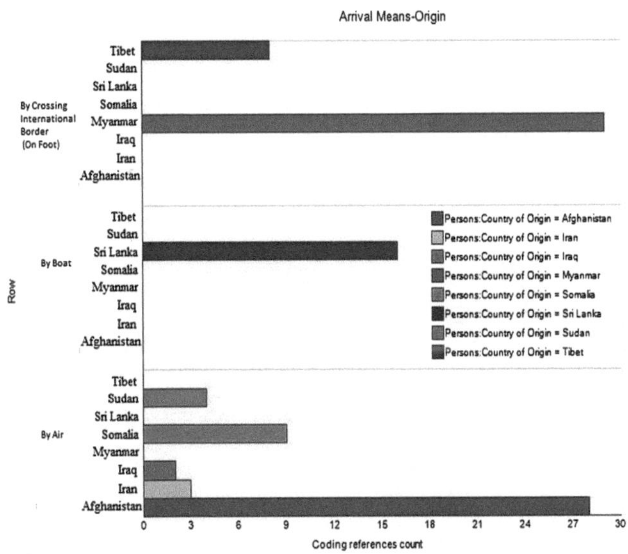

Fig. 4.6 Means of Arrival in India (origin-based query)

porous border has given refugees from neighboring countries the chance to cross the international border and arrive in India on foot or by boat. Refugees from countries that do not share a border with India have arrived by air.

The origin-based query in Fig. 4.6 and the religion-based query in Fig. 4.7 make clear that religion does not play a role in the choice of means of arrival in India. A closer look at Fig. 4.7 reveals that Buddhist, Christian, Muslim and Hindu refugees from neighboring countries with international borders with India have only entered on foot or by boat. At the same time, Muslim, Sikh and Hindu refugees from countries that do not share a border with India have arrived by air. Clearly, refugees' choice of means of travel to India is primarily based on convenience. However, concern about the non-possession of travel documents is one of the most important factors for determining convenience.

Figure 4.8 demonstrates the results of an origin-based query on possession of travel documents upon arrival of refugees in India. Significantly, it is found that most refugees from Tibet, Sri Lanka and Myanmar did not have any travel documents upon arrival in India. This

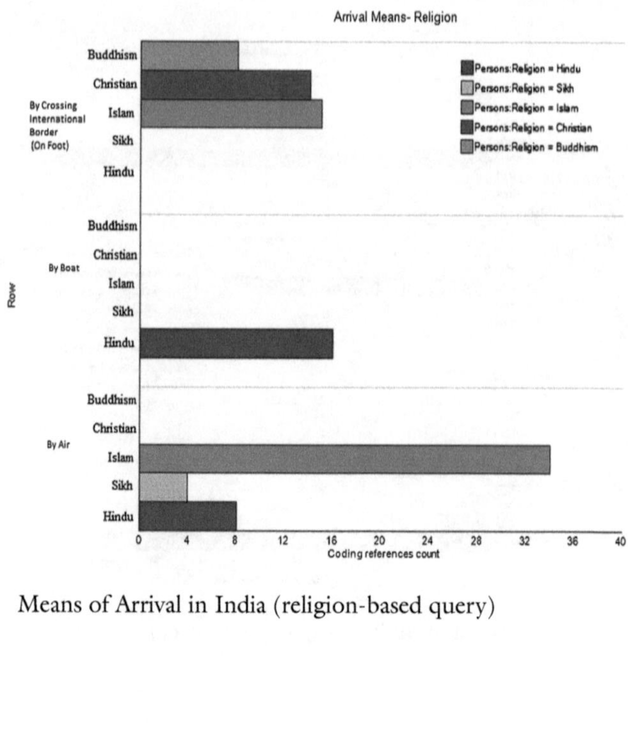

Fig. 4.7 Means of Arrival in India (religion-based query)

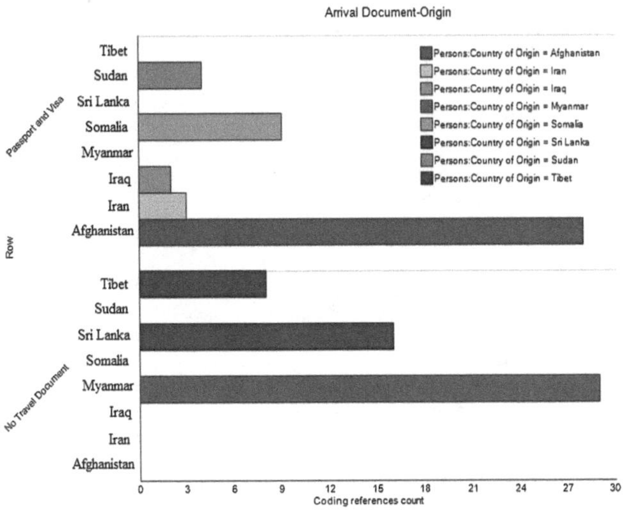

Fig. 4.8 Travel Documents upon Arrival (origin-based query)

trend of non-possession of travel documents upon arrival in India corroborates their answers shown in Figs. 4.6 and 4.7. Following the trend of arrival by air, refugees from Sudan, Somalia, Iraq, Iran and Afghanistan reported having a passport and visa at the time of arrival in India. In Fig. 4.9 the religion-based query extends the trends found in Figs. 4.6, 4.7 and 4.8.

When asked about their arrival in India, some Tibetan and Sir Lankan refugees reported having been born in India. This reveals that although some of these refugee children were born within the cut-off dates for citizenship by birth under the 1987 amendment of the Citizenship Act, 1955, they are still awaiting proper documentation of their right to Indian citizenship by birth. Several refugees reported that they were children of Tibetan parents who were also born in India, and one of the interviewed refugees also has a child who thus represents the fourth generation of a Tibetan refugee family living in India. The other refugee groups who have children born in India have experienced similar problems. Ignoring the facts and applicable laws that provide citizenship by birth has created further problems for the refugees in India that must be avoided when thinking of future political circumstances.

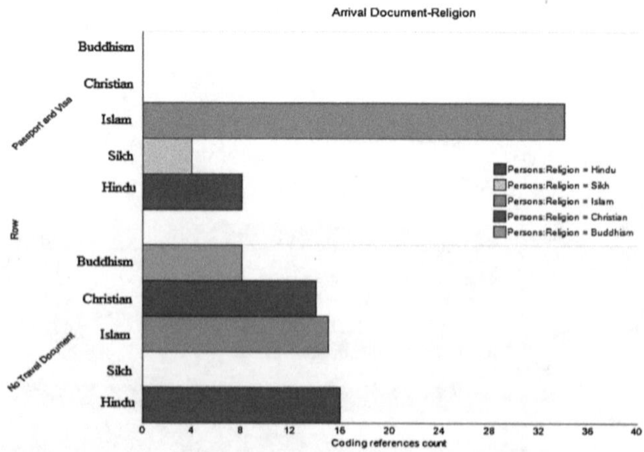

Fig. 4.9 Travel Documents upon Arrival (religion-based query)

4.2.3 Refugee Status in India

The interviews evidenced that there were two categories of status as determined by authorities in India. Refugees from Tibet and Sri Lanka have been given refugee status by the government as seen in Fig. 4.10. They have been issued documents by the Foreigners Registration Office—Registration Certificates for Tibetan refugees, and Refugee Identity Cards for Sri Lankan refugees. The validity of these documents is also extended by the Foreigners Registration Office in the place of residence of the refugees (Fig. 4.11).

The other refugee groups have been given refugee status by UNHCR in New Delhi as per the mandate of the 1951 Refugee Convention. These refugees are required to apply for registration with the Foreigners Registration Office after receiving a refugee certificate from UNHCR. The document provided by the Foreigners Registration Office is called the Residential Permit and Residential Certificate (RP&RC) (Fig. 4.12).

When obtaining the RP&RC, the visa for legal stay in India is also endorsed by the Foreigners Registration Office. The types of visas given to these refugees are the stay visa and the long-term visa. The stay visa is valid for one year, whereas the long-term visa is valid for between one and five years depending on various factors such as country of origin, religion and so forth. While most refugees are in possession of the

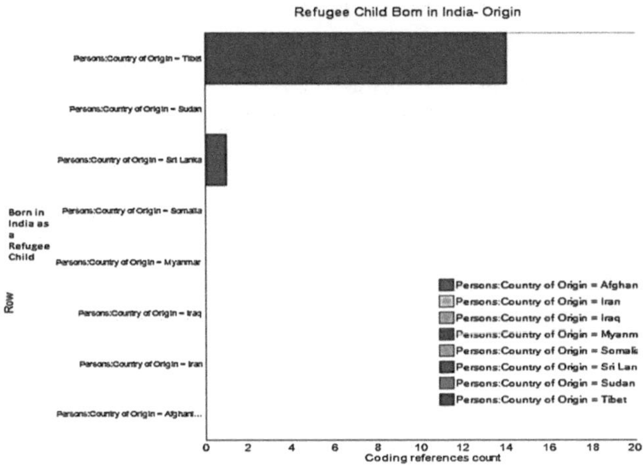

Fig. 4.10 Refugees Born in India (origin-based query)

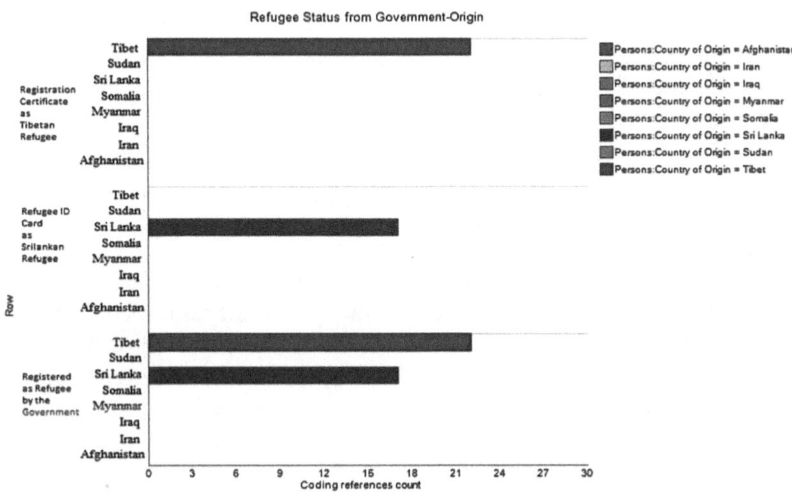

Fig. 4.11 Refugee Status from Government (origin-based query)

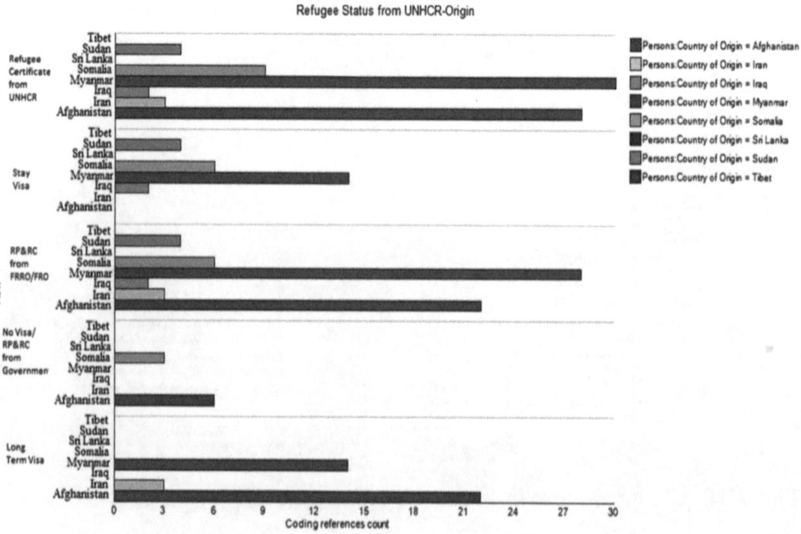

Fig. 4.12 Refugee Status from UNHCR (origin-based query)

UNHCR refugee certificate, RP&RC and visa, a very few refugees from Somalia and Afghanistan reported having no such documentation from the government, which means their stay in India is illegal per the existing laws.

4.2.4 Settlement in India

Upon arrival in a new country, finding a place to live is always a paramount concern. As shown in Fig. 4.13, refugees who have been granted refugee status usually live in rented housing. In addition, many refugees from Tibet, Sri Lanka and Afghanistan live in refugee camps. A distinct category emerged in the case of Tibetans, some of whom reported living in property leased by the government. These data are presented in Figs. 4.14 and 4.15.

Figure 4.14 represents a religion-based query about the place of residence of refugees in India, while Fig. 4.15 represents an origin-based query about the assistance received for rehabilitation. These charts indicate that only Tibetans have received leased property from the

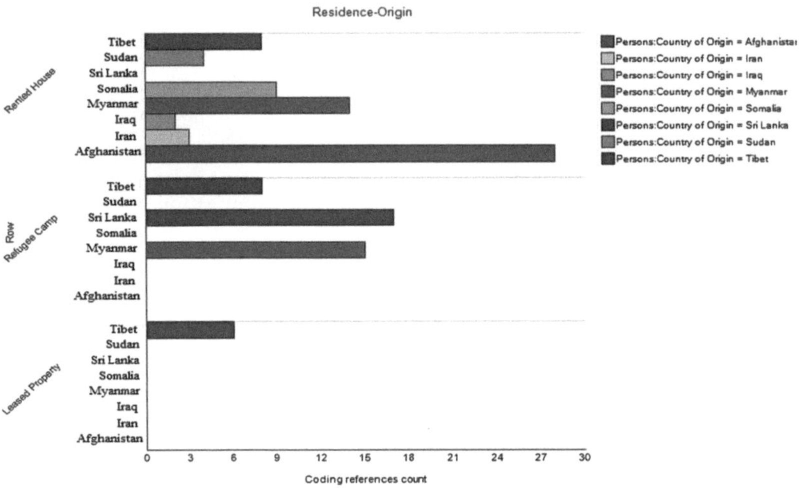

Fig. 4.13 Residence in India (origin-based query)

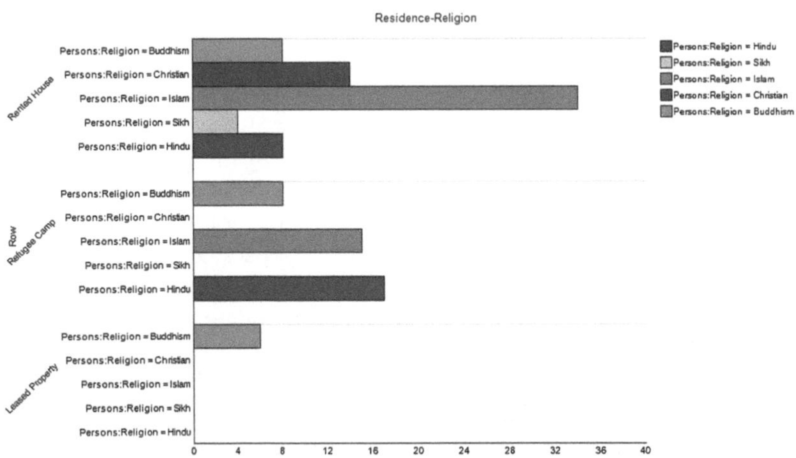

Fig. 4.14 Residence in India (religion-based query)

government for living in India. Refugees from Sri Lanka live primarily in camps set up by the government. Apart from that, it has been reported that several non-governmental organizations (NGOs) have assisted

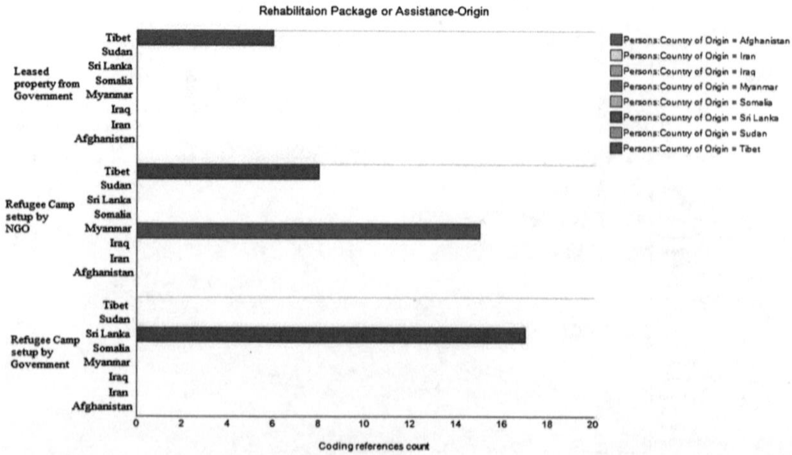

Fig. 4.15 Rehabilitation Package or Assistance (origin-based query)

refugees from Tibet and Myanmar (Rohingya refugees) in building refugee camps.

In case of the Tibetans in Darjeeling, the Tibetan Refugee Self Help Center has taken the initiative of building their own housing since 1959, whereas the Rohingya refugees from Myanmar who have been staying in camps set up by NGOs could not name any of the organizations that had helped them build camps in various places in Delhi. Refugees from Afghanistan, Sudan, Somalia, Iraq and Iran have not received any assistance for accommodation or any rehabilitation package, either from the government, UNHCR or any NGO. At the same time, Fig. 4.16 suggests that religious factors have played a role in determining the provision of rehabilitation assistance to refugees.

An important factor associated with place of residence, from which refugees in India have reported suffering, is restriction of movement. The results shown in Fig. 4.17 indicate that restriction of movement is experienced primarily by Sri Lankan refugees, who reported weekly roll calls at the government refugee camp. Though other refugees did not report any such incidents, one Afghan refugee reported threats from police for restriction of movement.

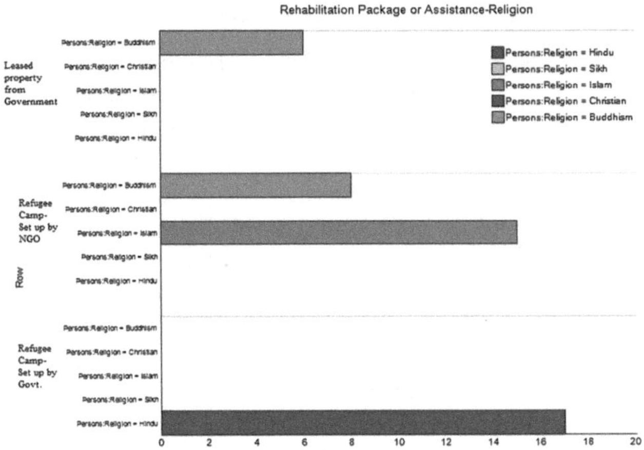

Fig. 4.16 Rehabilitation Package or Assistance (religion-based query)

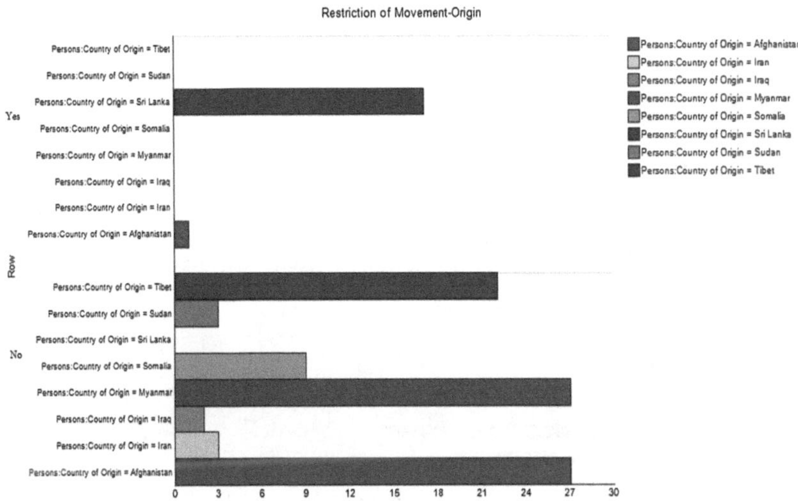

Fig. 4.17 Restriction of Movement (origin-based query)

4.2.5 *Livelihood*

In the country of refuge, it appears to be difficult to earn a livelihood if there is no clear policy of absorbing the refugee population into the labor market. In general, as per prevailing international standards, refugees must have the opportunity to work and earn their livelihood. The Indian policy seems very strange in this regard: while certain groups are required to have work permits, others do not need any work permit to continue their profession or occupation. However, in a vast country like India, where it is not always possible to enforce the rules regarding work permits, it is evident from Fig. 4.18 that most of the interviewed refugees are employed or doing business, though primarily in the informal sector. Only a small portion of the refugees reported not being employed and dependent on their family.

The possession of a work permit was not a concern for the Tibetan refugees interviewed—they all reported that a work permit is not a requirement for Tibetans to be employed or do business in India. The Tibetan Resettlement Policy, 2014 of the Ministry of Home Affairs

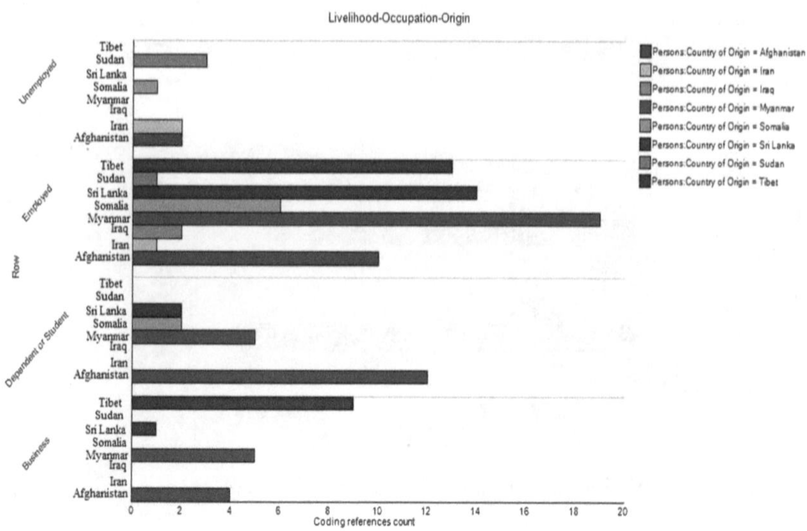

Fig. 4.18 Occupation in India (origin-based query)

established specific provisions for Tibetan refugees to take private sector employment and facilities of doing business. On the other hand, most of the interviewed refugees from other countries reported having no work permit. This trend of doing jobs without having a work permit as required by law raises questions about the validity of those laws, as the government has yet to understand the necessity of refugees (Fig. 4.19).

At the same time, assistance in finding a job or for self-employed activities for earning a livelihood is extremely minimal in nature, as shown in Fig. 4.20. Assistance from the government in the form of creating self-help groups or leasing land for agricultural purposes is available to the Sri Lankan and Tibetan refugees respectively. Assistance from UNHCR, as reported by interviewed refugees, is available only to refugees from Myanmar and Afghanistan in the form of grants for starting small businesses. Assistance from NGOs is restricted to learning local languages and computer applications.

An important concern has been raised by various refugee groups about the availability of a subsistence allowance for day-to-day living.

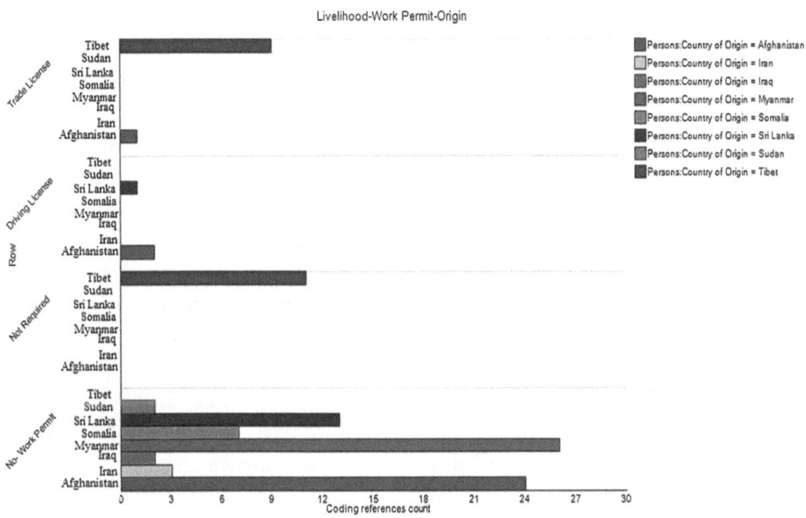

Fig. 4.19 Possession of Work Permit (origin-based query)

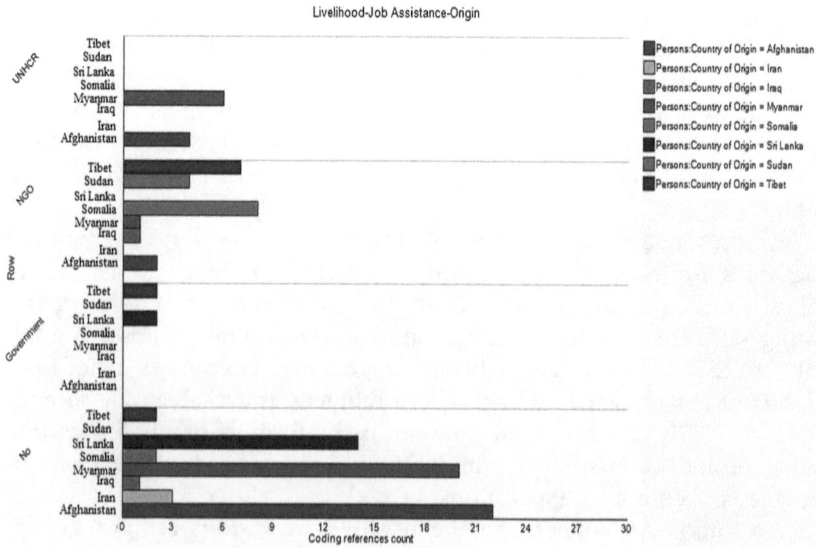

Fig. 4.20 Job Assistance (origin-based query)

After arrival in India, it takes quite a long time to obtain refugee status, find a place of stay and take up a job or self-employed activities. In interviews, refugees have appealed for the provision of a subsistence allowance during this initial period. The origin-based query represented in Fig. 4.21 shows that from among the interviewed refugees, only those from Sri Lanka, Sudan and Somalia receive a subsistence allowance, though their number is very low. Sri Lankan refugees receive a subsistence allowance from the government in the form of cash and essential food items at a very minimal rate, whereas the others receive a subsistence allowance from UNHCR in the form of cash.

In Fig. 4.22, the religion-based query on subsistence allowance clearly corroborates the claims of refugee groups that there may be a religious bias in determining the provision of subsistence allowances.

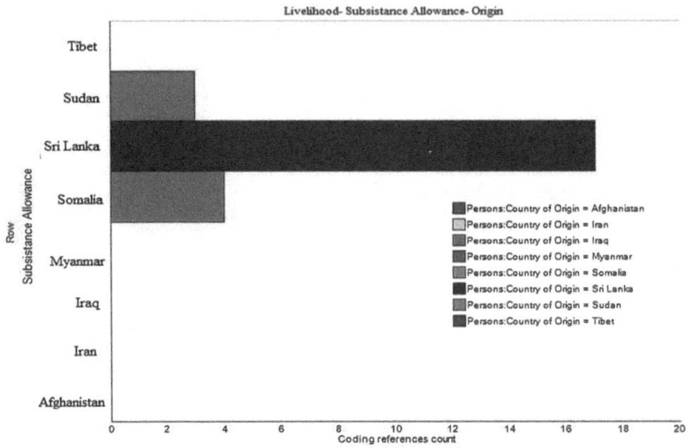

Fig. 4.21 Subsistence Allowance (origin-based query)

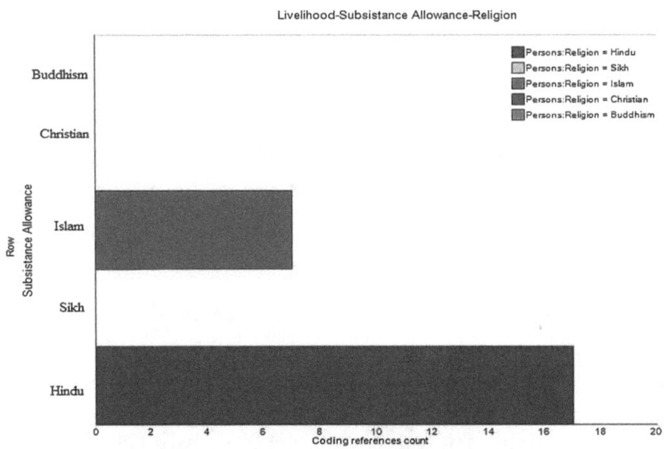

Fig. 4.22 Subsistence Allowance (religion-based query)

4.2.6 Education and Health Care

Most refugees interviewed reported having the opportunity to obtain an education for themselves or their children. A considerable number had not been able to access education mainly due to the absence of formal

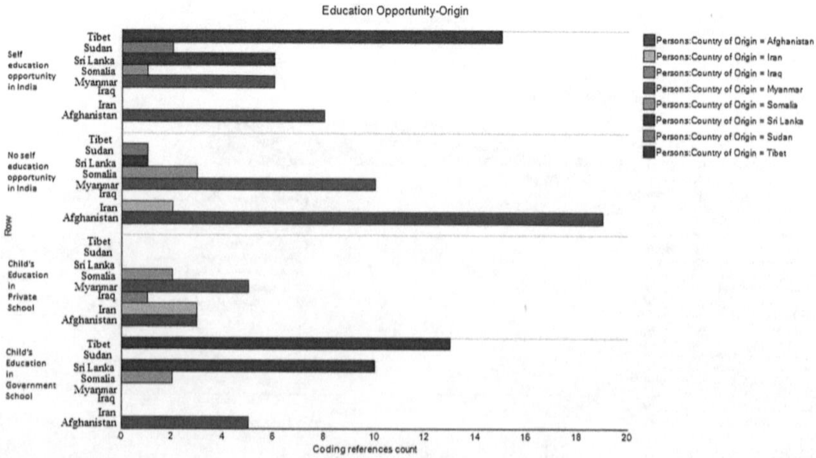

Fig. 4.23 Education Opportunity (origin-based query)

education in their country of origin. As seen in Fig. 4.23, it is primarily the refugee children from Tibet and Sri Lanka who have been educated or are receiving education in government schools. It is significant that in order to provide educational opportunities to Tibetan refugee children, the government established Central Tibetan Schools in various places in India, whereas no such facility is available for the Sri Lankan or other refugees.

The other refugee groups reported sending their children to private schools primarily due to denial of admission to government schools. Children of Sri Lankan refugees have received similar treatment to Indian citizens in the government schools in Tamil Nadu due to the generosity of the state government. They are entitled to free education up to the higher secondary level, free uniforms, books and prizes in case of extraordinary results in examinations (Fig. 4.24).

In accessing health care facilities, most of the refugees are dependent on government hospitals. The reason reported for this heavy dependence on government hospitals is lack of financial resources. It was also found that government hospitals did not make any distinction between refugees and Indian nationals. Some refugees holding UNHCR Refugee

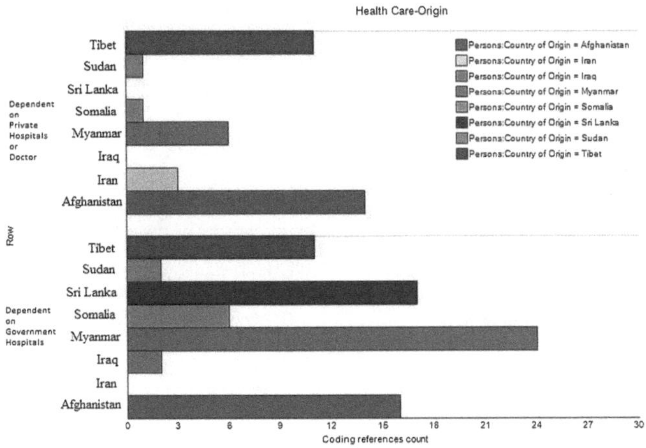

Fig. 4.24 Heath Care (origin-based query)

Certificates reported receiving free medicine from UNHCR. At the same time, some refugees in a better financial position visited private doctors or hospitals for treatment. However, none of the refugees held any medical or health insurance.

4.2.7 Detention, Deportation, Repatriation and Resettlement

Entry into Indian territory without valid travel documents is an offence under the Foreigners Act, 1948, and unauthorized stay after the expiry of such documents can result in detention or deportation. As most of the refugees in India entered Indian territory without the required travel documents, or with documents that expired after their entry, many refugees reported having been detained by the authorities.

The origin-based query illustrated in Fig. 4.25 shows the answers given by the interviewed refugees in these matters. Though none of the refugees reported any attempts at deportation or involuntary repatriation, refugees from Afghanistan, Iran and Myanmar reported verbal threats from the concerned government authorities. At the same time, Fig. 4.25 suggests that the trend of detention of refugees under the Foreigners Act, 1948 has decreased, which may be due to the rulings of

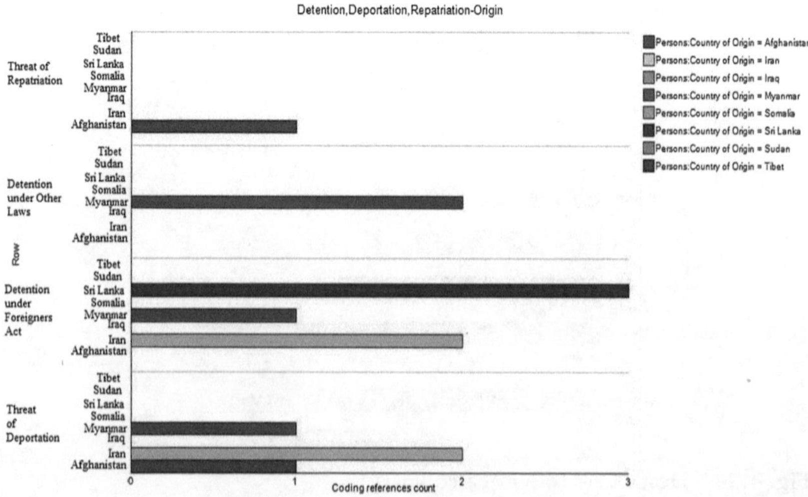

Fig. 4.25 Detention and Others (origin-based query)

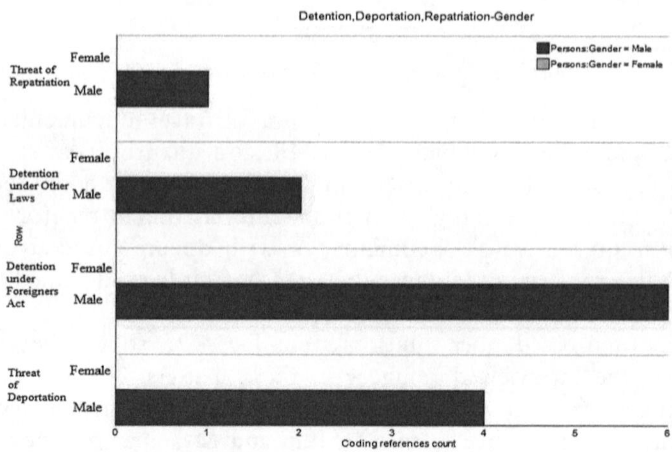

Fig. 4.26 Detention and Others (gender-based query)

various High Courts to enable refugees to appeal to UNHCR for refugee status succeeding in getting the charges dropped. Only a few refugees from Sri Lanka, Myanmar and Iran reported having been detained under the Foreigners Act, 1948. However, two refugees from Myanmar reported having been detained under information technology laws for campaigning online in favor of the Rohingya community of Myanmar. It is important to note that religious faith cannot be regarded as a factor in detention, whereas the gender-based query represented in Fig. 4.26 makes clear that from among the interviewed refugees, only male refugees have been subjected to detention or threat of deportation or repatriation.

In case of application for third country resettlement from India, refugees from Tibet, Sri Lanka and Afghanistan did not apply for third country resettlement; most such applications were made by refugees from Myanmar, irrespective of religious faith. Only two refugees from Somalia reported having obtained third country resettlement from among the interviewed refugees. A major issue raised by almost all refugees who had applied for third country resettlement was that UNHCR was not cooperative in this regard. The refugees need comprehensive information and assistance from UNHCR regarding application for third country resettlement.

4.2.8 Permanently Staying in India and Other Issues

Several refugee groups from Tibet, Sri Lanka, Afghanistan and Myanmar have been resident in India for long periods. Refugees from these groups expressed an interest in staying in India permanently and reported experiencing no discrimination by either the government or the citizens of India (Fig. 4.28).

It was mainly the refugees from Sudan, Somalia, Iraq, Iran and Myanmar (Chin community) who reported experiencing discrimination and who did not want to stay in India permanently. The religion-based query represented in Fig. 4.29 makes the scenario clearer that only those refugees adhering to Christianity (Myanmar citizens— Chin tribe) and Islam (African, Iraqi and Iranian) reported experiencing discrimination and did not wish to stay in India permanently. They highlighted differences in culture, language and physical orientation as reasons for the

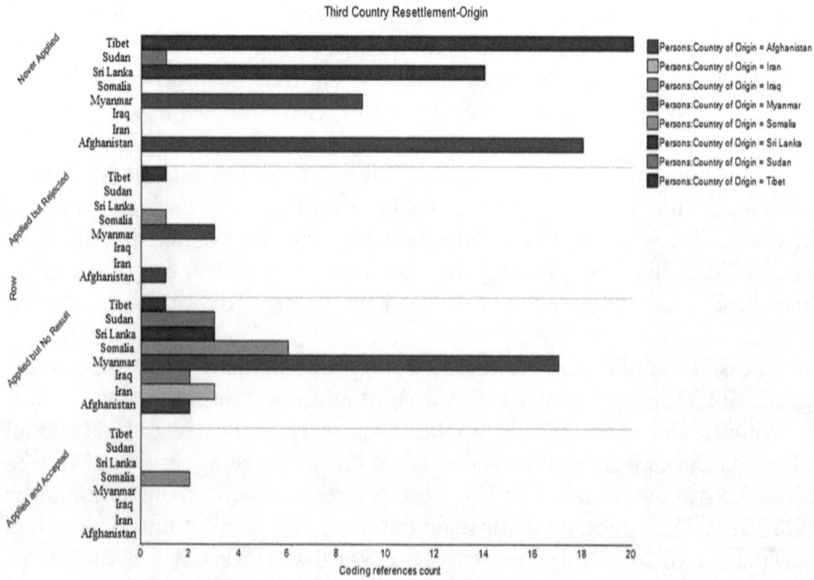

Fig. 4.27 Third Country Resettlement (origin-based query)

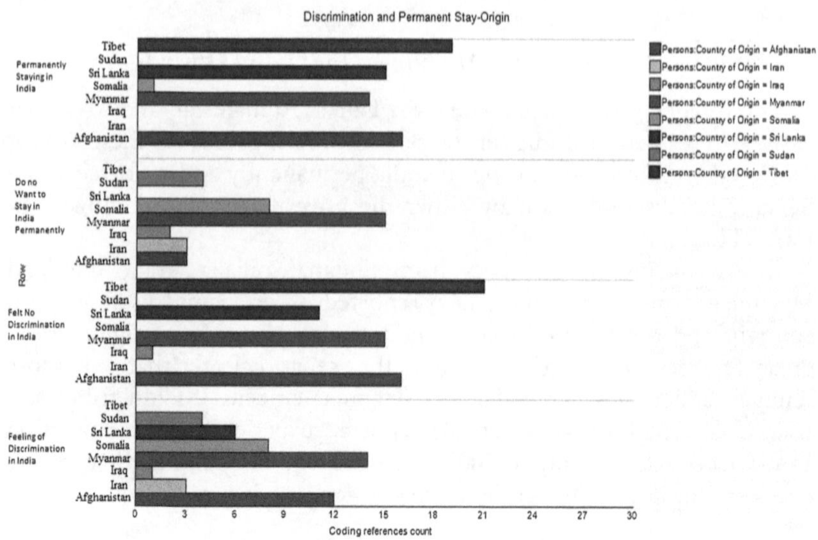

Fig. 4.28 Permanent Stay and Discrimination (origin-based query)

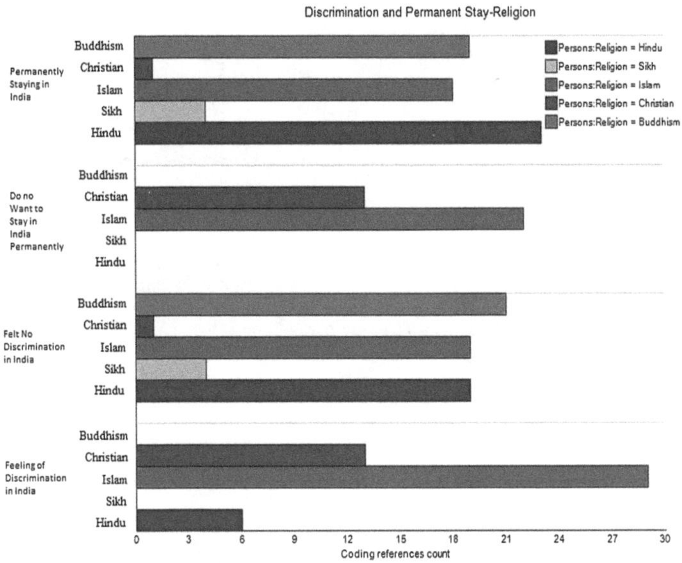

Fig. 4.29 Permanent Stay and Discrimination (religion-based query)

discrimination. These are the refugees who have applied for third country resettlement, as shown in Fig. 4.27.

Another important matter that came to light in the interviews concerned the possession of ration cards allowing refugees to obtain essential items from the ration shop at a lower rate. It was found that ration cards were only available to refugees from Tibet and Sri Lanka. The state government of Tamil Nadu has provided ration cards for Sri Lankan refugees, while the Tibetan Resettlement Policy, 2014 recommended the same for Tibetan refugees. However, it was also found that several refugees from Tibet were in possession of Indian voting cards while also holding Registration Certificates as refugees from the Foreigners Registration Office. Thus, several Tibetans were living in India as both Indian citizens and Tibetan refugees. This matter is very disturbing, as only citizens of India are entitled to voting cards(Fig. 4.30).

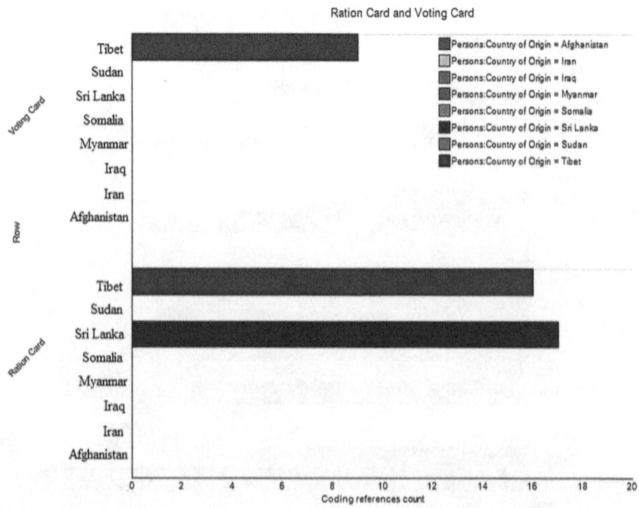

Fig. 4.30 Ration Card and Voting Card (origin-based query)

4.3 Conclusion

This empirical study seeks to answer questions regarding different factors in the lives of refugees in the state of refuge. Factors such as arrival, status determination, settlement, livelihood, education, health care, detention, deportation, repatriation, third country resettlement, feeling of discrimination and discriminative treatment, permanent stay and so forth touch upon many aspects of the life of a refugee in India. The answers given during the interviews have been analyzed using the qualitative data interpretation software NVivo 11. By using this software, queries have been made to analyze the difference in treatment and entitlements based primarily on origin and, where necessary, on religion and gender. It is evident from the analysis that there are differences in treatment as well as discrimination in terms of entitlements based on country of origin of refugees. The Government of India has treated Tibetan refugees as a high priority, providing them with various entitlements, sometimes on a par with or even beyond those received by Indian nationals; meanwhile, the treatment of and entitlements given to Sri Lankan refugees are somewhat half-hearted in nature. Those who have obtained refugee status from UNHCR have received little of significance from the government for their well-being in India except the documentation for legal stay. This kind of calculated kindness results in discrimination between refugee groups present in India. It is clear from this empirical study that refugees present in India are discriminated against based on their country of origin by the state machinery, which requires a normative change as per the principles of equality, justice and due process.

CHAPTER 5

International Standards of Refugee Protection

5.1 Refugees and Protection

It is notable that although India has long been home to refugees from different countries, the term refugee is not defined in any Indian law or administrative text. Despite the lack of an official definition, however, in practice the meaning of the term refugee can be said to be synonymous with the definition given in the 1951 Convention Relating to the Status of Refugees (hereinafter 1951 Refugee Convention) with regard to the Indian practice of providing asylum.[1] In India there are primarily three categories of refugees:

1. Refugees under the control and mandate of the Government of India who came from Tibet or Sri Lanka. Both of these refugee communities hold refugee identity documents issued by the government.
2. Refugees under the control of the Government of India who are from a minority community in Pakistan or Bangladesh. These

[1]Convention Relating to the Status of Refugees (adopted July 28, 1951, entered into force April 22, 1954) 189 United Nations Treaty Series 137 (1951 Convention); Protocol Relating to the Status of Refugees (entered into force October 4, 1967) 606 United Nations Treaty Series 267 (1967 Protocol); see how the definition of refugee is interpreted in the Western world in Daniel J. Steinbock, 'Interpreting the Refugee Definition' [1998] 19 Immigration and Nationality Law Review 733, 742.

S.P. Sarker, *Refugee Law in India*,
DOI 10.1007/978-981-10-4807-4_5

refugees hold long-term visas on the grounds of being a minority in their country of origin and/or based on extreme compassion. However, they do not hold documents identifying them as refugees provided by the government.

3. Refugees under the control and mandate of the United Nations High Commissioner for Refugees (UNHCR) in New Delhi who are mostly from Afghanistan, Myanmar, Somalia, Sudan, Iran, Iraq or another country. In other words, refugees from all countries except Tibet, Sri Lanka, Pakistan and Bangladesh are under the mandate of UNHCR in New Delhi.

It is important to note that the refugees in all three categories faced persecution in their country of origin due to various factors. The term refugee is internationally defined in the 1951 Refugee Convention, read with 1967 Protocol Relating to the Status of Refugees (1967 Protocol), as a person who,

owing to well founded fear of being persecuted for reasons of race, religion, nationality, membership of a particular social group or political opinion, is outside the country of his nationality and is unable or, owing to such fear, is unwilling to avail himself of the protection of that country; or who, not having a nationality and being outside the country of his former habitual residence as a result of such events, is unable or, owing to such fear, is unwilling to return to it.[2]

Individuals in the three categories indicated above have faced different procedures for obtaining refugee status or being regularized to stay in India as refugees under the various visa categories or residential permit. For example, the refugees indicated in the first category were part of a mass influx, and the Government of India provided them with refugee status (individually) using a less complicated administrative process along with several affirmative actions with regard to their staying in India. Those in the second category have primarily been treated on an individual or sometimes a family basis, where the process of granting of long-term visa is complicated as inputs from the concerned state government and intelligence agencies are required for this purpose by the central government before taking any decision. The third category is purely governed by the 1951 Refugee Convention by UNHCR, and a

[2] 1951 Refugee Convention, ibid., Article 1(A)(2).

formal process of determining individual refugee status is conducted by UNHCR in New Delhi.

When we discuss the protection of these refugees we are referring to legal protection, which is associated with entitlements under law and, for effective redress of grievances, mechanisms to vindicate claims in respect of those entitlements.[3] In Chap. 4 the findings of the empirical research made it clear that the way these three above-mentioned categories of refugees receive protection from the authorities, and the manner in which legal precepts are implemented, are different in terms of entitlements. The aim of this chapter is to identify the international standards of refugee protection, or prominent international practices of refugee protection mechanisms, which may be regarded as guiding texts in formulating a refugee law for India with necessary modifications.[4]

5.2 Standards of Protection Under the 1951 Refugee Convention

It is important to approach refugee protection from a legal perspective; as Atle Grahl-Madsen is quoted as saying, "discussion of the social and political dimensions of refugee flows while considered important, could not conclude the debate and would rarely lead to consistent and principled solutions."[5] The 1951 Refugee Convention is the first agreement of its kind in the modern era to provide protection for refugees and is highly regarded by most countries in the world.[6] This section of the chapter briefly analyzes the most important provisions of the 1951

---

[3]See Arthur C. Helton, 'What is Refugee Protection?' [1990] 2 International Journal of Refugee Law 119, 120; Antonio Fortin, 'The Meaning of Protection in the Refugee Definition' [2000] 12 International Journal of Refugee Law 548, 558.

[4]See generally James C. Hathaway [1991] 4(2) Journal of Refugee Studies 113, 124; O.B. Tshosa, 'National Refugee Laws in the Light of International Standards: Some Reflections on the Refugee (Recognition and Control) Act, 1967 of Botswana' [2007] 5 University of Botswana Law Journal 49, 76; Colleen V. Thouez, 'New Directions in Refugee Protection' [1998] 22 Fletcher Forum of World Affairs 89, 93.

[5]Dennis McNamara, *Foreword*, Commentary on the Refugee Convention 1951, Division of International Protection of the United Nations High Commissioner for Refugees, 1997.

[6]See James Kelley, 'Refugee Protection: Whose Responsibility Is it Anyway?' [1990] 2 International Journal of Refugee Law 277, 281; Pierre Bertrand, 'An Operational Approach to International Refugee Protection' [1993] 26 Cornell International Law Journal 495, 497.

Refugee Convention, which is the foundation for international practices of refugee protection mechanisms in various parts of the world.[7]

5.2.1 Non-Discrimination

The 1951 Refugee Convention was the first instrument for refugee protection to include an important provision on non-discrimination. The provision reads: "the contracting parties shall apply the provisions of this convention to refugees without discrimination as to race, religion and country of origin."[8] This particular provision can be said to be inspired by Article 2 of the Universal Declaration of Human Rights; however, the protection against discrimination in the 1951 Refugee Convention is limited in that it only prohibits discrimination between refugees.[9] There are several essential tenets of Article 3 of the 1951 Refugee Convention: the non-discrimination norm relates only to the provisions of the 1951 Refugee Convention; as per this norm states cannot differentiate between racial, religious or national groups among refugees; and the grounds on which non-discrimination is based are exhaustive in nature. In the case of refugee protection in India, discrimination in the provision of entitlements occurs on the basis of race, religion and country of origin, as shown in Chap. 4. Therefore, if a refugee law is to be enforced in India, the foremost provision should be to protect refugees from discrimination.[10] While this particular non-discrimination provision is the foundation for Chapter I of the 1951 Refugee Convention, there

---

[7]See David Kennedy, 'International Refugee Protection' [1986] 8 Human Rights Quarterly 1, 19; Karin Landgren, 'The Future of Refugee Protection: Four Challenges' [1998] 11(4) Journal of Refugee Studies 416, 428.

[8]1951 Refugee Convention (n 1) Article 3.

[9]Universal Declaration of Human Rights, G.A. Res. 217A (III), U.N. Doc A/810 at 71 (1948), Article 2: "Everyone is entitled to all the rights and freedoms set forth in this Declaration, without distinction of any kind, such as race, color, sex, language, religion, political or other opinion, national or social origin, property, birth or other status. Furthermore, no distinction shall be made on the basis of the political, jurisdictional or international status of the country or territory to which a person belongs, whether it be independent, trust, non-self-governing or under any other limitation of sovereignty."

[10]See James C. Hathaway & Anne K. Cusick, 'Refugee Rights are Non Negotiable' [2000] 14 Georgetown Immigration Law Journal 481, 593; Michael J. Parrish, 'Redefining the Refugee: The Universal Declaration of Human Rights as a Basis for Refugee Protection' [2000–2001] 22 Cardozo Law Review 223, 264.

are several other associated provisions such as general obligations of the country of refuge,[11] freedom to practice religion and religious education,[12] rights granted as aliens under other conventions and so on.[13]

5.2.2 Access to Legal Remedies

The provisions related to "access to courts" as contained in the 1951 Refugee Convention uphold the right to legal remedy for refugees.[14] It is sometimes the case that despite having the right to access the courts, refugees lack the necessary financial means in terms of cautio judicatum solvi and require legal aid. Thus this provision is an attempt to address such situations. All three provisions of Article 16 of the 1951 Refugee Convention extend to refugees the right to legal remedy by the court, for which purpose they shall be assimilated to nationals of the country in which they have their habitual residence.[15] However, Article 16 should have included some additional attributes within its scope, such as the right to a free and fair hearing, the assistance of an interpreter, the right against self-incrimination and so forth.

[11] 1951 Refugee Convention (n 1) Article 2: "Every refugee has duties to the country in which he finds himself, which require in particular that he conform to its laws and regulations as well as to measures taken for the maintenance of public order."

[12] 1951 Refugee Convention (n 1) Article 4: "The Contracting States shall accord to refugees within their territories treatment at least as favorable as that accorded to their nationals with respect to freedom to practice their religion and freedom as regards the religious education of their children."

[13] 1951 Refugee Convention (n 1) Article 5: "Nothing in this Convention shall be deemed to impair any rights and benefits granted by a Contracting State to refugees apart from this Convention."

[14] 1951 Refugee Convention (n 1) Article 16: "1. A refugee shall have free access to the courts of law on the territory of all Contracting States. 2. A refugee shall enjoy in the Contracting State in which he has his habitual residence the same treatment as a national in matters pertaining to access to the courts, including legal assistance and exemption from *cautio judicatum solvi*. 3. A refugee shall be accorded in the matters referred to in paragraph 2 in countries other than that in which he has his habitual residence the treatment granted to a national of the country of his habitual residence."

[15] See how decisions of courts affect the lives of refugees in Kate Ogg, 'A Sometimes Dangerous Convergence: Refugee Law, Human Rights Law, and the Meaning of 'Effective Protection'' [2013] 12 Macquarie Law Journal 109, 124.

5.2.3 *Access to Employment*

In general, states employ rules for aliens to obtain work permits in order to lawfully work in the country of residence. These rules for obtaining a work permit are sometimes restrictive in nature to protect the national labor market. However, considering the plight of refugees in a foreign land, the 1951 Refugee Convention codified three important provisions with regard to refugees earning a livelihood. Article 17(1) refers to states' mandatory obligation to allow refugees to engage in wage-earning employment.[16] The other provisions of Article 17 are for those refugees who have some special relation with the country of refuge through the duration of residence or through their spouse or children, and to protect those who have entered the country of refuge through labor recruitment or special immigration schemes.[17] The provision relating to self-employment of refugees is codified in the 1951 Refugee Convention through Article 18.[18] This is the first time that a refugee protection instrument has included a provision on self-employment to supplement the need of refugees for a wage-earning method apart from Article 17. Article 19 is far more progressive with regard to extending the possibilities of employment for refugees as it includes the practice of liberal professions.[19] In this provision the word "profession" suggests that the person concerned must possess certain qualifications from some institution, while the word "liberal" suggests that the person concerned acts on his/her own, not as an agent of the state or as a salaried employee. This provision, then, is

---

[16] 1951 Refugee Convention (n 1) Article 17: "The Contracting States shall accord to refugees lawfully staying in their territory the most favorable treatment accorded to nationals of a foreign country in the same circumstances, as regards the right to engage in wage-earning employment."

[17] 1951 Refugee Convention (n 1) Article 17(2) and Article 17(3).

[18] 1951 Refugee Convention (n 1) Article 18: "The Contracting States shall accord to a refugee lawfully in their territory treatment as favorable as possible and, in any event, not less favorable than that accorded to aliens generally in the same circumstances, as regards the right to engage on his own account in agriculture, industry, handicrafts and commerce and to establish commercial and industrial companies."

[19] 1951 Refugee Convention (n 1) Article 19: "1. Each Contracting State shall accord to refugees lawfully staying in their territory who hold diplomas recognized by the competent authorities of that State' and who are desirous of practicing a liberal profession' treatment as favorable as possible and, in any event, not less favorable than that accorded to aliens generally in the same circumstances."

meant to allow doctors, engineers, architects and lawyers to practice in their country of refuge.

5.2.4 *Access to Rationing, Housing and Education*

Provisions related to rationing, housing and education are included in Chapter IV of the 1951 Refugee Convention. In some countries residents are provided with essential items at a very low, subsidized price. Article 20 obligates states with rationing systems to include refugees in the scheme.[20] The provision related to housing obligates states to provide refugees with similar housing assistance or access to housing schemes as is provided to nationals.[21] Reflecting the spirit of Article 26(1) of the Universal Declaration of Human Rights, Article 22 of the 1951 Refugee Convention obligates states to treat refugees as nationals in cases of elementary education.[22] This Article also provides for the remission of fees in non-elementary education, awarding of scholarships and recognition of foreign degrees and diplomas in cases of admission matters.[23] Lastly, Chapter IV of the 1951 Refugee Convention added Article 23 for the provision of public relief to refugees and Article 24 for the inclusion of refugees in labor protection and social security schemes. The provisions discussed in this section are of great importance for the day-to-day life of a refugee in the country of refuge, along with the provision dealing with employment; without these fundamental rights of access, the lives of refugees could not be protected in the country of refuge.

---

[20] 1951 Refugee Convention (n 1) Article 20: "Where a rationing system exists, which applies to the population at large and regulates the general distribution of products in short supply, refugees shall be accorded the same treatment as nationals."

[21] 1951 Refugee Convention (n 1) Article 21: "As regards housing the Contracting States, in so far as the matter is regulated by laws or regulations or is subject to the control of public authorities, shall accord to refugees lawfully staying in their territory treatment as favorable as possible and, in any event, not less favorable than that accorded to aliens generally in the same circumstances."

[22] 1951 Refugee Convention (n 1) Article 22: "1. The Contracting States shall accord to refugees the same treatment as is accorded to nationals with respect to elementary education."

[23] 1951 Refugee Convention (n 1) Article 22(2).

5.2.5 *Non-Refoulement and Other Administrative Measures*

The prohibition against refoulement is at the center of all the provisions of the 1951 Refugee Convention. The provision states that "no Contracting State shall expel or return (*refouler*) a refugee in any manner whatsoever to the frontiers of territories where his life or freedom would be threatened on account of his race, religion, nationality, membership of a particular social group or political opinion."[24] This provision has now become a part of customary international law, which means it applies to a refugee who is present in the territory of any state irrespective of whether the entry of the refugee was lawful or unlawful. This provision in the 1951 Refugee Convention is further supplemented by Article 31, which stipulates that no penalties shall be imposed on a refugee for illegal entry or presence in the country of refuge. However, in cases of expulsion of refugees, the state has to follow due process and expulsion is permissible only on the grounds of national security or public order.[25] Another important provision regarding administrative measures is to provide refugees with assistance in assimilating in the country of refuge and becoming naturalized, and thus to no longer have the status of refugee.[26]

5.3 Extending Human Rights in Refugee Protection

The provisions of the 1951 Refugee Convention were indeed the pioneering guidelines for providing protection to refugees after World War II. It is important to note that the core provisions are still relevant for the protection of refugees, though a considerable period of time has passed since the entry into force of the 1951 Refugee Convention.[27] It can be argued that its provisions represent the minimum standard for protection of refugees, and considering the emergence of new conflicts

[24] 1951 Refugee Convention (n 1) Article 33(1).

[25] 1951 Refugee Convention (n 1) Article 32.

[26] 1951 Refugee Convention (n 1) Article 34: "The Contracting States shall as far as possible facilitate the assimilation and naturalization of refugees. They shall in particular make every effort to expedite naturalization proceedings and to reduce as far as possible the charges and costs of such proceedings."

[27] Bemma Donkoh, 'A Half-Century of International Refugee Protection: Who's Responsible, What's Ahead?' [2000] 18 Berkeley Journal of International Law 260, 263.

that generate refugees from several dimensions, some newer instruments have emerged.[28] These newer instruments are based primarily on the standards provided by the 1951 Refugee Convention, but they are modified to address the specific refugee situation along with the concerns of the country of refuge.[29] The behavior and divergent national interests of states may be seen to prevent the evolution of common patterns of protection standards.[30] These common patterns opened up a new avenue for protection which was unknown to previous conventions and ventured into areas that were considered political and beyond the scope of legal regulation.[31] In the 1960s, as Africans were resisting colonial domination, many victims of the turbulence fled their countries of origin. These people received some material assistance from UNHCR but were not considered refugees, and thus were not given international protection by UNHCR until the amendment of the 1951 UN Convention by the 1967 Protocol Relating to the Status of Refugees.[32] The African nations felt the need for a new mechanism as military dictatorships and single-party states were being formed, and because the 1967 Protocol to the 1951 Refugee Convention was inadequate to the situation.[33] The 1969 Organisation of African Unity (OAU) Convention Governing the Specific Aspects of Refugee Problems in Africa (OAU Convention) is an early but modified replica of the 1951 Refugee Convention that deals specifically with the definition of the term refugee, non-refoulement and

---

[28] See Ninette Kelley, 'International Refugee Protection Challenges and Opportunities' [2007] 19 International Journal of Refugee Law 401, 411; Guenet Guebre-Christos, 'State Building and Humanitarian Intervention: New Dimensions in Refugee Protection' [2001] 24 In Defense of the Alien 33, 36.

[29] Hugo Storey, 'EU Refugee Qualification Directive: A Brave New World?' [2008] 20 International Journal of Refugee Law 1, 13.

[30] Andres B. Johnsson, 'Two Decades of the 1969 OAU Convention Governing the Specific Aspects of the Refugee Problem in Africa' [1989] 1 International Journal of Refugee Law 557, 558.

[31] Ibid. 558.

[32] Emmanuel Opoku Awuxu, 'Refugee Movements in Africa and the OAU Convention on Refugees' [1995] 39 Journal of African Law 79, 80.

[33] Joe Oloka-Onyango, 'Human Rights, The OAU Convention and the Refugee Crisis in Africa: Forty Years After Geneva' [1991] 3 International Journal of Refugee Law 453, 454.

asylum.[34] Though it is a regional instrument on refugee protection, the extension of the definition of the term refugee is highly regarded by the world community, as the OAU Convention includes a new provision along with the definition given in the 1951 Refugee Convention. The extended definition of refugee includes a person who:

> owing to external aggression, occupation, foreign domination or events seriously disturbing public order in either part or the whole of his country of origin or nationality, is compelled to leave his place of habitual residence in order to seek refuge in another place outside his country of origin or nationality.[35]

This was the first time any instrument related to refugee protection directly addressed the causes of refugee movement. Giving due regard to the extended definition, the United Nations General Assembly further stated:

> Policies and practices of oppressive and racist regimes, as well as aggression, colonialism, apartheid, alien domination, foreign intervention and occupation are amongst the root causes of new and massive flows of refugees.[36]

Addressing the objective considerations of refugees leaving the country of nationality or habitual residence, and the United Nations General Assembly's reaffirmation of this, can be seen as opening up a new arena of human rights protection in which refugee protection and protection of the human rights of non-nationals have been merged. It is argued that the OAU Convention is significant in three definitive ways: the refugee definition is objective rather than subjective; within its framework, the

---

[34] OAU Convention Governing the Specific Aspects of Refugee Problems in Africa (adopted September 10, 1969, entered into force June 20, 1974) 14691 United Nations Treaty Series (OAU Convention). The main clauses of the Convention deal with the refugee definition (Article I), asylum (Article II), the prohibition of subversive activities (Article III), non-discrimination (Article IV), voluntary repatriation (Article V), travel documents (Article VI), and cooperation with the OAU and UNHCR (Articles VII and VIII), see W.J.E.M. van Hdvell tot Westerflier, 'Africa and Refugees: The OAU Refugee Convention in Theory and Practice' [1989] 7 Netherlands Quarterly of Human Rights 172, 174.

[35] Ibid. Article I(2).

[36] United Nations General Assembly, Resolution No: A/RES/36/148, December 16, 1981 http://www.un.org/documents/ga/res/36/a36r148.htm accessed December 12, 2016.

cause of harm and motive for flight is indeterminate; and the refugee definition is such that it can be used as a group definition.[37]Another significant provision that was added by the OAU Convention is that on asylum.[38] This provision is important as it forbids a signatory state to reject the entry of refugees even if the concerned state does not intend to provide asylum. At the same time, the signatory state is obligated to provide temporary refuge until another country grants permanent refuge to these temporary refugees.

On the other side of the world, in Latin America, where the practice of providing political asylum has a long history, outbreaks of violence in the 1980s forced many people to flee their country of origin, and state mechanisms as well provisions of the 1951 Refugee Convention and the 1967 Protocol were not sufficient for managing this regional displacement.[39] At a colloquium in 1981, several academicians and experts on refugee law looked into refugee protection mechanisms at the regional and global level. The colloquium called for a regional instrument for Latin American states embodying the principles of international refugee law with necessary additions required to manage the Latin American refugee crisis. The final result was the 1984 Cartagena Declaration on Refugees (Cartagena Declaration).[40] The Cartagena Declaration established and consolidated

[37]Micah Bond Rankin, 'Extending the Limits or Narrowing the Scope? Deconstructing the OAU Refugee Definition Thirty Years On' [2005] 21 South African Journal on Human Rights 406, 410.

[38]OAU Convention (n 34) Article II (3–5): "3. No person shall be subjected by a Member State to measures such as rejection at the frontier, return or expulsion, which would compel him to return to or remain in a territory where his life, physical integrity or liberty would be threatened for the reasons set out in Article I, paragraphs 1 and 2. 4. Where a Member State finds difficulty in continuing to grant asylum to refugees, such Member State may appeal directly to other Member States and through the OAU, and such other Member States shall in the spirit of African solidarity and international co-operation take appropriate measures to lighten the burden of the Member State granting asylum. 5. Where a refugee has not received the right to reside in any country of asylum, he may be granted temporary residence in any country of asylum in which he first presented himself as a refugee pending arrangement for his resettlement in accordance with the preceding paragraph."

[39]Eduardo Arboleda, 'The Cartagena Declaration of 1984 and its Similarities to the 1969 OAU Convention-A Comparative Perspective' [1995] 7 International Journal of Refugee Law 87, 91.

[40]Cartagena Declaration on Refugees, Adopted by the Colloquium on the International Protection of Refugees in Central America, Mexico and Panama, November 22, 1984.

the humanitarian practices and principles of refugee protection for the Latin American states. Interestingly, the Cartagena Declaration is not a legally binding instrument or an officially sanctioned statement. However, the declaration became significant when countries in Latin America adopted its principles in their own domestic law. The main contribution of the Cartagena Declaration is the adoption of a wider definition of refugee than the OAU Convention when it endorsed:

> in addition to containing the elements of the 1951 Convention and the 1967 Protocol, includes among refugees persons who have fled their country because their lives, safety or freedom have been threatened by generalized violence, foreign aggression, internal conflicts, massive violation of human rights or other circumstances which have seriously disturbed public order.[41]

Using terms such as generalized violence, foreign aggression, internal conflicts and massive violation of human rights have a significant effect by respecting and promoting the principles of basic human rights in refugee protection, keeping in view the modern political polity.[42] It is also felt that following the steps taken by the OAU Convention and the Cartagena Declaration, the definition of refugee should be enlarged in the 1951 Refugee Convention.[43] Given the emergence of new models of conflict in the current world order and new forms of persecution, the extended definition should have a significant impact on the practices of providing international protection.

5.4 Common European Asylum System

In the Special Meetings of the European Council in Tampere in 1999, the need to establish a Common European Asylum System (CEAS) was taken into consideration for the first time.[44] The CEAS is based on the

[41] Ibid. Part III, Article 3.

[42] See James C. Hathaway, 'Reconceiving Refuge Law as Human Rights Protection' [1991] 4 Journal of Refugee Studies, 113, 123.

[43] Jill I. Goldenziel, 'Regulating Human Rights: International Organizations, Flexible Standards, and International Refugee Law' [2013–2014] 14 Chicago Journal of International Law 453, 464.

[44] Presidency Conclusions, Tampere European Council, October 15–16, 1999 http://www.europarl.europa.eu/summits/tam_en.htm#a accessed December 2, 2015.

full and inclusive approach of the 1951 Refugee Convention, with more clarity about the process for member states of the European Union (EU) to follow in cases of granting asylum. Today the CEAS forms the body of the EU Asylum Law through directives and regulations of the EU and looks into common standards for recognition and refugee status and subsidiary protection through the Qualification Directive[45]; a fair and efficient asylum procedure through the Asylum Procedures Directive[46]; conditions of reception through the Reception Conditions Directive[47]; temporary protection through the Temporary Protection Directive[48]; and regulations on identification and the member state responsible for providing international protection. The first phase of the process of creating a harmonized protection mechanism ran from 1999 to 2005 with the previous versions of the directives and regulations mentioned above, and was finally transformed into the CEAS from July 21, 2015. The following sections of this chapter briefly analyze the core directives of the CEAS.

5.4.1 *Qualification Directive*

The Qualification Directive was adopted by the Council of the European Union on April 29, 2004 after extended negotiations.[49] It entered into force on October 20, 2004 and member states had until

[45] Directive on Standards for the Qualification of Third-country Nationals or Stateless Persons as Beneficiaries of International Protection, for a Uniform Status for Refugees or for Persons Eligible for Subsidiary Protection, and for the Content of the Protection Granted (recast), 2011/95/EU of the European Parliament and of the Council, December 13, 2011.

[46] Directive on Common Procedures for Granting and Withdrawing International Protection (recast), 2013/32/EU of the European Parliament and of the Council, June 26, 2013.

[47] Directive on Laying Down Standards for the Reception of Applicants for International Protection (recast), 2013/33/EU of the European Parliament and of the Council, June 26, 2013.

[48] Council Directive on Minimum Standards for Giving Temporary Protection in the Event of a Mass Influx of Displaced Persons and on Measures Promoting a Balance of Efforts between Member States in Receiving such Persons and Bearing the Consequences Thereof, 2001/55/EC of the European Council, July 20, 2001.

[49] See Helene Lambert, 'The EU Asylum Qualification Directive, Its Impact on the Jurisprudence of the United Kingdom and International Law' [2006] 55 International and Comparative Law Quarterly 161, 161.

October 10, 2006 to implement its provisions in their national legislation. Meanwhile, they had a duty not to adopt measures contrary to this directive, and in those countries that had already implemented the Qualification Directive, the judiciary would need to ensure compliance.[50] The present version of the Qualification Directive is a recast version adopted in 2011, which has now been implemented throughout the EU since July 21, 2015 as the previous version maintained divergence in national asylum legislation and practices. The core of the Qualification Directive is the inclusion of other persons entitled to asylum as per provisions of international human rights law, as the directive combines refugee protection and subsidiary protection to institutionalize a common EU definition of persons in genuine need of international protection and to provide a status for these persons.[51]

In the Qualification Directive the term "international protection" is defined as refugee status or subsidiary protection status.[52] The definition of refugee in the Qualification Directive is similar to the definition given in the 1951 Refugee Convention. It is important that the extended definition of international protection includes the term "subsidiary protection," which is available to a person who is a

third-country national or a stateless person who does not qualify as a refugee but in respect of whom substantial grounds have been shown for believing that the person concerned, if returned to his or her country of origin, or in the case of a stateless person, to his or her country of former habitual residence, would face a real risk of suffering serious harm.[53]

The term "serious harm" further refers to any of the following: death penalty or execution, torture or inhuman or degrading treatment, and threat to civilian life in situations of armed conflict.[54]

---

[50] Ibid.

[51] Ibid. 162; see also R. Piotrowizc and C. van Eck, 'Subsidiary Protection and Primary Rights' [2004] 53 International and Comparative Law Quarterly 107, 115.

[52] Qualification Directive (n 45) Article 2(a); For internal protection see generally Jonah Eaton, 'The Internal Protection Alternative Under European Union Law: Examining The Recast Qualification Directive' [2012] 24 International Journal of Refugee Law 765, 777.

[53] Qualification Directive (n 45) Article 2(f); see also Jane McAdam, 'The European Union Qualification Directive: The Creation of a Subsidiary Protection Regime' [2005] 17 International Journal of Refugee Law 461, 469.

[54] Qualification Directive (n 45) Article 15.

In the 1951 Refugee Convention the term "persecution" is not defined, and "it seems as if the drafters have wanted to introduce a flexible concept which might be applied to circumstances as they might arise; or in other words, that they capitulated before the inventiveness of humanity to think up new ways of persecuting fellow men."[55] However, the Qualification Directive defines several specific acts as persecution, including[56]

1. serious or repeated violation of basic human rights;
2. physical, mental or sexual violence;
3. discriminatory measures taken by the state machinery;
4. disproportionate or discriminatory treatment, and the denial of redress by judicial measures;
5. prosecution and punishment for refusal to perform military service;
6. harm intended to a specific gender or to children.

At the same time, the Qualification Directive includes a provision about the perpetrators of persecution or serious harm.[57] The provision refers to three perpetrators of persecution or serious harm: the state, parties or organizations controlling the state, and non-state actors. The Qualification Directive also asserts that protection from persecution or serious harm must be effective and non-temporary in nature, and the parties responsible for providing protection are listed as the state and the parties or organizations or international organizations controlling the state.[58] Articles of Qualification Directive discussed above have set the standard of the Qualification Directive to a higher place than the 1951 Refugee Convention as novelty and reasonableness for a better protection is given due consideration.[59]

The Qualification Directive also defines the contents of international protection, which mean the rights acquired through refugee status or subsidiary protection status. Rights granted under these provisions of the Qualification Directive are set to be effective without prejudice to the

[55] Alte Grahl-Madsen, *The Status of Refugees in International Law* (1966) 193.

[56] Qualification Directive (n 45) Article 9.

[57] Qualification Directive (n 45) Article 6.

[58] Qualification Directive (n 45) Article 7.

[59] Storey (n 29) 3.

rights granted under the 1951 Refugee Convention.[60] The contents of protection under the Qualification Directive are listed below:

1. Protection from refoulement[61]: Member states of the EU are obliged to respect the principle of non-refoulement with respect to their international obligations. It is noteworthy that all the member states of the EU are signatories of the 1951 Refugee Convention and hence are bound by the rules provided there. Thus the Qualification Directive only complements the obligations contained in the 1951 Refugee Convention in terms of the right against refoulement. However, the Qualification Directive provides grounds on which a member state can *refoul* a refugee, such as when the refugee poses a danger to the security of the state or in the case of conviction by a court for having committed a serious crime against the community of the concerned state.[62]
2. Receiving of information and language[63]: The beneficiaries of international protection under the Qualification Directive are to receive information in a language that they understand. The information will include their rights and obligations as a refugee.
3. Family unity[64]: Another very interesting extension of protection is the provision relating to the maintenance of family unity. It is often the case that not all family members are entitled to international protection under the Qualification Directive as a result of not meeting the requirements mentioned to qualify for refugee or subsidiary protection status. However, under the Qualification Directive, states are obliged to ensure the family unity of persons who have received international protection. In this case, all the rights which are available to the persons having international protection will also be applicable to the family members. It is noteworthy that family members may include both immediate family members and persons who lived as family members as dependents.

---

[60] Qualification Directive (n 45) Article 20.

[61] Qualification Directive (n 45) Article 21.

[62] For effective remedy see Marcelle Reneman, 'Access to an Effective Remedy in European Asylum Procedures' (2009) 1 Amsterdam Law Forum 65, 70.

[63] Qualification Directive (n 45) Article 22.

[64] Qualification Directive (n 45) Article 23.

4. Issue of residence permit[65]: The issuing of a residence permit for third-country nationals is key to receiving other civic amenities in the EU. The Qualification Directive sets out provisions for issuing residence permits to refugees or persons covered under subsidiary protection. Refugees are to receive a residence permit valid for 3 years with a provision of extension. Persons covered under the subsidiary protection status are to receive a residence permit valid for a year and in case of renewal for 2 years. In both cases, family members of the concerned persons are also to receive residence permits. However, the residence permit can be revoked in case of a threat to the security of the state or association with serious crime.
5. Issue of travel document[66]: It is frequently the case that refugees do not have travel documents of their own, or that their documents have expired. The Qualification Directive makes it obligatory for member states to issue travel documents as per the provisions of the 1951 Refugee Convention. At the same time, a person covered under the subsidiary protection status who does not have a passport or was not able to obtain a passport from his/her country of nationality can also get a travel document from the EU member state where he/she is under subsidiary protection.
6. Access to employment[67]: The Qualification Directive obliges the member states of the EU to provide full access to employment and self-employment to persons covered under the international protection status. At the same time, training and vocational education are to be made available to persons having international protection status under the same conditions as nationals.
7. Access to education[68]: Access to education under the same conditions as nationals for persons who have been granted international protection status is included in the Qualification Directive. Minors are to have full access to education, and other persons are to have access to the general education system.

[65] Qualification Directive (n 45) Article 24.
[66] Qualification Directive (n 45) Article 25.
[67] Qualification Directive (n 45) Article 26.
[68] Qualification Directive (n 45) Article 27.

8. Recognition of degree and diploma[69]: Beneficiaries of international protection are to be treated the same as nationals with regard to recognition of degrees and diplomas obtained in other countries. This is to ensure that the previous education of a beneficiary of international protection is not wasted in the country of refuge.
9. Social welfare[70]: The member states of the EU are obliged to provide beneficiaries of international protection with the same access to social welfare schemes as nationals. However, in the case of subsidiary protection status, states may limit assistance to the core benefits of the social welfare system.
10. Health care[71]: It is obligatory for the member states of the EU to provide beneficiaries of international protection with full access to health care facilities under the same conditions as nationals. At the same time, special attention must be given to pregnant women, disabled persons, children and other persons who have suffered from any form of violence.
11. Best interest of unaccompanied minors[72]: The best interest of unaccompanied minors has to be considered as per the Qualification Directive. Unaccompanied minors are to be provided with all necessary care through a legal guardian. The guardianship of an unaccompanied minor can be given to his/her adult relatives, or to a foster family or center specializing in the protection of minors. Another important aspect of this provision is that the state is responsible for locating the family of the minor for reunion, and all information in this regard or any act in this regard should be done confidentially to protect the minor as well as the family.

12 Access to accommodation[73]: Member states are obliged to provide access to accommodation to beneficiaries of international protection under the same conditions as for third-country nationals.

[69] Qualification Directive (n 45) Article 28.
[70] Qualification Directive (n 45) Article 29.
[71] Qualification Directive (n 45) Article 30.
[72] Qualification Directive (n 45) Article 31.
[73] Qualification Directive (n 45) Article 32.

13. Freedom of movement[74]: Member states are obliged to allow beneficiaries of international protection the freedom of movement within their territory under the same conditions as provided for legal residents from any third country.
14 Integration facilities[75]: Integration facilities have to be provided to beneficiaries of international protection to enable them to participate in the community. Access to various integration programs and language courses is generally provided under this provision.
15. Repatriation[76]: In case of voluntary repatriation, member states may provide such facilities as required by beneficiaries of international protection.

It can be argued that the Qualification Directive refers to a "uniform status" for beneficiaries of international protection and to "standards" instead of "minimum standards" on qualification for status.[77] The main aims in coming up with the Qualification Directive were to ensure a fully inclusive application of the 1951 Refugee Convention and compliance with human rights law, raise the standard of protection, increase the degree of harmonization and improve the effectiveness of the asylum law within the EU.[78] Some critics argue that while the Qualification Directive has gone a long way towards the first aim of a fully inclusive application of the 1951 Refugee Convention and compliance with human rights law, it has failed on other issues.[79] However, considering the strategic ambiguity of the refugee protection procedure followed in India, it could learn from the codification of combined protection under the 1951 Refugee Convention along with international human rights standards.

[74] Qualification Directive (n 45) Article 33.

[75] Qualification Directive (n 45) Article 34.

[76] Qualification Directive (n 45) Article 35.

[77] Steve Peers, 'Legislative Update 2011, EU Immigration and Asylum Law: The Recast Qualification Directive' [2012] 14 European Journal of Migration and Law 204, 204.

[78] Ibid. 220.

[79] Ibid. 221.

5.4.2 *Asylum Procedures Directive*

The recast Asylum Procedures Directive was adopted on June 26, 2013 by the European Parliament and the European Council. Most of the provisions of the Asylum Procedures Directive had entered into force by July 20, 2015.[80] The purpose of the Asylum Procedures Directive is to establish common procedures for granting and withdrawing international protection pursuant to the Qualification Directive.[81]

Access to the procedures under the Asylum Procedures Directive is available to applicants for international protection at the borders or in the territorial waters or transit zones of the member states of the EU.[82] The Asylum Procedures Directive makes it mandatory that whenever any third-country national wishes to apply for international protection, irrespective of his/her presence in a detention center or at a border post, the members states of the EU are obliged to provide the prospective applicant for international protection information related to the process and counseling.[83] At the same time, applicants for international protection have the right to remain in the territory of the concerned member state until a decision is made on the application.[84] Member states must ensure that an application for international protection is duly examined by the determining authority empowered to do so irrespective of the time taken by the applicant to make the application, and the determining authority must ensure that individual decisions are objective and impartial.[85] The determining authority will preliminarily determine whether the applicant qualifies for refugee status, and if not whether the applicant qualifies for subsidiary protection status. To make the decision, the determining authority will conduct a personal interview with the applicant, although in cases where the medical condition of the applicant is such that a personal interview is not possible, the determining authority

---

[80] Asylum Procedure Directive (n 46) Article 51(1); for detailed negotiation process, see Doede Ackers, 'The Negotiations on the Asylum Procedures Directive' [2005] 7 European Journal of Migration and Law 1–33

[81] Asylum Procedure Directive (n 46) Article 1; see Maria Panezi, 'The 2005 Asylum Procedures Directive: Developing the European Asylum Law' [2006–2007] 13 Columbia Journal of European Law 501, 505.

[82] Asylum Procedure Directive (n 46) Article 3.

[83] Asylum Procedure Directive (n 46) Article 8.

[84] Asylum Procedure Directive (n 46) Article 9.

[85] Asylum Procedure Directive (n 46) Article 10.

may not conduct the interview.[86] The decision on the application for international protection must be communicated to the applicant in writing, and in cases where international protection is denied, the reasons in fact and in law along with the process for appealing that decision must be stated in the written communication.[87] At the same time, while the determination process is under way the member state will guarantee that all communication is in the language understood by the applicant, and it will provide the applicant with the services of an interpreter if required as well as the chance to communicate with UNHCR or other organizations providing legal advice to applicants and the chance to be represented by a legal practitioner and free legal services.[88] As per the Asylum Procedures Directive , member states are not allowed to detain an applicant for international protection solely on the grounds that decision on the application is pending.[89] Member states will ensure that the decision of an application is taken within six months of its submission, and in the case of complexity of law and fact with regard to one application, or a high volume of applications received by the determining authority, this term of 6 months can be extended to a further term of 9 months.[90]

With regard to the admissibility of applications for international protection, there are several grounds on the basis of which an application can be considered inadmissible.[91] The grounds for inadmissibility include: protection has been granted by another member state; any country except a member state is considered as a first country of asylum for the applicant; any country except a member state is considered a safe third country for the applicant; a subsequent application has no significant grounds; and so forth.[92] The concepts used in the inadmissibility provision that are exclusively used in the Asylum Procedures Directive are important in terms of a properly governed refugee protection system as well as in the prevention of secondary movement. The concept

[86] Asylum Procedure Directive (n 46) Article 14–17.

[87] Asylum Procedure Directive (n 46) Article 11.

[88] Asylum Procedure Directive (n 46) Article 12.

[89] Asylum Procedure Directive (n 46) Article 26.

[90] Asylum Procedure Directive (n 46) Article 31.

[91] See Cathryn Costello, 'The Asylum Procedures Directive and the Proliferation of Safe Country Practices: Deterrence, Deflection and the Dismantling of International Protection?' [2005] 7 European Journal of Migration and Law 35, 39.

[92] Asylum Procedure Directive (n 46) Article 33.

of "first country of asylum" is the one where the present applicant for international protection in any member state of the EU has already been granted legal status allowing the person to remain as an asylum seeker or refugee.[93] The provision in the Asylum Procedures Directive further directs that a country can be termed a "first country of asylum" for an applicant for international protection if the applicant is enjoying status as a refugee in that country, receiving protection in that country, or enjoying protection including benefit of the non-refoulement principle in that country. In contrast, the concept of "safe third country" refers to a country where the person could have found protection, but did try to get it.[94] The provision of "safe third country" further refers to the grounds for determination, such as when the life and liberty of the applicant is not threatened in that country, there is no risk of serious harm, the principle of non-refoulement is respected in that country, prohibition of removal is respected in that country, and the process to apply for refugee status in that country and a genuine chance to receive refugee status are available. Apart from these two procedural matters in terms of inadmissibility, the concept of "safe country of origin" is also regarded as one of the important pillars of exclusion. Member states are obliged to make a list of "safe countries of origin" in their national legislation.[95]

The various provisions of the Asylum Procedures Directive have laid out a better procedure to be followed and guaranteed some procedural rights for applicants in the member states of the EU in terms of standards provided by various international law instruments.[96] At the same time, the concepts of inadmissibility have significance in terms of balancing refugee flow and protection vis-à-vis overall refugee governance in terms of international burden-sharing and maintaining human rights standards.[97]

---

[93] Asylum Procedure Directive (n 46) Article 35; see Costello (n 79) 39.

[94] Asylum Procedure Directive (n 46) Article 38.

[95] Asylum Procedure Directive (n 46) Article 36.

[96] For a detailed discussion, see Pieter Boeles and Ashley Terlouw, 'Minimum Guarantees for Asylum Procedures' [1997] 9 International Journal of Refugee Law 472, 478.

[97] Panezi (n 81) 512; see also Kay Hailbronner, 'The Right to Asylum and Future of Asylum Procedures in the European Community' [1990] 2 International Journal of Refugee Law 341, 358.

5.4.3 Reception Conditions Directive

The purpose of the Reception Conditions Directive is to set standards for the reception of applicants for international protection in member states of the EU.[98] It ensures that applicants have access to housing, food, health care and employment, as well as medical and psychological care. Reception conditions are defined as the full set of measures granted to applicants for international protection by the member states of the EU.[99] Again, "material reception conditions" include housing, food and clothing provided in kind, or as financial allowances or vouchers, or a combination of the three, and a daily expenses allowance.[100]

Under the Reception Conditions Directive, member states are obliged to provide for the various needs of applicants for international protection. These needs are primarily material and welfare based. The material conditions have to be ensured for each applicant for international protection to provide an adequate standard of living for applicants, which guarantees their subsistence and protects their physical and mental health.[101] In cases where member states provide financial allowances, the amount will be determined by the member states by law or by practice. While the member states have provided with housing facility that be on the form of premises used for the purpose of housing applicants during the examination of an application or accommodation centers or private houses adapted for housing applicants.[102] There shall be provision for schooling facilities for minors under similar conditions as nationals, and in case of necessity such education opportunity can be provided in the accommodation center.[103] It is also obligatory for member states to provide health care facilities to applicants for international protection.[104]

As per the Reception Conditions Directive, access to employment must be provided to applicants for international protection within nine months of the application, and this access will continue until a final

[98] Reception Conditions Directive (n 47) Article 1; See also Nicola Rogers, 'Minimum Standards for Reception' [2002] 4 European Journal of Migration and Law 215, 228.

[99] Reception Conditions Directive (n 47) Article 2(f).

[100] Reception Conditions Directive (n 47) Article 2(g).

[101] Reception Conditions Directive (n 47) Article 17.

[102] Reception Conditions Directive (n 47) Article 18.

[103] Reception Conditions Directive (n 47) Article 14.

[104] Reception Conditions Directive (n 47) Article 19.

decision is made on the eligibility of the applicant for international protection.[105] At the same time, access to vocational training can also be granted to applicants for international protection by member states.[106]

Detailed common rules have been adopted on the issue of detention of asylum seekers, ensuring that their fundamental rights are fully respected under the Reception Conditions Directive. The grounds for detention are documented and any detention that does not fulfill any of the grounds will be illegal.[107] At the same time, it restricts the detention of vulnerable persons, provides free legal assistance, requires specific reception conditions at detention centers and so on.[108]

It is important that a new regime for refugee protection includes an entire directive on the standards of reception conditions. Reception conditions may not be considered as important as qualification or asylum procedures, but it must be understood that the essentials of daily life are extremely important during a refugee's first days in a foreign land.[109]

5.4.4 Temporary Protection Directive

The Temporary Protection Directive was adopted on July 20, 2001, but the provisions of this directive have not yet been applied by the member states of the EU. It was adopted as a special procedure for times of mass influx with an aim to protect the displaced. The purpose of this directive is to establish minimum standards for giving temporary protection in the event of a mass influx of people from third countries who are unable to return to their country of origin.[110]

Temporary protection is defined as a

procedure of exceptional character to provide, in the event of a mass influx or imminent mass influx of displaced persons from third countries who are unable to return to their country of origin, immediate and temporary protection to such persons, in particular if there is also a risk that

---

[105] Reception Conditions Directive (n 47) Article 15.

[106] Reception Conditions Directive (n 47) Article 16.

[107] Reception Conditions Directive (n 47) Article 8.

[108] Reception Conditions Directive (n 47) Article 9–11.

[109] Rogers (n 98) 230.

[110] Temporary Protection Directive (n 48) Article 1; for a detailed discussion on mass influx, see Karoline Kerber, 'The Temporary Protection Directive' [2002] 4 European Journal of Migration and Law 193, 196.

the asylum system will be unable to process this influx without adverse effects for its efficient operation, in the interests of the persons concerned and other persons requesting protection.[111]

The prerequisites for making this directive operational are a mass influx situation, when persons are unable to return to their country of origin, and when there is a possibility that the normal asylum system will be overwhelmed. Again, displaced persons are divided into two categories: those who have fled armed conflict or endemic violence, and those who are or have been victims of a serious violation of their human rights in systematic or generalized form.[112] The directive defines mass influx as the arrival of large numbers of displaced persons from one country or geographical area irrespective of spontaneous or aided arrival.[113] The directive guarantees temporary protection for a year initially and may be extended to one more year, and in the case of a grave situation the Council may extend the protection to one more year.[114]

The Temporary Protection Directive in Chapter III Articles 8–16 defines the obligations towards beneficiaries of temporary protection. Chapter III of the directive refers to the "obligations" of member states and not the "rights of persons enjoying temporary protection," implying that member states are internationally obliged to grant temporarily protected persons a certain minimum of treatment.[115] However, temporarily protected persons have no subjective rights towards member states that can be judicially enforced.[116] Member states are required to provide for beneficiaries of temporary protection as per Article 8 of the directive for the entire term of their stay.

Persons enjoying temporary protection will be permitted to engage in employed or self-employed activities during the temporary protection regime subject to the rules applicable to the profession, and member states shall take all necessary measures in this regard.[117] Member states shall also take effective measures to provide accommodation or

[111] Temporary Protection Directive (n 48) Article 2(a).
[112] Temporary Protection Directive (n 48) Article 2(c).
[113] Temporary Protection Directive (n 48) Article 2(d).
[114] Temporary Protection Directive (n 48) Article 4.
[115] Kerber (n 110) 201.
[116] Ibid.
[117] Temporary Protection Directive (n 48) Article 12.

the means to obtain housing to beneficiaries of temporary protection.[118] Apart from that, member states shall be required to act upon social welfare and medical care, education and opportunity of family reunification, and so on.[119] With these provisions the Temporary Protection Directive makes it a part of the CEAS, above all in situation of mass influx the protection according to human rights standards makes this Directive the most notable among the CEAS. Following the armed conflict in the former Yugoslavia the EU was in favor of providing a common system in times of mass influx, though during the present Syrian refugee crisis this directive has not been applied.

5.5 Conclusion

An examination of protection standards for refugees reveals that after the 1951 Refugee Convention, the OAU Convention, the Cartagena Declaration and the newest of all, the CEAS, provide the most developed and detailed standards for protection of refugees. Introducing the norm of protecting human rights as included in the OAU Convention and the Cartagena Declaration opened a new frontier in the realm of refugee protection. At the same time, it is important to note that the CEAS, apart from including refugees under the protection framework, also included a separate category of "subsidiary protection" for other persons in need of protection from serious harm. This novel provision actually removes the barrier between refugee protection and protection given for securing human rights. This bridge between refugee protection and the protection of human rights could become the model for a twenty-first-century protection regime. At the same time, the CEAS throughout emphasizes several essential elements required for living a life of adequate standard, such as material reception conditions, housing, education, health care, residence permit, opportunity for employment or self-employment and so on. Lastly, it can be argued that the CEAS provisions can be taken into consideration by those who are trying to formulate a refugee protection regime based on cosmopolitan traditions, human rights protection, and balancing security and state practice.

[118] Temporary Protection Directive (n 48) Article 13.

[119] Temporary Protection Directive (n 48) Article 13–16.

CHAPTER 6

A Comparative Study on National Refugee Law of South Africa, Brazil and Canada

6.1 States and National Laws on Refugee Protection

The standards for refugee protection contained in the 1951 Convention Relating to the Status of Refugees (hereinafter 1951 Refugee Convention), the 1969 Organisation of African Unity (OAU) Convention Governing the Specific Aspects of Refugee Problems in Africa (hereinafter OAU Convention), the 1984 Cartagena Declaration on Refugees (hereinafter Cartagena Declaration) and the newest of all, the Common European Asylum System (hereinafter CEAS), have evolved over time. The state parties have taken varied approaches to following the provisions laid down in these conventions, and several states have incorporated these provisions in their national laws on refugee protection.[1] At the same time, several Western and Pacific countries have begun providing resources to help states serving as routes of refugee movement to Europe and Australia so that the refugees are able to settle in those states and their further movement can be restricted. This kind of operational measure on the part of

[1] G. Loescher, *Beyond Charity: International Cooperation and Global Refugee Crisis* (Oxford University Press, New York 1993) 59–60; See also Guy S. Goodwin-Gill, 'The Politics of Refugee Protection' in Helene Lambert (ed), *International Refugee Law* (Ashgate Publishing Limited 2010) 145–160; M. R. Marrus, *The Unwanted: European Refugees in the Twentieth Century* (Oxford University Press, New York 1985) 317–324.

S.P. Sarker, *Refugee Law in India*,
DOI 10.1007/978-981-10-4807-4_6

countries of the Global North can also be termed a mechanism of calculated kindness.[2] It is therefore necessary to analyze the spirit of the refugee protection legislation of states that has been in operation for a considerable period of time and thus can be regarded as a model for its region. However, the practice of implementation of this legislation by the respective states will not be discussed here, as the principal aim of this research is to look at the spirit of the laws. The selection of states for this comparative study is based on region, or more specifically on the divide between the Global South and the Global North: South Africa and Brazil represent the Global South, while Canada represents the Global North. In terms of continental representation, South Africa belongs to Africa, Brazil belongs to South/Latin America and Canada belongs to North America. In terms of legal systems followed, Canada follows common law, Brazil follows civil law and South Africa follows a mixed system of civil and common law.

6.2 Refugee Protection in South Africa

South Africa over the years has experienced refugee movement at a higher rate than expected by the authorities. The causes of refugee movement in South Africa were both micro (psychological, individual and familial) and macro (for example, social class, political, regional and global) in nature.[3] South Africa has witnessed how issues of political economy shape the selection of specific targets in refugee-generating conflicts—having massive impacts on individuals, families and

[2] See Gil Loescher and John A. Scanlan, 'Calculated Kindness: Refugees and America's Half Open Door, 1945 to the Present' *The Free Press* (New York 1986) 210; K. Solomon, *Refugees in the Cold War: Toward a New International Refugee Regime in the Early Post-War Era* (Lund University Press, Lund 1991) 53; "Countries in which the largest number of people have taken refuge are precisely those that have supported war and terrorism," see Robert E. Mazur, 'The Political Economy of Refugee Creation in Southern Africa: Micro and Macro Issues in Sociological Perspective' [1989] 2(4) Journal of Refugees Studies 441, 461.

[3] T. Hart & C. M. Rogerson, 'The Geography of International Refugee Movements in Southern Africa' [1982] 64(2) South Africa Geographical Journal 125, 135. See also Robert E. Mazur, 'Linking Popular Initiative and Aid Agencies: The Case of Refugees' [1987] 18(4) Development and Change 437, 440.

communities—which permits the transformation of the regional political economy. Its sociological and political economy perspectives, which are complementary and essential ingredients in understanding processes of change in the refugee-related crises in Southern Africa, reveal the dynamic interaction between macro- and micro-level phenomena and their mutual transformation.[4] Historically the refugee problem is to be situated in the context of class practices and the class struggle in South Africa. This means it is a multidimensional struggle, not only because of the multiplicity of social ensembles (basically classes) that take part in it, but also because of the multiplicity of levels at which it is waged—economic, political and ideological, as well as national, regional and global.[5] However, the nodal point of the class struggle takes various forms in various countries and regions at specific historical moments. The moment of the global class struggle can be captured by a number of national and global processes.[6] South Africa has witnessed a complex conjuncture of the class struggle because of the intricate mix of class and racial factors involved. This class struggle is mirrored by a number of conditions that

[4]Robert E. Mazur, 'Refugees in Africa: The Role of Sociological Analysis and Praxis' [1988] 36(2) Current Sociology 43, 49; See also Tiyanjana Maluwa, 'The Refugee Problem and the Quest for Peace and Security in Southern Africa' [1995] 7 International Journal of Refugee Law 653, 670.

[5]A. Richmond, 'Sociological Theories of International Migration: The Case of Refugees' [1988] 36(2) Current Sociology 7, 21; See also Peter Anyangnyongo & Justus Abonyo Nyangaya, 'Comprehensive Solutions to Refugee Problems in Africa: Bilateral, Regional and Multilateral Approaches' [1995] 7 International Journal of Refugee Law 164, 166.

[6]Okechukwu Ibeanu, 'Apartheid, Destabilization and Displacement: The Dynamics of the Refugee Crisis in Southern Africa' [1990] 3(1) Journal of Refugees Studies 47, 51; Okechukwu writes four major instances prevailing in South Africa, these are: polarization of the world (both within and among nations) into a rich minority and a poor-majority, a process which is organically related to problems of exploitation, poverty, inequity, discrimination and under development; political repression and the militarization of social life; exclusivity and factionalism especially within ruling groups; and denial of the right of people to control their social and bio-physical environments, for their own benefit and as they see fit. This gives rise to external intervention in national and regional problems, as well as to the denial of the genuine right of nationalities to self-determination. See also Obonye Jonas, 'Reflections on the Refugee Protection Regime in Africa: Challenges and Prospects' [2012] 14 University of Botswana Law Journal 71, 76.

have directly generated population displacement and relocation, such as apartheid, destabilization of neighbors and liberation struggles.[7]

It is in the context of these conditions and their connection to the displacement and relocation of people in the region that the South African refugee protection law will be evaluated. It is generally understood that the aims of any refugee protection law are to create decent and orderly reception, provide safety and mitigate suffering. The Aliens Control Act, 1991 of South Africa failed on many levels to provide adequate guarantees to applicants.[8] Thereafter the entire process of refugee reform was initiated, leading to the development of the Refugees Act, 1998,[9] followed by the Immigration Act, 2012 (which repealed the Alien Control Act, 1991).[10] South Africa's national refugee legislation incorporates the basic principles of refugee protection, including freedom of movement, the right to work and access to basic social services. The South African government has made important strides in protecting people who have been compelled to leave their countries of origin as a result of well-founded fear of persecution, violence or conflict. However, there are questions with regard to the implementation the refugee protection legislation and rigidity in several aspects.[11] South Africa is a party to the 1951 Refugee Convention and the OAU Convention. The conflicts that

---

[7] id. 53; Ahmednasir M.Abdullahi, 'The Refugee Crisis in Africa as a Crisis of the Institution of the State' [1994] 6(4) International Journal of Refugee Law 562, 566.

[8] Jonathan Klaaren & Chris Sprigman, 'Refugee Status Determination Procedures in South African Law', in Jeff Handmaker, Lee Anne de la Hunt & Jonathan Klaaren, *Advancing Refugee Protection in South Africa* (Berghahn Books, New York 2007) 61–88.

[9] Refugees Act, 1998 (No. 30 of 1998, South Africa).

[10] Immigration Act, 2002 (No. 13 of 2002, South Africa).

[11] Audie Klotz, *Migration and National Identity in South Africa 1860–2010* (Cambridge University Press, New York 2013) 202–215; See also J. Garvey, 'Toward a Reformulation of International Refugee Law' [1985] 26 Harvard International Law Journal 483; J. Hathaway, 'A Reconsideration of the Underlying Premise of Refugee Law' [1991] 31 Harvard International Law Journal 129.

accompanied the end of the colonial era in Africa led to a series of large-scale refugee movements. These population displacements prompted the drafting and adoption of not only the 1967 Refugee Protocol but also the OAU Convention.[12] The OAU Convention follows the refugee definition of the 1951 Convention with the inclusion of some objective considerations specific to Africa from the international human rights instruments.[13] As a result, persons fleeing civil disturbances, widespread violence and war are entitled to claim the status of refugee in states that are parties to the OAU Convention, regardless of whether they have a well-founded fear of persecution.[14]

The proposal to introduce refugee legislation in South Africa came in 1996, with the preparation of an initial draft refugee bill by the Department of Home Affairs. This was followed by the circulation of drafts, which received critical public comments, and thereafter, with certain substantial changes involving public debates and meetings with civil societies, the draft received a consensus vote from the National Assembly on November 5, 1998.[15] Though the policy-making process or legislative process may sometimes be controversial, it is always recommended that the approach continue

---

[12] Bonaventure Rutinwa, 'The End of Asylum? The Changing Nature of Refugee Policies in Africa' in Helene Lambert (ed.), *International Refugee Law* (Ashgate Publishing Limited 2010) 35; See also 'Prohibited Persons, Abuse of Undocumented Migrants, Asylum-Seekers, and Refugees in South Africa' *Human Rights Watch* (New York 1998) 221.

[13] W.J.E.M. van Hdvell tot Westerflier, 'Africa and Refugees: The OAU Refugee Convention in Theory and Practice' [1989] 7 Netherlands Quarterly of Human Rights 172, 174; See also Alice Edwards, 'Refugee Status Determination in Africa' [2006] 14 African Journal of International and Comparative Law 204, 205

[14] Michael Kingsley Nyniah, 'Reflections on the Institution of Asylum, Refugee Criteria, and Irregular Movements in Southern Africa' [1995] 7(2) International Journal of Refugee Law 291, 293; See also Joe Oloka-Onyango, 'Human Rights, The OAU Convention and the Refugee Crisis in Africa: Forty Years After Geneva' [1991] 3 International Journal of Refugee Law 453, 455.

[15] Ingrid van Beek, 'Prima Facie Asylum Determination in South Africa', in Jeff Handmaker, Lee Anne de la Hunt & Jonathan Klaaren (eds.), *Perspectives on Refugee Protection in South Africa* (Pretoria: Lawyers for Human Rights 2001) 17–59; See J. Handmaker, 'Who Determines Policy? Promoting The Right of Asylum in South Africa' [1999] 11(2) International Journal of Refugee Law 291, 292.

to focus on enhancing strategic partnerships and strengthening coordination in its main areas of intervention for better protection of refugees.[16]

6.2.1 *Refugee Definition, Exclusion and Cessation*

The Refugees Act, 1998 is South Africa's legislation regarding refugee protection. The Refugees Act, 1998 establishes the institutions and procedures to offer refuge and protection to those who are facing persecution and instability in their home countries. However, the Immigration Act, 2002 deals with the regulation of entry, stay and documentation of non-nationals in South Africa. These two pieces of legislation differ in their scope and application. Immigration law is ruled by the principle of sovereignty, where every state is free to design and implement its own immigration policies, while refugee law is characterized by various international obligations based on international human rights law. As a sovereign state, South Africa has the right to detain and deport those who violate its immigration laws—a power that allows the state to govern and control its borders.[17] On the other hand, the Refugees Act is the primary piece of legislation that ensures the safety, well-being and dignity of asylum seekers and refugees. It provides for the reception into the country of asylum seekers and regulates the application for and recognition of refugee status. The matters concerning asylum seekers and refugees are outside the purview of immigration laws. The integrity of the legal regime underpinning refugee protection would be at risk if asylum policies were considered a subset of migration management strategies that are governed by security concerns. Thus the sections of this chapter will be concerned with refugees and the laws governing them, leaving aside the aspect of immigration.

For a person to qualify for refugee status in South Africa, he/she must conform to the definition of a refugee provided in the Refugees Act, 1998. South Africa follows an individual refugee status determination procedure. An asylum seeker is defined as a person who has lodged or intends to lodge an asylum application and who is awaiting a decision on his/her asylum claim.[18] An asylum seeker qualifies as a refugee under the Refugees Act, 1998 if that person:

---

[16] Jeff Handmaker, 'No Easy Walk: Advancing Refugee Protection in South Africa' [2001] 48(3) Indiana University Press 91, 92; Michael Kingsley-Nyinah, 'Reflections on the Institution of Asylum, Refugee Criteria, and Irregular Movements in Southern Africa' [1995] 7 International Journal of Refugee Law 291, 310.

[17] Section 3(1)(g), The Immigration Act, 2002.

[18] Section 1, The Refugees Act, 1998.

1. Owing to a well-founded fear of being persecuted by reason of his or her gender, race, tribe, religion, nationality, political opinion or membership of a particular social group, is outside the country of his or her nationality and is unable or unwilling to avail himself or herself of the protection of that country, or, not having the nationality and being outside the country of his or her former habitual residence is unable or, owing to such fear, is unwilling to return to it; or
2. Owing to external aggression, occupation, foreign domination, or other events seriously disturbing public order in either a part or the whole of his or her country of origin or nationality, is compelled to leave his or her place of habitual residence in order to seek refuge in another place outside his or her country of origin or nationality; or
3. Is a spouse or dependant of a person contemplated in paragraph (i) or (ii).[19]

Asylum seekers are also protected under the umbrella concept of refugee even though they are not expressly included in the definition. Though asylum seekers are protected by the law, their legal position or status is somehow unclear. This multiplicity of criteria used to determine who is a refugee leads to multiple interpretations, causing an avalanche of changes to an individual's material and social situation.[20] An asylum seeker will not qualify for refugee status under South African law if he/she has committed acts such as international crime, any non-political crime punishable in South Africa, acts committed against the United Nations or OAU, or if he/she enjoys the protection of any other country.[21] A person ceases to qualify for refugee status if he/she avails him/herself of the protection of the country of his/her nationality, or if circumstances in connection with which he/she has been recognized as a refugee have ceased to exist and no other circumstances have arisen to justify his/her continued recognition as a refugee.[22] The provision related to cessation contains a proviso which states that refugee status does not cease for a refugee "who is able to invoke compelling reasons

[19] Section 3, Refugees Act, 1998.

[20] Daniel J. Steinbock 'The Refugee Definition as Law: Issues of Interpretation' in Nicholson and Twomey (eds.), *Refugee Rights and Realities: Evolving International Concepts and Regimes* (Cambridge University Press, Cambridge 1999) 20.

[21] Section 4, Refugees Act, 1998.

[22] Section 5, The Refugees Act, 1998.

arising out of previous persecution for refusing to avail himself of the protection of the country of nationality."[23]

6.2.2 Procedure and Determining Authorities

An application for refugee status has to be submitted to a Refugee Reception Officer at any Refugee Reception Office as per the law.[24] The Refugee Reception Officer is bound to accept the application and in case of necessity he/she will assist the applicant to comply with the requirements of application.[25] The Refugee Reception Officer will then forward the application to the Refugee Status Determination Officer after necessary enquiry as he/she deems fit.[26] At the same time, the Refugee Reception Officer will issue an asylum seeker permit to the applicant that allows him/her to temporarily reside in South Africa, and that permit will be regularly extended until a decision has been reached.[27] After receiving the application from the Refugee Reception Officer, the Refugee Status Determination Officer may ask for further information either from the forwarding officer or from the United Nations High Commissioner for Refugees (UNHCR) representative to reach a decision.[28] The Refugee Status Determination Officer will conduct a hearing with the applicant and may grant asylum.[29] In some cases the Refugee Status Determination Officer may refer any question of law related to the application to the Standing Committee for their determination.[30] The Refugee Status Determination Officer may also reject the application

[23] Section 5(2), The Refugees Act, 1998; This again is a copy of the exception from the 1951 Convention and confirms the potential need for continued refugee protection for some refugees. See also Jeremy R. Tarwater, 'Analysis and Case Studies of the 'Ceased Circumstances' Cessation Clause of the 1951 Refugee Convention' [2001] 15 Georgetown Immigration Law Journal 563, 601.

[24] Section 21(1), Refugee Act 1998; For critique, see Roni Amit, 'No Refuge: Flawed Status Determination

and the Failures of South Africa's Refugee System to Provide Protection' [2011] 23 International Journal of Refugee Law 458–488.

[25] Section 21(2)(a), 21(2)(b) and 21(3), Refugees Act, 1998.

[26] Section 21(2)(c) and 21(2)(d), Refugees Act, 1998.

[27] Section 22(1) and 22(3), Refugees Act, 1998.

[28] Section 24(1), Refugees Act, 1998.

[29] Section 24(3)(a), Refugees Act, 1998.

[30] Section 24(3)(d), Refugees Act, 1998.

if he/she finds that the application is manifestly unfounded, abusive or fraudulent.[31]

The Refugees Act, 1998 provides for the establishment of Refugee Reception Offices throughout South Africa.[32] In every Refugee Reception Office there must be one Refugee Reception Officer and one Refugee Status Determination Officer functioning under this Act.[33] Both of these officers will have experience and knowledge in dealing with refugee matters and they will serve as the officers of the department. Above the Refugee Reception Office in the hierarchy is an independent Standing Committee consisting of a Chairperson and such other members as determined by the Minister.[34] The Standing Committee is primarily responsible for formulating and implementing the procedures under this Act and other acts, including supervising the work of the Refugee Reception Offices, reviewing and monitoring the decisions of the Refugee Status Determination Officer, deciding any questions of law referred by the Refugee Status Determination Officer, and liaising with the Minister and the representatives of UNHCR and non-governmental organizations.[35] The Refugees Act, 1998 also provides for the establishment of an independent Refugee Appeal Board consisting of one Chairperson and two other members appointed by the Minister.[36] The Refugee Appeal Board is empowered under this Act to make its own rules of practice and procedure, and to determine questions of law referred to the Board, determine any appeal against rejection and advise the Minister on matters related to the implementation of the Act.[37]

Under the Refugees Act, 1998 the power to review the decisions of the Refugee Status Determination Officer, in the case of the rejection of an application for asylum on the grounds that it is manifestly unfounded, abusive or fraudulent, has been given to the Standing Committee.[38] At the same time, the Standing Committee is empowered to decide on any question of law referred to it by the Refugee Status Determination

[31] Section 24(3)(b) and 24(3)(c), Refugees Act, 1998.

[32] Section 8(1), Refugees Act, 1998.

[33] Section 8(2), Refugees Act, 1998.

[34] Section 9 and 10, Refugees Act, 1998.

[35] Section 11, Refugees Act, 1998.

[36] Section 12 and 13, Refugees Act, 1998.

[37] Section 14, Refugees Act, 1998.

[38] Section 25(1) and 24(3)(b), Refugees Act, 1998.

Officer, and the Standing Committee will prepare a directive on this matter which is binding for the Refugee Status Determination Officer.[39] The Standing Committee, after a hearing and collecting information as required, will confirm or set aside the order made by the Refugee Status Determination Officer and communicate its decision as prescribed by the rules.[40] The power to decide an appeal against an order of a Refugee Status Determination Officer on the grounds of rejection of an asylum application as unfounded rests with the Refugee Appeal Committee.[41] The Appeal Board, after hearing the appeal application and upon collection of the required information as deemed necessary by it, will confirm, set aside or substitute the order made by the Refugee Status Determination Officer.[42]

6.2.3 *Rights Granted to Refugees*

There is a general prohibition on refusal of entry, expulsion, extradition or return to another country for refugees in the Refugees Act, 1998.[43] It is not an absolute prohibition, but from the point of view of protection standards, when the national law of a state contains such provisions it demonstrates the spirit of the legislation and its impact on the civil society at large.[44] There is also a restriction on starting proceedings in case of unlawful entry to or presence in South Africa if the person concerned

[39] Section 25(3)(b), 24(3)(d) and 25(5), Refugees Act, 1998.

[40] Section 25(3) and Section 25(4), Refugees Act, 1998.

[41] Section 26(1) and Section 24(3)(c), Refugees Act, 1998.

[42] Section 26(2) AND Section 26(3), Refugees Act, 1998.

[43] Section 2, The Refugees Act, 1998: 'Notwithstanding any provision of this Act or any other law to the contrary, no person may be refused entry into the Republic, expelled, extradited or returned to any other country or be subject to any similar measure, if as a result of such refusal, expulsion, extradition, return or other measure, such person is compelled to return to or remain in a country where—(a) he or she may be subjected to persecution on account of his or her race, religion, nationality, political opinion or membership of a particular social group; or (b) his or her life, physical safety or freedom would be threatened on account of external aggression, occupation, foreign domination or other events seriously disturbing or disrupting public order in either part or the whole of that country.' See also Obeng Mireku, 'South African Refugee Protection System: An Analysis of Refugee Status, Rights and Duties' (2002) 35(3) Law and Politics in Africa, Asia and Latin America 399, 410.

[44] Jeff Handmaker, 'Advocating Accountability: The Reforming of a Refugee Rights Discourse in South Africa' (2007) 25 Netherlands Quarterly of Human Rights 53, 68; See also Willem H. Olivier, 'The New Asylum Law in South Africa' (2002) 4 Journal of South African Law 650, 658.

applies for refugee status.[45] This is the best guarantee for a refugee who is entering a country without travel documents. Refugees are entitled to a written document with regard to their status, an identity document and a travel document as per the law.[46] Basic education and medical facilities on a par with the citizens of the country are also guaranteed to refugees under the law.[47] Refugees are also granted the right to seek employment and an immigration card (permanent residence) after a continuous stay of 5 years in South Africa.[48] With regard to removal of refugees from South Africa, this is allowed only in cases of maintaining national security and public order, and such order of removal has to be signed by the Minister after consideration has been given to national laws and international human rights.[49] At the same time, the refugee will be given a reasonable amount of time to get approval from the country to which he/she wants to be removed.[50]

From this point it can be argued that the primary needs of a refugee are limited to access to documentation, a fair and functioning asylum system, basic social services, occasional emergency assistance for the most vulnerable including shelter and food, and social integration in case of prolonged stay. The South African refugee legislation is silent on the matter of shelter and food during the initial days following arrival; on the other hand, the possibility of obtaining an immigration permit after a stay of 5 years is the most significant achievement of this legislation. The Refugees Act, 1998 also contains provisions related to restrictions on detention for more than thirty days,[51] provisions of special assistance for unaccompanied children and mentally disabled persons,[52] and provisions for the dependents of a refugee to apply for and retain refugee status even after divorce or the death of the head of the refugee family.[53]

---

[45] Section 21(4), Refugees Act, 1998.

[46] Section 27(a), 27(d), 27(e), 30, 31 Refugees Act, 1998.

[47] Section 27(g), Refugees Act, 1998.

[48] Section (f) and 27(c), Refugees Act, 1998.

[49] Section 28(1) and Section 28(2), Refugees Act, 1998.

[50] Section 28(5), Refugees Act, 19980.

[51] Section 29, Refugees Act, 1998.

[52] Section 32, Refugees Act, 1998.

[53] Section 33, Refugees Act, 1998.

6.2.4 *Mass Influx Situation*

An important contribution of the South African refugee protection law is the incorporation of provisions dealing with a mass influx situation.[54] The development of these provisions came with the understanding that the normal individual refugee status determination system would be unable to cope with the workload in cases when the state concerned faced an influx of many persons likely to qualify for refugee status. The Refugee Act, 1998 provides that the Minister may grant refugee status to any group or category of persons who are already in the territory of South Africa unconditionally or with such conditions as required.[55] The Minister may also seek consultation with UNHCR and the local administration to finalize the temporary reception conditions for large groups of asylum seekers.[56]

6.3 Refugee Protection in Brazil

Brazil granted ordinary migrant status to those refugees who arrived in Brazil during World War I and World War II. Brazil's commitment to the protection of refugees began in the early 1950s when it became party to the 1951 Refugee Convention.[57] Thereafter refugee protection policies emerged at the end of the 1970s in Brazil, with its constitutional guarantees to provide asylum to aliens backed by a federal law regulating immigration issues in general, including asylum, preserving human rights, cooperation among peoples for the progress of humanity and the granting of political asylum.[58] A national council subordinate to the Ministry of Labor, which is in charge of coordinating immigration activities in

[54] Handmaker (n 16) 102; Olivier (n 44) 652.

[55] Section 35(1), Refugees Act, 1998.

[56] Section 35(2), Refugees Act, 1998.

[57] Brazil ratified the 1951 Refugee Convention in 1960 and its 1967 Protocol in 1972 but legal and political reasons prevented non-European refugees from enjoying asylum in Brazil. Brazil is a party to both the 1954 Convention on the Status of Stateless Persons and the 1961 Convention on the Reduction of Statelessness. See Liliana Lyra Jubilut, 'Refugee Law and Protection in Brazil: A Model in South America' [2006] 19(1) Journal of Refugee Studies 22.

[58] ibid. See generally Jose H. Fischel De Andrade, 'Refugee protection in Brazil (1921–2014): An Analytical Narrative of Changing Policies' in David James Cantor et al (ed) *A Liberal Tide? Immigration and Asylum Law and Policy in Latin America* (London 2015) 153, 167.

the country, issues regulations establishing the requirements for obtaining refugee or asylum status.[59] The Brazilian Refugee Act, 1997 defines the mechanisms for implementing refugee status (through the protection mechanisms of the 1951 Convention and 1967 Protocol, and incorporating the wider refugee definition contained in the 1984 Cartagena Declaration) in the country and created a national committee under the Ministry of Justice to deal with refugee matters.[60] Drafted in close collaboration with UNHCR, the law started operation from July 1997. The Brazilian Refugee Act, 1997 was the first comprehensive national refugee law in South America. Under this authority, the committee issued a normative resolution detailing the procedures for the request and processing of refugee applications. Permanent residency and citizenship are available to holders of asylum and refugee status, provided that certain requirements are met.

As per Brazil's commitments to a resettlement policy, it views resettlement as a protection tool and durable solution, aiming at allowing refugees to integrate into Brazilian society and to achieve self-sufficiency as quickly as possible.[61] The Brazilian Resettlement Program (BRP) relies on a tripartite structure that involves government, civil society and UNHCR in specific roles in accordance with the macro agreement for the resettlement of refugees in Brazil, signed in 1999. The Brazilian Refugee Act, 1997 guarantees basic documentation for refugees, including identity cards and work permits, freedom of movement and other civil rights. Government authorities, just like in any other sovereign country, are mainly responsible for the provision of documentation and public services for refugees both at national and local levels. With the exception of access to political rights, refugees benefit from equal conditions with nationals, accessing the same public policies available to Brazilians through an extensive network of governmental offices.[62] As discussed earlier, having a specific act concerning refugee protection is desirable as it allows for better correspondence between legal provisions, local conditions and the needs of refugees.

---

[59] Jose H. Fischel De Andrade, 'Regional Policy Approaches and Harmonization: A Latin American Perspective' [1998] 10(3) International Journal of Refugee Law 389, 395.

[60] The Brazilian Refugee Act, 1997 (Law 9474/97 of 22 July, 1997); see also Andrade (n 58) 168.

[61] Jubilut (n 57) 37.

[62] Jose H. Fischel de Andrade & Adriana Marcolini, 'Brazil's Refugee Act: Model Refugee Law for Latin America?' [2002] 12 Forced Migration Review 37, 38.

6.3.1 Refugee Definition, Exclusion, Termination, Cessation and Loss

The creation of a specific and comprehensive act on refugee status determination and protection paved the way for a network for the protection of human rights of refugees in Brazil.[63] Further, considering its association with other South American countries, it is important to understand the distinction made between the legal institutions of domestic asylum and refuge in this part of the world.[64] The harmonious concurrence of these two institutions in the South American continent can be explained by the fact that the states, while desiring closer integration with the international community via the incorporation of international regulations on refuge, wanted and needed to maintain their tradition of granting protection to persecuted people who are either outside the definition of a refugee according to the 1951 Convention, or to whom granting refuge was not a wise political move.[65] In defining a refugee, the Act adopts the same criteria as the 1951 UN Convention but with different wording and with the addition of the human rights perspective of the 1984 Cartagena Declaration. A person can claim refugee status under Brazilian law if:

> I—due to well founded fears of persecution for reasons of race, religion, nationality, social group or political opinions, he or she is out of his or her country of nationality and cannot or does not wish to rely on the protection of such country;
> II—having no nationality and being out of the country where he or she had previously retained permanent residence, cannot or does not wish to return to such country based on circumstances mentioned in item I above;
> III—due to severe and generalized violation of human rights, he or she is compelled to leave his or her country of nationality to seek refuge in a different country.[66]

---

[63] Jubilut (n 57) 27.

[64] Andrade and Marcolini (n 62) 38.

[65] Jubilut (n 57) 29; See also Catherine Tinker and Laura Madrid Sartoretto, 'New Trends in Migratory and Refugee Law in Brazil: The Expanded Refugee Definition' [2015] 3(3) & 3(4) Panorama of Brazilian Law 145, 149.

[66] Article 1, The Brazilian Refugee Act, 1997.

With regard to the exclusion clauses, the Act adds that a person shall not benefit from the condition of refugee if he/she enjoys the protection of any agency of the United Nations except UNHCR; if, as a resident of Brazil, he/she enjoys the rights and obligations of a Brazilian national; if he/she is guilty of acts against the purposes and principles of the United Nations; or if he/she has committed a serious non-political crime or international crime.[67] In this law the exclusion provision adds to the 1951 UN Convention the possibility of denying refuge to people who have committed terrorism or been involved in drug trafficking.[68] This could be regarded as an effort to update and refine the original text of the 1951 UN Convention insofar as both terrorism and drug trafficking come under the category of serious non-political crimes or acts contrary to the purposes and principles of the UN—an effort within the realm of International Refugee Law.

The Act contains a cessation clause defining reasons for losing refugee status, which are largely dependent on the objective situation in the state of origin or residence of the refugee.[69] Such a situation is subject to changes or improvements such that the need for protection may cease to exist. Further, any misconduct (gross violation of international law) on the part of the refugee could lead to loss of refugee status. Ordinary criminal offences are not listed in the Act's exclusion clause, as is the case in most national legislation in the South American states.[70] If refugee status ends or is lost, the individual is placed under the general system of rules for foreigners in Brazil. The Act has a provision which is in tune with the concept of the rule of law under which an exclusion clause can only be applied when the person asking for refugee status has actually committed an act, and not when there are serious reasons for considering that the person has done so.[71]

[67] Article 3, The Brazilian Refugee Act, 1997.

[68] Article 3 (III), The Brazilian Refugee Act, 1997.

[69] Article 38 and 39, The Brazilian Refugee Act, 1997.

[70] Jubilut (n 57) 33–34.

[71] Maria Beatriz Nogueira & Carla Cristina Marques, 'Brazil: Ten Years of Refugee Protection' [2008] 30 Forced Migration Review 58, 59.

6.3.2 Procedure and Determining Authority

For entry of refugees into Brazil, the Act assures the opportunity to request refuge from any immigration authority, and a person who has asked for refuge may not be deported until the conclusion of the refugee status determination procedure.[72] The Act also establishes that irregular entry does not prejudice the possibility of asking for refugee status.[73] Further, any criminal and administrative procedures arising from illegal or irregular entry into Brazil that could result in the deportation or expulsion of the refugee are adjourned until after the determination of refugee status has been made, and are terminated in the event that the request for refugee status is approved.[74]

A refugee applicant has to be present before the authority to which he/she will submit the formal application.[75] The refugee will receive information about the commencement of proceedings and in case of necessity will receive assistance from an interpreter and UNHCR.[76] After receipt of the application from the refugee applicant, the Federal Police of Brazil will issue a pass to allow the applicant and his/her family members to stay in Brazil legally.[77] On the basis of this pass the refugee applicant will be able to apply for an employment card from the Ministry of Labor for engaging in paid employment. The pass given by the Federal Police will be valid until a decision on refugee status has been taken.[78] The Act provides for the establishment of a National Committee for Refugees, under the control and supervision of the Ministry of Justice, for determining refugee status.[79] The National Committee for Refugees is empowered to take decisions on any asylum application at the first instance and to take any other steps necessary under this Act to protect refugees.[80] The committee comprises seven representatives

---

[72] Article 7, The Brazilian Refugee Act, 1997; See also Liliana Lyra Jubilut & Silvia Menicucci de Oliveira Selmi Apolinario, 'Refugee Status Determination in Brazil: A Tripartite Enterprise' [2008] 25(2) Refugee 30.

[73] Article 8, The Brazilian Refugee Act, 1997.

[74] Article 10, The Brazilian Refugee Act, 1997.

[75] Article 17, The Brazilian Refugee Act, 1997.

[76] Article 18, The Brazilian Refugee Act, 1997.

[77] Article 21, The Brazilian Refugee Act, 1997.

[78] Article 21 and 22, The Brazilian Refugee Act, 1997.

[79] Article 11, The Brazilian Refugee Act, 1997.

[80] Article 12, The Brazilian Refugee Act, 1997.

including one each from the Ministry of Justice, the Ministry of Foreign Affairs, the Ministry of Labor, the Ministry of Health, the Ministry of Education and Sports, the Federal Police Department and a non-governmental organization involved in refugee protection in Brazil.[81] UNHCR is invited to be part of the meeting of the National Committee for Refugees, with a right to participate in the dialogue but without any right to vote.

As soon as the National Committee for Refugees comes to a decision on the application for asylum, the decision is communicated to the Federal Police Department and the applicant.[82] If the decision is in favor of the applicant, the Federal Police follow the formal process of providing the refugee with an identity card and complete the process with the signing of documents on his/her obligations as a refugee.[83] If the decision is not in favor of the applicant, the applicant has the right to appeal before the Minister of State of Justice within fifteen days of the communication of the order.[84] The decision of the Minister of State of Justice is final and cannot be appealed.[85] After rejection of the appeal, the decision is communicated to the National Committee for Refugees and Federal Police for further administrative processing. However, the refugee applicant shall not be sent back to any country where his/her life, physical integrity or liberty will be at risk.

6.3.3 *Rights and Obligations of Refugees*

The provisions of the Act are innovative in that they extend the right to refugee status to the family of the refugee in Brazil.[86] Further, it broadens the classic definition of refugee to include gross violations of human rights as a legitimate reason for granting refuge.[87] This inclusion demonstrates human solidarity, a consciousness of Brazil's international responsibilities and recognition of the bonds of international refugee law and

[81] Article 14, The Brazilian Refugee Act, 1997.

[82] Article 26 and Article 27, The Brazilian Refugee Act, 1997.

[83] Article 28, The Brazilian Refugee Act, 1997.

[84] Article 29, The Brazilian Refugee Act, 1997.

[85] Article 31, The Brazilian Refugees Act, 1997.

[86] Article 2, The Brazilian Refugee Act, 1997.

[87] Article 1 (III), The Brazilian Refugee Act, 1997, which is in tune with the definition of refugee status adopted in the Cartagena Declaration 1984.

international human rights law.[88] However, with the continued influx of refugees and forced migrants, new methods of addressing these concerns have been adopted by the government authorities.[89] An ad hoc complementary protection system addresses such an emergency situation and protects those migrants who arrive by means of a humanitarian visa instrument which covers forced migrants who do not fulfill the necessary requirements of the 1951 UN Convention.[90]

However, this approach lacks consistency and binding force and relies heavily on the discretionary power of administrative bodies. This Act also exposes the state's and international organizations' preference for granting weaker subsidiary protection rather than recognition of full refugee status for individuals. The mechanism of complementary systems, though set within the municipal limits of the state, has the potential to expand the narrow content of the 1951 Refugee Convention and introduce new grounds for protection, taking into account human rights instruments as well as humanitarian law in order to protect more people from violations of human rights and generalized violence.

Once a temporary haven for asylum seekers, Brazil has became a refugee-receiving country as it has developed a democratic process and human rights approach, including the drafting of a Plan on Human Rights, since its emergence from dictatorship in the mid-1980s. The Refugee Act is a modern and coherent legal instrument, in harmony both with the practice carried out by the national authorities and with international and regional norms. The Act's resettlement provisions are the basis of a new phase in refugee protection in Brazil. Many hope that it will serve as a starting point for harmonizing policies and legal instruments for refugee protection throughout Latin America.[91] The Act contemplates new initiatives in the form of a voluntary character of

---

[88] Article 48, The Brazilian Refugee Act, 1997, which stipulates that refugee law has to be interpreted in keeping with the Universal Declaration of Human Rights, the 1951 UN Convention and its 1967 Protocol, as well as any international Human Rights documents—to which Brazil is committed.

[89] Tinker and Sartoretto (n 65) 144.

[90] Tinker and Sartoretto (n 65) 157; See also David. James Cantor and Stefania Eugenia Barrichello, 'The Inter-American Human Rights System: A New Model for Integrating Refugee and Complementary Protection?' [2013] 17(5–6) The International Journal of Human Rights 690.

[91] See generally Jubilut and Apolinario (n 72) 35; Jubilut (n 57) 40–41; Tinker and Sartoretto (n 65) 164

resettlement and the need for planning, coordination and determination of responsibilities.[92]

Further, the Act forbids the extradition of refugees and applicants for refugee status pending a decision on their cases, with the exception of cases where national security or a threat to public order are involved, in which case the refugee or applicant cannot be sent to the country of their origin or residence or to a place where life, liberty or welfare may be at peril. Several other documents such as a refugee identity card, labor card and travel document are made available to refugees in Brazil under the law.[93]

6.4 Refugee Protection in Canada

Canada's refugee protection is regulated mainly by the Immigration and Refugee Protection Act, 2001,[94] and consists of the Refugee and Humanitarian Resettlement Program for refugees seeking protection from outside as well as within the Canada.[95] Canada is a party to the 1951 Refugee Convention and its 1967 Protocol, and is committed to advancing the cause of international human rights through the work of the United Nations.[96] Canada's refugee law aims to provide assistance to refugees on the basis of their needs. Allocations to refugees are supported by the Government Assisted Refugee Program where either the Government of Canada or the province of Quebec provides the initial support and assistance to refugees being resettled in Canada. In addition, Canada allows private organizations or persons to identify and sponsor individuals who meet the admissibility and eligibility requirements under Canadian law. Canada works closely with UNHCR along with private sponsors to identify refugees for resettlement. Canada continues

[92] Article 45 and 46, The Brazilian Refugee Act, 1997.

[93] Article 5, The Brazilian Refugee Act, 1997.

[94] Immigration and Refugee Protection Act, 2001 (SC 2001, c. 27, Canada), Last Amended on: 01-07-2015

[95] Catherine Dauvergne, 'Evaluating Canada's New Immigration and Refugee Protection Act in its Global Context' [2003] 41(3) Alberta Law Review 725, 742.

[96] James C. Hathaway, 'Selective Concern: An Overview of Refuge Law in Canada' [1987–1988] 33 McGill Law Journal 667, 682; See also A. E. Gotlieb, 'Canada and the Refugee Question in International Law' [1975] 13 Canadian Yearbook of International Law 3, 7.

to be amongst the top destinations for refugees in the world—possibly as a result of the reform of its law and asylum policies.[97] Immigration has had a major impact on Canadian society. Canada has adopted a refugee screening procedure that is thorough, rigorous and multi-staged in response to a widespread sense that immigration is not economically beneficial for the country. Stoffman argues that immigration flows are too high, too concentrated in urban areas and make only a small contribution to meeting Canada's growing demand for skilled workers.[98] Its refugee system is regulated by the Immigration and Refugee Protection Act, 2001 which implements the 1951 Refugee Convention and 1967 Protocol. The refugee resettlement program is administered by Citizenship and Immigration Canada (CIC), which manages both the processing of applications and resettlement assistance. The refugee status determination system and other areas of the Canadian refugee protection and management system were altered by the Balanced Refugee Reform Act, 2010 which amended or replaced several provisions of the Immigration and Refugee Protection Act, 2001.[99] Further, as a result of the enactment of the Protecting Canada's Immigration System Act, 2012,[100] which amends or replaces several provisions of both the Immigration and Refugee Protection Act, 2001 and the Balanced Refugee Reform Act, 2010, the government is of the view that these changes will respond to delays, backlogs, weaknesses and inefficiencies in the refugee status determination process.[101] The Immigration and Refugee Protection Act, 2001 undeniably contains many changes, including new and expanded objectives.[102] These objectives present a complex situation for the government, serving best for the mere purpose

[97] Peter Li, *Destination Canada: Immigration Debates and Issues* (Oxford University Press, Toronto 2003) 48.

[98] See generally Daniel Stoffman, *Who Gets In? What's Wrong with Canada's Immigration System and How to Fix It* (Macfarlane Walter and Ross, Toronto 2002) 3; Martin Collacott, *Canada's Immigration Policy: The Need for Major Reform* (The Fraser Institute, Vancouver 2002) 6–10.

[99] Balanced Refugee Reform Act (S.C. 2010, c. 8, Canada), Assented to 29-06-2010.

[100] Protecting Canada's Immigration System Act (S.C. 2012, c. 17, Canada), Assented to 28-6-2012.

[101] See also Emily Bates, Jennifer Bond and David Wiseman, 'Troubling Signs: Mapping Access to Justice in Canada's Refugee System Reform' [2016] 47(1) Ottawa Law Review 1, 17.

[102] Section 3, Immigration and Refugee Protection Act, 2001.

of announcement alone. There appear some structural as well as procedural changes in the functioning of the Immigration and Refugee Board, as the Immigration and Refugee Protection Act, 2001 defines family in a new way, alters the points system which provides the central logic for independent immigrant screening, and redefines skilled worker migration.[103] It also provides a tighter framework for discretionary decision-making and for delegated legislative power, and it expands the jurisdiction of the Refugee Protection Division of the Immigration and Refugee Board. The Immigration and Refugee Protection Act, 2001 limits the right to appeal (largely due to an excess of applications)[104] and brings more stringent enactments pertaining to human smuggling,[105] human trafficking,[106] and criminal inadmissibility.[107]

6.4.1 Refugee Definition, Ineligibility and Cessation

A refugee in Canada can be a person from two different classes: a convention refugee or a person in need of protection.[108] The definition of convention refugee is same as the definition given in the 1951 Refugee Convention but is divided into two parts:

> A Convention refugee is a person who, by reason of a well-founded fear of persecution for reasons of race, religion, nationality, membership in a particular social group or political opinion,
> (a) is outside each of their countries of nationality and is unable or, by reason of that fear, unwilling to avail themself of the protection of each of those countries; or
> (b) not having a country of nationality, is outside the country of their former habitual residence and is unable or, by reason of that fear, unwilling to return to that country.[109]

---

[103] Section 151, Immigration and Refugee Protection Act, 2001.

[104] Section 64, Immigration and Refugee Protection Act, 2001.

[105] Section 11, Immigration and Refugee Protection Act, 2001.

[106] Section 12, Immigration and Refugee Protection Act, 2001.

[107] Section 33–43, Immigration and Refugee Protection Act, 2001.

[108] Section 95(1)(a) and Section 95(2), Immigration and Refugee Protection Act, 2001.

[109] Section 96, Immigration and Refugee Protection Act, 2001.

The second category of refugee in Canada is a person in need of protection and is defined as:

> A person in need of protection is a person in Canada whose removal to their country or countries of nationality or, if they do not have a country of nationality, their country of former habitual residence, would subject them personally
> (a) to a danger, believed on substantial grounds to exist, of torture within the meaning of Article 1 of the Convention Against Torture; or
> (b) to a risk to their life or to a risk of cruel and unusual treatment or punishment if
> (i) the person is unable or, because of that risk, unwilling to avail themself of the protection of that country,
> (ii) the risk would be faced by the person in every part of that country and is not faced generally by other individuals in or from that country,
> (iii) the risk is not inherent or incidental to lawful sanctions, unless imposed in disregard of accepted international standards, and
> (iv) the risk is not caused by the inability of that country to provide adequate health or medical care.[110]

The objectives enshrined in the Immigration and Refugee Protection Act, 2001 reflect the country's humanitarian concerns and convey its commitment to offer maximum assistance to refugees.[111] The definition of convention refugee takes into account the fear of persecution, which is reviewed at the time of the examination of the refugee application.[112] The government official must determine whether the applicant has a well-founded fear of persecution after assessing the reasons provided by the applicant. The applicant must also establish that the fear is reasonable and, if the applicant provides more than one basis for persecution, it is the duty of the officer, not the applicant, to identify the reasons for

---

[110] Section 97(1), Immigration and Refugee Protection Act, 2001.

[111] Elena Fiddian-Qasmiyeh, Gil Loescher, Katy Long, and Nando Sigona (eds), *The Oxford Handbook of Refugee and Forced Migration Studies* (Oxford University Press, Oxford, 2014) 679.

[112] Ibid.

the persecution.[113] In addition, they must be referred by UNHCR or another referral organization, or be sponsored by a private group.[114] Furthermore, both eligibility and admissibility requirements must be met before an application can be accepted.[115] The Immigration and Refugee Protection Act, 2001 also includes certain provisions concerning cessation. A claim for refugee protection can be rejected under certain circumstances, such as voluntarily re-availing oneself of the protection of the country of nationality, re-acquiring nationality, acquiring a new nationality, re-establishing in the country of nationality or habitual residence, or any other reason that the need for protection has ceased to exist.[116] At the same time, persons from designated countries of origin—those that do not normally produce refugees and that respect human rights and offer state protection—may not be eligible for refugee status in Canada.[117]

6.4.2 *Claim for Protection and Determining Authorities*

Protection as a refugee may be claimed as per the Immigration and Refugee Protection Act, 2011 from inside or outside of Canada.[118] It is noteworthy that a person from outside Canada can make a claim by applying for a visa at a Canadian Consulate as a convention refugee or as a person in similar circumstances.[119] South Africa and Brazil do not

[113] See Section 12, Immigration and Refugee Protection Act, 2001; See also Citizenship and Immigration Canada (CIC), *Guidance on Interpreting the Definition of a Convention Refugee*, Government of Canada, http://www.cic.gc.ca/english/resources/tools/refugees/resettlement/eligibility/definitions.asp accessed 3 August 2016.

[114] See Citizenship and Immigration Canada (CIC), *Resettlement from Outside Canada*, Government of Canada, http://www.cic.gc.ca/english/refugees/outside/ Accessed 3 August 2016.

[115] Section 101 and Section 102, Immigration and Refugee Protection Act, 2001.

[116] Section 108, Immigration and Refugee Protection Act, 2001.

[117] Section 109, Immigration and Refugee Protection Act, 2001 read with amendment made under Section 12, Balanced Refugee Reform Act, 2010 and Section 58, Protecting Canada's Immigration System Act, 2012.

[118] Section 99(1) Immigration and Refugee Protection Act, 2001; For the history of refugee status determination system in Canada, see R. G. L. Fairweather, 'Canada's New Refugee Determination System' [1989] 27 Canadian Yearbook of International Law 295–308.

[119] Section 99(2), Immigration and Refugee Protection Act, 2001.

include such a provision in their refugee protection legislation, which essentially extends the border of Canada for the purposes of entry to the country to the respective consulates.

A claim for refugee protection inside Canada can also be made at the port of entry or after entry to a designated officer by furnishing all information regarding the grounds of the claim.[120] The officer to whom a claim is made from inside Canada must determine whether the claim is eligible to refer to the Refugee Protection Division within three days, and in case of non-referral by the officer, the claim will be deemed referred to the Refugee Protection Division within three days unless it is suspended or ineligible.[121] Unless the claimant requests an early interview, the Refugee Protection Division will fix a date for hearing after fifteen days of receiving of the claim, and the burden of proof will rest on the claimant.[122] After this hearing the Refugee Protection Division will accept the claim in case the claimant is determined to be a convention refugee or a person in need of protection, and in case of rejection the reasons for finding no credible basis or that the claim is manifestly unfounded will be stated.[123] The Immigration and Refugee Protection Act`, 2001 provides for the establishment of an Immigration and Refugee Board.[124] The Board consists of a Chairperson and such other members as necessary for the proper functioning of the Board.[125] There are two divisions under the Immigration and Refugee Board: the Refugee Protection Division is primarily in charge of deciding claims in

---

[120] Section 99(3) and 99(3)(1), Immigration and Refugee Protection Act, 2001.

[121] Section 100(1) and Section 100(3), Immigration and Refugee Protection Act, 2001.

[122] Section 100(1)(1) and Section 100(4), Immigration and Refugee Protection Act, 2001 read with amendment made under Section 11, Balanced Refugee Reform Act, 2010.

[123] Section 107, Immigration and Refugee Protection Act, 2001 read with amendment made under Section 11, Balanced Refugee Reform Act, 2010 and Section 57, Protecting Canada's Immigration System Act, 2012.

[124] 151, Immigration and Refugee Protection Act, 2001.

[125] Section 152, Immigration and Refugee Protection Act, 2001.

hearings,[126] and the Refugee Appeal Division[127] is responsible for hearing appeals.[128]

6.4.3 *Rights and Obligations of Refugees*

The principle of non-refoulement is recognized as a protection requirement under the Immigration and Refugee Protection Act, 2001. However, this protection is not available to those persons who are inadmissible on the grounds of serious criminality, security, or violating human and international rights.[129] Recognized refugees can either be permanent residents or temporary residents in Canada subject to other rules and processes relating to residency. Right of refugees as a permanent resident or temporary resident remains as much as favorable like a Canadian citizen.[130] At the same time, all persons in the territory of Canada are protected by the Bill of Rights starting from equality, due process, speech, assembly and associations.

6.5 Conclusion

By and large, governments initially have failed to deal with waves of refugee movement in Latin America, Asia, Europe and Africa. Instead of acknowledging the skills and productivity that refugees can contribute to host nations, and supporting investment that boosts economic growth and job creation to the benefit of refugees and host communities,

---

[126] Section 169.1, Immigration and Refugee Protection Act, 2001 read with amendment made under Section 26, Balanced Refugee Reform Act, 2010.

[127] Section 171, Immigration and Refugee Protection Act, 2001 read with amendment made under Section 28, Balanced Refugee Reform Act, 2010 and Section 28, Protecting Canada's Immigration System Act, 2012.

[128] Section 170 and Section 171, Immigration and Refugee Protection Act, 2001 read with amendment made under Section 28, Balanced Refugee Reform Act, 2010 and Section 52, Protecting Canada's Immigration System Act, 2012; For critique on the appeal system, see Angus Grant & Sean Rehaag, 'Unappealing: An Assessment of the Limits on Appeal Rights in Canada's New Refugee Determination System' [2016] 49 University of British Columbia Law Review 203, 212–214; Jon B. Gould, Colleen Sheppard, and Johannes Wheeldon, 'A Refugee from Justice? Disparate Treatment in the Federal Court of Canada' [2010] 32 Law and Policy 454, 460.

[129] Section 115, Immigration and Refugee Protection Act, 2001.

[130] Section 27–32, Immigration and Refugee Protection Act, 2001.

countries have focused on increasing funding for refugee needs and social protections in host nations. The determination of *sui juris* people to construct their own future despite hardships and trauma should not be underrated. There is a need for collective agreement on an action plan, firstly to ensure peace and prosperity in host nations, and secondly to develop a common strategy to resettle people who are forced to flee to neighboring countries that recognizes the rights of refugees to be part of a formal economy with requisite labor, social, political and cultural rights, including the freedom to associate, and enact measures to make these rights a reality. This chapter's comparative study of South Africa, Brazil and Canada has shown how three nation-states have taken up the responsibility of protection and at the same time ensured their own national interest. In these cases, refugees are provided with both an established system to follow in the host country, and several essential rights based on the humanitarian role of the concerned countries.

The world as a whole has a responsibility to recognize the worst refugee crisis since World War II and use this experience as an opportunity to strengthen existing humanitarian provisions of laws to demand that states recognize and resettle refugees and offer full asylum to those arriving in their territories. This should include affording them the right to work in the formal economy and granting them full social, political and cultural rights, as well as providing the necessary funding to deliver on these commitments. States must stand up and extend their support for humanity. However, right across Europe and indeed in other continents we are witnessing a lack of generosity and an unwillingness to accept greater numbers of refugees despite the economic evidence that asylum represents a neutral cost over time and that employment migration represents a net gain. The reality is that it is no longer possible to distinguish between categories of refugees seeking safety and security in another nation. It is further argued that such solidarity and support for both safe haven and social protection must also be afforded to developing economies struggling to cope with millions of additional people. The world as a whole must demonstrate leadership in upholding the value of human life and triumph over fear and xenophobia.

CHAPTER 7

Visualization of a Refugee Law for India

7.1 Analyzing the MNLR and the Pending Bills

The drafting of the Model National Law on Refugees (hereinafter MNLR) was the first attempt at setting a consistent regime of refugee protection in India.[1] Though drafted in 1997, it has not yet been given any significant consideration by the Indian Government. After eighteen years, new initiatives have been taken by introducing the Asylum Bill, 2015 (hereinafter Asylum Bill);[2] the National Asylum Bill, 2015 (hereinafter National Bill);[3] and the Protection of Refugees and Asylum Seekers Bill, 2015 (hereinafter Refugee Bill)[4] in the Lok Sabha. At the same time it is significant that the National Human Rights Commission (NHRC) supported formulation of a national law in line with the MNLR.[5] These important events, along with various judgments of the Supreme Court of

[1] 'Model National Law on Refugees' [2001] 19 ISIL Yearbook of International Humanitarian and Refugee Law, http://www.worldlii.org/int/journals/ISILYBIHRL/2001/19.html accessed March 19, 2015.

[2] The Asylum Bill, No. 334 of 2015 (India), Introduced in Lok Sabha by Dr. Shashi Tharoor, MP (hereinafter Asylum Bill).

[3] The National Asylum Bill, No. 341 of 2015 (India), Introduced in Lok Sabha by Feroze Varun Gandhi, MP (hereinafter National Bill).

[4] The Protection of Refugees and Asylum Seekers Bill, No. 290 of 2015 (India), Introduced in Lok Sabha by Rabindra Kumar Jena, MP (hereinafter Refugee Bill).

[5] For detailed discussion see Section 3.2 in Chapter 3.

S.P. Sarker, *Refugee Law in India*,
DOI 10.1007/978-981-10-4807-4_7

India and the High Courts, have highlighted the need for a consistent, non-discriminative, equal protection regime for refugees in India.[6]

The texts of these proposed laws could be regarded as a guide for the drafting of a refugee law for India. There will be several differences in the resulting provisions due to the evolving nature of international refugee protection, the development of new standards, the difference of time and finally differences in the mindsets of the persons who drafted or initiated them. The MNLR was drafted by the Eminent Persons Group in 1997. The Asylum Bill was introduced in the Lok Sabha by Dr. Shashi Tharoor, MP and drafted in association with the members of Ara Legal Initiative, a center for refugee studies in India, who have experience working with international organizations in refugee protection. The National Bill was introduced in the Lok Sabha by Feroze Varun Gandhi, MP, and the Refugee Bill by Rabindra Kumar Jena, MP. It is significant to note that these three Members of Parliament are from different political parties and from different parts of the country, but they have all recognized the need for the protection of refugees in India. It should also be noted that all three bills in the Lok Sabha were introduced as private members' bill, which means they were not drafted by the Ministry that deals with foreigners and refugees in India. In view of these factors, it is unlikely that any of these bills will become a law made by the Parliament. The following sections analyze the MNLR and the three newly introduced bills.

7.2 The Model National Law for Refugees

The MNLR was drafted in response to the need for a consistent, non-discriminative and equal protection regime for refugees in India.[7] The preamble of the law asserts India's tradition and experience in dealing with refugee crises, its faith in the non-refoulement principle, its commitment to uphold the principles of international human rights, and the judgments of the Supreme Court and High Courts in upholding refugee rights under the Indian Constitution.[8] At the same time, the granting of

[6] For detailed discussion see Section 2.2 and Section 2.4 in Chapter 2.

[7] See V. Suryanarayan, 'Need for National Refugee Law' [2001] 1 ISIL Yearbook of International Humanitarian and Refugee Law 254, 257.

[8] Model Law (n 1) Preamble.

refugee status has been regarded as a peaceful and humanitarian conduct which makes India away to be a part of international political game plays. The MNLR is analyzed according to different key categories in the following sections.

7.2.1 Definition of Refugee, Exclusion and Cessation

The MNLR is named as Refugees and Asylum Seekers Protection Act, 2000 extending its effect to the whole of India.[9] It is significant to note that the definition of refugee given in the MNLR is an extended version of the definition found in various regional refugee protection instruments.[10] The inclusion of "sex" and "ethnic identity" as grounds for well-founded fear of persecution makes the definition innovative in terms of protecting women refugees and ethnic groups.[11] The MNLR also includes external aggression, occupation, foreign domination, serious violation of human rights or other events seriously disrupting public order in the country of origin as grounds for seeking refugee protection.[12] It is clear from the definition that both "well-founded fear" and "persecution" have to be substantiated for refugee status, but no explanation or definition has been provided with regard to the term "persecution" in the MNLR. The reasons for excluding a person from refugee status mainly include conviction for international crimes such as war crimes, crimes against peace, crimes against humanity and commission of serious non-political crime.[13] It is ironic to note that conviction for international crimes and commission of non-political crimes are not equally weighty matters, which has been overlooked by the drafters.[14] The MNLR includes five grounds for cessation of refugee status:

---

[9] Model Law (n 1) Section 1(a) and Section 1(b).

[10] OAU Convention Governing the Specific Aspects of Refugee Problems in Africa, adopted: September 10, 1969, entry into force: June 20, 1974, United Nations Treaty Series No. 14691. Cartagena Declaration on Refugees, Adopted by the Colloquium on the International Protection of Refugees in Central America, Mexico and Panama, November 22, 1984.

[11] Model Law (n 1) Section 3(a).

[12] Model Law (n 1) Section 3(b).

[13] Model Law (n 1) Section 4.

[14] For detailed discussion see Arun Sagar & Farrah Ahmed, 'The Model Law for Refugees: An Important Step Forward?' [2005] 17 Student Bar Rev. 74–91.

voluntarily re-availing oneself of the protection of the country of origin, taking Indian citizenship, taking the citizenship of some other country, re-establishing in the country of origin and when the need for protection no longer exists.[15]

7.2.2 *Status Determination and Procedure*

The provisions for refugee status determination that have been included under the MNLR leave some questions unanswered. As per the MNLR, the applicant is permitted to apply for refugee status at the time of entry to India or subsequently and shall be directed or assisted to apply to the Commissioner for Refugees.[16] The provision is vague as it does not clearly state which authorities are charged with assisting the applicant, nor does it specify the time frame for subsequent application. It must be understood that in the Indian scenario most refugees will have entered Indian territory without valid a travel document and/or visa, and applicants who have entered India through a recognized port of entry will be handled by different authorities than those who have arrived without authorization. At the same time, while the application for refugee status is pending, no restriction on movement is allowed, except for reasons of sovereignty and integrity or maintaining public order, under the MNLR.[17] This provision also does not make clear the time restrictions, or what legal action can or cannot be taken against undocumented persons who have not yet applied for refugee status or who are about to apply. These practical considerations should have been addressed before drafting a law for refugees in India, considering India's open and long borders with several neighboring states. An applicant for refugee status will be interviewed by the Commissioner of Refugees to determine the status of his/her application as per the MNLR.[18] This provision includes some facilities which will be given to the applicant during the interview process, such as the services of a competent interpreter, the opportunity to contact a UNHCR representative, the services of a legal practitioner, time to appeal the order of the Refugee Commissioner, an order in

[15] Model Law (n 1) Section 12.

[16] Model Law (n 1) Section 6(a).

[17] Model Law (n 1) Section 6(b).

[18] Model Law (n 1) Section 9(a).

writing including the reasons for denial of refugee status and appropriate certification in case of the granting of refugee status.[19]

7.2.3 *Determining Authorities*

The MNLR is unclear with regard to the formation of authorities for refugee status determination and further appeal. The authority that will deal with refugee status determination is the Commissioner of Refugees. The President of India is empowered to appoint the Commissioner of Refugees, Deputy Commissioners of Refugees and other members of staff in consultation with the Commissioner.[20] To be appointed as a Commissioner of Refugees the concerned person must be a sitting or retired High Court judge, and for Deputy Commissioners of Refugees the person should be qualified to be appointed as a High Court judge.[21] In both these cases the appointment should be done in consultation with the Chief Justice of India. The appellate authority against the decision of the Commissioner of Refugees will be the Refugee Committee, consisting of one Chairperson and three other members. The Chairperson will be a retired judge of the Supreme Court of India, and the other three members will be sitting or retired High Court judges and two independent members with knowledge and experience of refugee issues and refugee law respectively.[22]

7.2.4 *Rights of Refugees*

The most important of all refugee rights, that of non-refoulement, has been recognized in the MNLR but not as an absolute right.[23] The refugee or asylum seeker cannot be returned home or expelled from India unless he/she has been convicted of a war crime, crime against peace or crime against humanity, and there are reasonable grounds to believe that the concerned person is a threat to the sovereignty and integrity of

[19] Model Law(n 1) Section 9(b)–9(g).

[20] Model Law (n 1) Section 7(a).

[21] Model Law (n 1) Section 8(a)–8(b).

[22] Model Law (n 1) Section 8(c)–8(d).

[23] Model Law (n 1) Section 5(a).

India.[24] The principle of non-refoulement is now considered a rule of customary international law, and the inclusion of this rule in the national laws of many countries has become common.[25] At the same time, the MNLR also restricts the government from imposing a penalty on refugees for illegal entry to Indian territory and their immediate act to present themselves before the authorities.[26] However, this provision refers only to refugees and not to asylum seekers, making the provision inoperative in practice, as at the time of entry every applicant for refugee status is considered an asylum seeker. Several other rights are granted by the MNLR, such as employment opportunity, health care, education, travel document and rights guaranteed under the Constitution of India.[27] However, the provisions are skeletal in nature and do not provide any detailed framework for accessing these rights by the refugees.

7.2.5 *Mass Influx and Other Provisions*

The MNLR also makes provision for mass influx situations. The provision extends authority to the government in case of mass influx to consider allowing refugees to stay in India without going through the individual status determination procedure.[28] The refugees who have been allowed to stay in India due to mass influx will receive all the rights mentioned in this law except the right to free movement.[29] The provision relating to voluntary repatriation echoes the desirable solution supported by the Indian Government.[30] As per the current international standards, repatriation is not the only possible solution; integration and naturalization are considered more durable solutions. It must be accepted that the MNLR is a pioneer attempt at a refugee law in India, though the provisions are skeletal in nature. The MNLR may not stand the test of time in light of developments in international standards of protection and procedure, but its significance lies in its acceptance by the National Human

---

[24] Model Law (n 1) Section 5(b).

[25] Guy S. Goodwin-Gill, 'Non-Refoulement and the New Asylum-Seekers' [1986] 26 Virginia Journal of International Law 897, 901.

[26] Model Law (n 1) Section 15.

[27] Model Law (n 1) Section 13.

[28] Model Law (n 1) Section 14(a).

[29] Model Law (n 1) Section 14(b).

[30] Model Law (n 1) Section 16; see also Sagar & Ahmed (n 27) 90.

Rights Commission, as well as scholars and practitioners of refugee law, as a guiding text for enacting a refugee law for India.

7.3 The Asylum Bill, 2015

The Asylum Bill was tabled in the Lok Sabha to establish an effective protection framework and appropriate legal means by which the various standards applicable to refugees and asylum seekers will be consolidated, harmonized and streamlined.[31] The preamble also refers to the constitutional mandate of equality, fairness and due process of law, extension of certain fundamental rights to refugees and asylum seekers, India's acceptance of and commitment to norms of international law and human rights, and its long tradition of providing humanitarian assistance to refugees and asylum seekers. The preamble of the Asylum Bill echoes the tone set by the MNLR which ultimately posed the common necessity of a law like this. The following sections provide further analysis of the Asylum Bill.

7.3.1 Important Definitions and Principles of Protection

It is important for any national refugee law to include a definition of refugee. The Asylum Bill defines a refugee as a person who has been deemed such by the Commission or Appellate Board under the criteria provided under Section 4, or who has been classified as a refugee in a situation of mass influx under Section 30.[32] Under the determining criteria there are two different situations: the first includes the conventional criteria to define a refugee along with the inclusion of sex and ethnicity as factors for well-founded fear of persecution,[33] while the second situation refers to serious and indiscriminate threat, generalized violence and serious disturbances of public order that have prompted the applicant to leave the country of origin.[34] In fact, developments in the international standards of refugee protection vis-à-vis the EU's Qualification Directive have inspired the Asylum Bill to include a very broad definition

[31] Asylum Bill (n 2) Preamble.

[32] Asylum Bill (n 2) Section 2(u).

[33] Asylum Bill (n 2) Section 4(a).

[34] Asylum Bill (n 2) Section 4(b).

of refugee that might attract scrutiny from the political or administrative side. The provision also allows the dependents of refugees, including the spouse, children and infirm family members, to be declared refugees.[35] In instances where the person has more than one nationality, the term "country of origin" refers to each of the countries of which he/she has nationality, though different definitions have been provided for the terms "country of origin"[36] and "nationality"[37] under the Asylum Bill.[38] Unlike the MNLR, the Asylum Bill provides a definition of mass influx as "a situation where considerably large numbers of people from a specific country or geographical area, arrive at, or cross, an international border of India."[39] This definition is also inspired by the EU's Temporary Protection Directive.

The Asylum Bill includes seven distinct considerations on the basis of which the powers under the law are to be operative.[40] These are the following:

1. the applicant has faced or may face persecution in the country of origin that results in the entry to India, irrespective of arrival from the country of origin directly or indirectly;
2. support for the principle of non-refoulement;
3. fair and transparent refugee status determination system;
4. interim protection for asylum seekers;
5. consideration of refugees and asylum seekers as vulnerable persons;
6. voluntary and informed repatriation in a safe and dignified manner;
7. maintenance of family unity.

[35] Asylum Bill (n 2) Section 4(2) and 2(l).

[36] Asylum Bill (n 2) Section 2(k): "Country of origin means the country of nationality of the refugee or asylum seeker, or, if he has no nationality, the country of his former ordinary residence."

[37] Asylum Bill (n 2) Section 2(q): "'nationality' means the status of a person who is attached to a state by the tie of allegiance and includes but is not limited to citizenship, membership of an ethnic, linguistic or racial group."

[38] Asylum Bill (n 2) Section 4(3).

[39] Asylum Bill (n 2) Section 2(o).

[40] Asylum Bill (n 2) Section 3.

7.3.2 *Exclusion, Cessation, Cancellation and Removal*

The Asylum Bill, unlike the MNLR, includes detailed and broad provisions regarding "exclusion,"[41] "cessation"[42] and "cancellation"[43] of refugee status. The clauses under the exclusion provision include international criminal law, non-political crimes and crimes committed in India as grounds for exclusion from protection. Most importantly, they also include instigating, aiding or abetting any international crime, non-political crime or inhumane act as grounds for exclusion. The grounds for cessation echo those found in the MNLR, and the grounds for cancellation deal primarily with error, fraud and mistakes during the process of granting refugee status. The provision of removal of a refugee from India grants wide power to the central government to make a decision in this regard.[44] At the same time, it enables the refugee to obtain information about the removal and a chance to appeal the removal.[45] It also provides the refugee the chance to be removed to a third country other than the country of origin, and for this the concerned refugee will be afforded a reasonable amount of time to get approval from that third country.[46]

7.3.3 *Determining Authority*

The Asylum Bill proposes to establish a National Commission for Asylum mainly for the purpose of determination, cessation and cancellation of refugee status.[47] The Commission will comprise one Chief Commissioner and not more than six other Commissioners, to be appointed by the central government.[48] The Chief Commissioner can be appointed in consultation with the Chief Justice of India from among persons who have been High Court judges.[49] The other Commissioners can be appointed in consultation with the Chief

---

[41] Asylum Bill (n16) Section 5.
[42] Asylum Bill (n16) Section 6.
[43] Asylum Bill (n16) Section 7.
[44] Asylum Bill (n16) Section 9.
[45] Asylum Bill (n16) Section 9(2).
[46] Asylum Bill (n16) Section 9(5).
[47] Asylum Bill (n16) Section 2 and Section 18.
[48] Asylum Bill (n 2) Section 17(1).
[49] Asylum Bill (n 2) Section 17(2).

Commissioner from among persons with more than ten years of experience in refugee law and policy or experience in human rights litigation.[50] The Commission shall be guided by the principles of natural justice and shall have the power to regulate its own proceedings, along with powers of a civil court under the Code of Civil Procedure, 1908.[51] For the purpose of appeal against the order of the Commission, the Asylum Bill provides for establishing an Appellate Board consisting of one Chairperson and no fewer than four members, to be appointed by the central government.[52] The Chairperson can be appointed from among persons who have been judges on the Supreme Court of India, in consultation with the Chief Justice of India.[53] The four other members of the Appellate Board can be appointed from among persons who have been High Court judges, been a Commissioner of Refugees for five years, or had fifteen years of experience in refugee law and policy.[54] The Appellate Board shall have the power to examine, confirm, modify or set aside any order of the Commission *suo moto* or on the basis of application.[55] The Appellate Board shall also be guided by the principles of natural justice and regarded as a civil court under the Code of Civil Procedure, 1908.[56] Apart from these main provisions on the determining authorities, there are detailed provisions about the terms and conditions of service,[57] removal provisions,[58] appointment of employees and so forth.[59] All proceedings of the Commission and the Appellate Board will be regarded as judicial proceedings under the Asylum Bill.[60]

[50] Asylum Bill (n 2) Section 17(3).

[51] Asylum Bill (n 2) Section 19(1) and Section 19(4).

[52] Asylum Bill (n 2) Section 21(1).

[53] Asylum Bill (n 2) Section 21(2).

[54] Asylum Bill (n 2) Section 21(3).

[55] Asylum Bill (n 2) Section 22.

[56] Asylum Bill (n 2) Section 23.

[57] Asylum Bill (n 2)Section 24, Section 27 and Section 28.

[58] Asylum Bill (n 2) Section 25.

[59] Asylum Bill (n 2) Section 26.

[60] Asylum Bill (n 2) Section 29.

7.3.4 *Procedures to Apply for Refugee Status*

The right to apply for asylum in India has been proposed under the Asylum Bill to the National Commission for Asylum.[61] The application must be made within sixty days of arrival in India; however, the Commission, on considering the reasons for non-filing, may admit the application after the said sixty days.[62] The asylum seeker is also permitted to apply on behalf of accompanying family members, who may or may not be his/her dependents.[63] Upon application, the Commission will be required to issue one registration document free of cost to the concerned asylum seeker that includes all identity information, which will be valid for a period of six months.[64] If the status determination process is not completed within six months, there is a provision to extend the validity of the registration document sixty days at a time until a decision has been made by the Commission. It has also been provided that the asylum seeker will not be subjected to any detention or penalty due to illegal entry while the application for asylum is pending, and any police officer or other official who has intercepted a foreigner in any port of entry or international border for seeking entry to India to apply for asylum shall not deny the entry and shall provide the necessary information and assistance for the application.[65] However, the provision is not clear about the consequences if the police or other officials intercept the foreigner after the entry is made, that is, within Indian territory and not at the port of entry or on the international border.

As soon as an application for asylum is made, the Commission will provide the applicant with an opportunity for a hearing in the form of an interview, if necessary with the help of an interpreter or lawyer, and provide an adequate opportunity to present evidence in support of the claim.[66] After conclusion of the hearing, the Commission is required to carry out further inquiry and make a decision on the matter within three months.[67] If the decision of the Commission is against the asylum

---

[61] Asylum Bill (n 2) Section 10(1).

[62] Asylum Bill (n 2) Section 10(3).

[63] Asylum Bill (n 2) Section 10(4).

[64] Asylum Bill (n 2) Section 10(6).

[65] Asylum Bill (n 2) Section 10(5) and Section 10(2).

[66] Asylum Bill (n 2) Section 11(1), Section 11(2), Section 13(1) and Section 15.

[67] Asylum Bill (n 2) Section 11(1) and Section 11(3).

seeker, he/she may choose to appeal it before the Appellate Board within sixty days of the passing of the impugned order.[68] The Appellate Board, on receipt of the appeal, will give the asylum seeker an opportunity for a hearing and carry out an inquiry as necessary, then make a decision by confirming, modifying or setting aside the order of the Commission within three months of concluding the hearing.[69] The Asylum Bill also makes it mandatory that the decisions of the Commission and Appellate Board shall be in writing and cite proper reasons for arriving at the decision.[70] If the decision of the Commission or the Appellate Board is in favor of the asylum seeker, then the Commission will issue a refugee certificate as per the provisions.[71]

7.3.5 *Voluntary Repatriation*

The Asylum Bill specifies the process of voluntary repatriation as an activity carried out by the central government in cooperation with international organizations, public institutions and civil society organizations.[72] It requires the refugee to make a written application before the Commission for voluntary repatriation.[73] Afterwards, the order of the central government will be scrutinized by the Commission as to the genuineness of the consent of the refugee and the possibility of repatriation in a safe and dignified manner to the country of origin.[74]

7.3.6 *Rights of Refugees*

Like the MNLR, the Asylum Bill regards non-refoulement as a right accorded to refugees but not to asylum seekers.[75] However, the amplitude of the provision of non-refoulement is further narrowed by the

---

[68] Asylum Bill (n 2) Section 12(1).

[69] Asylum Bill (n 2) Section 12(3) and 12 (5).

[70] Asylum Bill (n 2) Section 11(5), Section 12(7) and Section 14(1).

[71] Asylum Bill (n 2) Section 11(4) and Section 12(5).

[72] Asylum Bill (n 2) Section 34(1) and Section 34(2).

[73] Asylum Bill (n 2) Section 34(3).

[74] Asylum Bill (n 2) Section 34(4), Section 34(5) and Section 34(6).

[75] Asylum Bill (n 2) Section 8.

provisions on removal of refugees and asylum seekers from India under Section 9. Apart from this, the Asylum Bill echoes the MNLR in granting the same rights and obligations to refugees and asylum seekers, such as identity documents,[76] travel documents[77] residence permits,[78] freedom from discrimination,[79] due process,[80] employment,[81] health care,[82] education,[83] and access to courts.[84]

7.3.7 *Provisions Related to Mass Influx Situations*

The power to designate certain groups or persons as refugees under mass influx has been given to the central government under the Asylum Bill, and the provisions echo the MNLR in this regard.[85] Those persons who have been recognized as refugees under mass influx situations can be subjected to several restrictions as per the provisions.

7.4 The National Asylum Bill, 2015

The National Bill was introduced in the Lok Sabha to provide rules for citizenship for refugees and asylum seekers.[86] Although the name of the bill suggests the establishment of a lawful system of providing asylum, the preamble suggests the provision of citizenship without acknowledging the need for a status determination system at first instance. On the other hand, the bill stresses India's commitment to refugee protection and the misery of refugees throughout the world. The following sections analyze the provisions of the bill.

---

[76] Asylum Bill (n 2) Section 35(1)(b) and Section 36(1)(a).

[77] Asylum Bill (n 2) Section 35(1)(c) and Section 37.

[78] Asylum Bill (n 2) Section 35(1)(d).

[79] Asylum Bill (n 2) Section 35(1)(e) and Section 36(1)(e).

[80] Asylum Bill (n 2) Section 35(1)(f).

[81] Asylum Bill (n 2) Section 35(1)(h) and Section 36(1)(b).

[82] Asylum Bill (n 2) Section 35(1)(i) and Section 36(1)(c).

[83] Asylum Bill (n 2) Section 35(1)(j) and Section 36(1)(d).

[84] Asylum Bill (n 2) Section 35(1)(k) and Section 36(1)(f).

[85] Asylum Bill (n 2) Section 30(1).

[86] National Bill (n 3) Preamble.

7.4.1 *Definitions and Cessation*

The National Bill in the first instance defines several important elements in a law for refugees and asylum seekers. The bill defines asylum seeker as a foreigner who is looking for recognition as a refugee.[87] The bill defines refugee in a manner similar to the 1951 Refugee Convention but excludes persons with no nationality.[88] The bill is very skeletal in nature as far as providing proper definitions of many other terms frequently used in refugee situations. Several grounds have been listed for the cessation of refugee status under the National Bill, such as re-availing oneself of the protection of the country of nationality, acquiring new nationality, re-establishing in the country of nationality with protection, committing international crimes and so forth.[89] A closer look at this provision reveals that it is repetitive on several objectives.

7.4.2 *Status Determination and Procedure*

The National Bill provides for application for recognition as a refugee at the port of entry to India or subsequently after entering India.[90] After receiving a request from the asylum seeker, the registration authority will decide whether the applicant is a refugee or not as per the definition. In this regard, no further provision has been inserted to indicate either an objective or a subjective basis for the decision by the registration authority. Extending the rule-making power under this bill to the government may seem innocent in nature,[91] but in terms of matters that should have been included in the provisions for establishing a proper status determination system, the use of this rule-making power might be unbalanced and arbitrary. At the same time, the National Bill is silent about any appeal procedure on behalf of the refugee in case of rejection of refugee status. However, only in cases of application for citizenship status by a refugee, the Refugee Committee shall have the power to receive appeal from a refugee.[92]

---

[87] National Bill (n 3) Section 2(a).

[88] National Bill (n 3) Section 2(d).

[89] National Bill (n 3) Section 5.

[90] National Bill (n 3) Section 3.

[91] National Bill (n 3) Section 13.

[92] National Bill (n 3) Section 4(1)(b).

7.4.3 Determination Authority

The MNLR and the Asylum Bill include provisions regarding the status determination authority. Unlike those two texts, the National Bill seeks to appoint a registrar of refugees to receive and take decisions on refugee status.[93] Again, unlike the texts of the MNLR and Asylum Bill, the National Bill does not stipulate any time frame for the receiving and determination procedure. The qualifications of the registrar of refugees will be prescribed as per rules made under this bill. The appellate authority for the determination of claims for citizenship status by refugees has been given to the Refugee Committee.[94] The Committee will comprise a retired judge of High Court appointed in consultation with the Chief Justice of India, and two other members having experience in refugee-related matters. As per the National Bill, this Refugee Committee will be an appellate authority to receive and consider applications for refugee status. It is significant that no provisions regarding the establishment of the determination authority and their functions and powers were inserted into the National Bill, making it unsuitable as per the prevailing international standards under conventions or national laws discussed in previous chapters.

7.4.4 Rights and Obligations of Refugees

The National Bill does not include extensive sections on refugee rights. More specifically, the principle of non-refoulement as a rule has not been inserted into the provisions. As per the provisions, the rights granted to refugees are of freedom of religious practice and religious education on a par with Indian citizens.[95] The obligations of the refugee are to abide by the laws of the land, and the government is obliged to maintain the principle of non-discrimination in terms of applying the provisions of this bill.[96]

---

[93] National Bill (n 3) Section 4(1)(a).

[94] National Bill (n 3) Section 4(1)(b).

[95] National Bill (n 3) Section 6(3).

[96] National Bill (n 3) Section 6(1) and 6(2).

7.4.5 *Citizenship Rights and Mass Influx Situations*

Given the many skeletal provisions, the National Bill is very humane in terms of providing citizenship to refugees. It specifies that any refugee living in India for more than five years shall be eligible to apply for Indian citizenship.[97] It is not clear from the text under which law the refugee will apply for Indian citizenship. The National Bill has a provision for overriding all other legislation, and the authority for granting refugee status is the Refugee Committee, so it seeks to provide a parallel regime of citizenship along with the Citizenship Act, 1955. However, in the case of children of refugees born in India, the citizenship granting process will be covered under the Citizenship Act.[98] The National Bill includes one provision with regard to mass influx which empowers the officers of the Office of Refugee Registrar to register refugees at the point of entry.[99] The provision regarding mass influx situations is also silent about how the government is to decide which situations will be designated mass influx.

7.5 The Protection of Refugees and Asylum Seekers Bill, 2015

The Refugee Bill seeks to provide an appropriate legal framework to deal with matters relating to forced migration, determination of refugee status, protection from refoulement and treatment during stay in India in the interest of upholding the values of international human rights.[100] The preamble echoes with the MNLR and the Asylum Bill. The bill recognizes the need for an administrative procedure free from arbitrariness for refugee protection, the need for a framework in the form of a law considering the refugee crisis in Europe and uniformity of rights of refugees during their stay in India. As in the MNLR, the granting of refugee status is considered a humanitarian matter.

[97] National Bill (n 3) Section 8(1).

[98] National Bill (n 3) Section 8(2).

[99] National Bill (n 3) Section 7.

[100] Refugee Bill (n 4) Section Preamble.

7.5.1 *Definitions, Objectives, Exclusion and Cessation*

The provisions dealing with definitions of important terms under the Refugee Bill seem to be illustrative and objective. The definition of refugee comes under two major criteria. Firstly, the conventional definition of refugee, extended by the MNLR with the inclusion of "sex" and "ethnic identity," is included in the Refugee Bill.[101] Secondly, the Refugee Bill echoes the 1969 Organisation of African Unity (OAU) Convention Governing the Specific Aspects of Refugee Problems in Africa (hereinafter OAU Convention) by extending the definition to include "external aggression, occupation, foreign domination, serious violation of human rights or other events seriously disrupting public order" as grounds for leaving the country of origin.[102] It is noteworthy that the Asylum Bill echoes the EU's Qualification Directive in extending the refugee definition, while the MNLR and the Refugee Bill keep faith with the OAU Convention in terms of their definition of refugee. Again the term "country of origin" is defined as the country of nationality or, in case of no nationality, the country of former habitual residence.[103] In a definite sense, the definition provided in the Refugee Bill also applies to a stateless person. Another important term, "refugee children," is defined in the Refugee Bill as "children below the age of eighteen years who are seeking refuge or where protection is extended by the State to children under article 22 of the Convention on the Rights of the Child, 1989."[104] None of the other bills discussed in this chapter include a definition of "refugee children," which can be regarded as a novelty of this bill. Apart from defining the key terms, the Refugee Bill specifically states the objectives of the proposed legislation, including:

1. establishment of an appropriate legal framework through adherence to an administrative system free from arbitrariness under Articles 37 and 253 of the Constitution of India;
2. implementation of international human rights treaties and India's commitment to do so;
3. granting of refugee status as a peaceful and humanitarian action.

[101] Refugee Bill (n 4) Section 3(e)(i).
[102] Refugee Bill (n 4) Section 3(e)(ii).
[103] Refugee Bill (n 4) Section 3(c).
[104] Refugee Bill (n 4) Section 3(g).

The Refugee Bill provides detailed provisions regarding exclusion from refugee status.[105] The grounds included under this provision include committing international crime or suspicion thereof, and committing non-political crime contrary to the South Asian Association for Regional Cooperation (SAARC) Regional Convention on Suppression of Terrorism. In both of these cases, if there is reason to believe that these acts have been committed, this will be sufficient to exclude the person from refugee status. The provision, while including the term "reason to believe," actually provides the determination authority with unlimited power to exclude a person from refugee status. Apart from that, there is a provision in the Refugee Bill dealing with cessation of refugee status which is also in line with the MNLR and the Asylum Bill.[106]

7.5.2 *Procedure and Determination*

The Refugee Bill proposes a system in which the refugee applicant may apply at the point of entry to India or subsequently after entering India.[107] As soon as an application for refugee status is received by any authority of the state, that authority will assist and direct the refugee applicant to apply to the Commissioner of Refugees. However, it is not clear what authorities will be responsible for assisting and directing the refugee applicant to the Commissioner for Refugees, nor how long after entering India an application for refugee status can be made. It is provided that when an application is pending for determination of refugee status, the government may impose restrictions based on the sovereignty, integrity and public order of India.[108] Another important provision seeks to protect child refugees from vulnerable situations immediately as per the laws related to child protection prevailing in India.[109] Apart from that, the local Legal Services Authority or any authority responsible for the protection of an unaccompanied child is permitted to apply on his/her behalf.[110]

---

[105] Refugee Bill (n 4) Section 4.

[106] Refugee Bill (n 4) Section 12.

[107] Refugee Bill (n 4) Section 6(1).

[108] Refugee Bill (n 4) Section 6(2).

[109] Refugee Bill (n 4) Section 6(4).

[110] Refugee Bill (n 4) Section 6(5).

After making the application to the Commissioner of Refugees, the refugee applicant will have the opportunity for a hearing for determination of status as provided by the Refugee Bill.[111] For the purpose of the hearing before the Commissioner of Refugees, the refugee applicant will receive the following facilities as needed[112]:

1. the services of an interpreter;
2. a reasonable opportunity to present evidence in support of his/her claim;
3. an opportunity to contact representatives of UNHCR;
4. a list of competent legal practitioners;
5. an opportunity to select a legal practitioner from that list if he/she wishes.

After the hearing the Commissioner of Refugees is required to provide reasons for the decision if the refugee applicant failed to prove his/her claim.[113] A copy of the decision will be made available to the applicant by the Commissioner of Refugees.[114] If the claim is rejected by the Commissioner of Refugees, the applicant will have a reasonable amount of time to file an appeal with the Refugee Committee. If an applicant is recognized as a refugee, he/she will be provided with the necessary documentation confirming refugee status.[115]

7.5.3 Determination Authorities

Similar to the MNLR, the Refugee Bill deals with the formation of authorities for refugee status determination and further appeal. The authority to deal with refugee status determination is the Commissioner of Refugees. The President of India is empowered to appoint the Commissioner of Refugees, Deputy Commissioners of Refugees and other members of staff in consultation with the Commissioner.[116] To be

[111] Refugee Bill (n 4) Section 9(1).
[112] Refugee Bill (n 4) Section 9(2)–9(5).
[113] Refugee Bill (n 4) Section 6(7).
[114] Refugee Bill (n 4) Section 6(6).
[115] Refugee Bill (n 4) Section 6(8).
[116] Refugee Bill (n 4) Section 7(1).

appointed as a Commissioner of Refugees, the concerned person must be a sitting or retired High Court judge, and for Deputy Commissioners of Refugees the person should be qualified to be appointed as a High Court judge.[117] In both cases the appointment should be made in consultation with the Chief Justice of India. The appellate authority under the Refugee Bill is the Refugee Committee, consisting of one Chairperson and three other members. The Refugee Committee is empowered to hear appeals against the orders of the Commissioner of Refugees and at the same time to hear *suo moto* applications for status determination.[118] The Chairperson will be a retired judge of the Supreme Court of India, and the other three members will be sitting or retired High Court judges plus two independent members with knowledge and experience of refugee issues and refugee law respectively.[119]

7.5.4 Rights and Obligations

The Refugee Bill in the first instance makes it obligatory for the state to observe the principle of non-refoulement.[120] However, the state is not bound by this core principle of refugee protection if the refugee applicant is convicted by a judgment of any court for international crimes, poses a danger to the community, or there are grounds to believe the/she may pose a threat to the sovereignty and integrity of India.[121] Another important obligation listed in the Refugee Bill is non-culpability in cases of illegal and unlawful entry directly from the place of persecution in cases when the refugee applicant reports his/her presence to the authorities without delay.[122] These two provisions can be said to be at the core of the protection strategy of the Refugee Bill. At the same time, the government is bound to provide the refugee with fair and due treatment without discrimination based on race, religion, sex, nationality,

[117] Refugee Bill (n 4) Section 8(1)–8(2).
[118] Refugee Bill (n 4) Section 11 and Section 8(5).
[119] Refugee Bill (n 4) Section 8(3)–8(4).
[120] Refugee Bill (n 4) Section 5(1).
[121] Refugee Bill (n 4) Section 5(2).
[122] Refugee Bill (n 4) Section 15.

ethnic identity, membership of a particular social group or political opinion.[123]

The Refugee Bill also includes provisions for access to several other rights essential for dignified living, such as[124]:

1. same treatment as per the Constitution or any other law;
2. the opportunity to seek employment to maintain livelihood;
3. special consideration for refugee women and children to ensure their protection and material well-being;
4. choice of a place of residence and the ability to move freely within the territory of India, subject to any regulation applicable to refugees generally in the same circumstances;
5. access to identity documents;
6. access to travel documents;
7. access to education, health care and other related services.

7.5.5 *Mass Influx Situations*

The Refugee Bill, like the MNLR and the Asylum Bill, includes a provision relating to mass influx in consideration of the past experiences of India. Under this provision the central government is empowered to allow mass influx refugees to stay in India for a certain time as fixed by the government or as necessity requires.[125] It also provides that in case of mass influx refugees, the government does not need to follow the individual status determination system. There is also a provision for special assistance to refugee women and children in a mass influx situation.

7.6 Conclusion

The chapter analyzed four texts, namely the MNLR of 1997, the Asylum Bill of 2015, the National Bill of 2015 and the Refugee Bill of 2015. With the exception of the MNLR, these bills were introduced in the Lok Sabha in 2015 by MPs. Whatever the variations in the provisions of these bills and the MNLR, their significance lies with the necessity of India to

[123] Refugee Bill (n 4) Section 13(1).
[124] Refugee Bill (n 4) Section 13(2).
[125] Refugee Bill (n 4) Section 14.

have one national law for refugees. It is noteworthy that since the drafting of the MNLR in 1997, there has been no effort for eighteen years to come up with a draft for a national law for India. The provisions of these texts vary in several aspects, but the principle of non-refoulement, a status determination procedure, appeal procedure, rights and obligations of refugees and the mass influx situation provisions suggest a possible basic structure for a national law for refugees in India. In Chapter 8, considering these aspects of the basic structure of a national law for refugees in India along with international standards developed through conventions, declarations and national laws, an attempt is made to propose the principle points of a new refugee protection law.

CHAPTER 8

The Call for a New Law

8.1 Towards an End to the Era of Strategic Ambiguity

The previous chapters provided analysis of the philosophical discourses on refugee protection, India's policies and practices of refugee protection, and the judgments of Indian courts and other organizational efforts to make these policies and practices equally protective for every refugee in India; further, the data collected in a field-based study through interviews with refugees in India brought to light the prevailing unequal protection standards and entitlements in India.

The philosophy behind the protection of refugees has been shown to be one of the cosmopolitan principles of the "right to hospitality," which it is argued should be extended to political membership in the society of refuge. The protection framework developed by the 1951 Convention Relating to the Status of Refugees (hereinafter 1951 Refugee Convention) has been adapted within new frameworks, for example in Africa with the introduction of the 1969 Organisation of African Unity (OAU) Convention Governing the Specific Aspects of Refugee Problems in Africa (hereinafter OAU Convention), in Latin America with the 1984 Cartagena Declaration on Refugees (hereinafter Cartagena Declaration) and in the European Union (EU) with the introduction of the Common European Asylum System (CEAS) in 2015. The newest of all these standards, the CEAS deals with each aspect of the life of a refugee in a foreign land, such as qualification to become a refugee, procedures to be followed by determining

S.P. Sarker, *Refugee Law in India*,
DOI 10.1007/978-981-10-4807-4_8

authorities while deciding an application for protection, housing, health care, financial aid, education, detention procedures and rules, residence permit, opportunity to obtain employment or self-employment, and finally temporary protection. The protection framework under the 1951 Refugee Convention, the OAU Convention, the Cartagena Declaration and the CEAS came into existence following the negotiations between state parties discussed in Chap. 7. It has also been shown that these international standards were influential in the development of national refugee legislation in South Africa, Brazil and Canada, although each state modified the standards to fit their own administrative mechanisms.

It is significant that the CEAS is now applicable throughout the EU and sets the common minimum standards to be followed by member states. At present there are 28 member states in the EU, all of whom are obliged to follow the CEAS and if required to implement the provisions in their national laws. It should be noted that the CEAS is the result of negotiations between all these members states vis-à-vis the European Parliament,[1] the European Council,[2] the Council of the European Union,[3] and the European Commission.[4] The importance of the CEAS in terms of accepting the spirit of protection of refugees is paramount, along with the commitment of all 28 member states to uphold the protection framework. If a consensus had not been reached among the member states, there would be no protection framework such as the CEAS operating throughout the EU. Thus the CEAS clearly illustrates the importance of upholding of the spirit of the protection of refugees and the commitment to the protection framework or provisions.

The previous chapters have shown that India has neither the courage to uphold the spirit of equal protection of refugees nor a commitment to

[1]The European Parliament is the **law-making body of the EU**. It is directly elected by European voters every 5 years with legislative, supervisory and budgetary responsibilities.

[2]The European Council brings together **EU leaders** to set the EU's **political agenda**. It represents the **highest level** of political cooperation between EU countries.

[3]In the Council, **government ministers from each EU country** meet to discuss, amend and adopt laws, and coordinate policies. Together with the European Parliament, the Council is the **main decision-making body** of the EU.

[4]The European Commission is the EU's **politically independent executive arm**. It alone is responsible for drawing up proposals for new European legislation, and it implements the decisions of the European Parliament and the Council of the EU.

any existing protection framework. This has led India to retain a policy of strategic ambiguity over the decades.[5] Significantly, in the Lok Sabha the Government of India has given eight reasons, which can be classified according to three distinct categories, for not signing the 1951 Refugee Convention or the Protocol.[6] However, no sufficient reason for not yet having enacted a national law for the protection of refugees has been provided.

In the first category of reasons for rejecting the 1951 Refugee Convention and the Protocol, the government pointed out that they represent only a partial regime as neither instrument deals with situations of mass influx. If India's initiative in cases of mass influx is compared with its approach to individual entry, it becomes clear that in cases of mass influx the Indian Government has always taken a humanitarian stand to support refugees, providing long-term settlement options to Tibetans and Sri Lankans and temporary settlement to Bangladeshi refugees who arrived during the 1971 war.[7] But in cases of individual entry, though not a signatory to the 1951 Refugee Convention, the Indian Government has allowed UNHCR to conduct status determination for refugees from non-neighboring countries. These two different approaches to providing protection certainly highlight the ambiguous nature of India's approach to refugees.[8] If a national law is formulated by the Government of India, it is possible that both individual and mass influx cases may be covered under its provisions.

The second category of reasons for rejecting the 1951 Refugee Convention and Protocol is associated with their failure to address the situation faced by developing countries with regard to the entry of economic migrants. In this regard the counter argument would be that the 1951 Refugee Convention and the Protocol deal exclusively with

---

[5] See B.S. Chimni, 'Status of Refugees in India: Strategic Ambiguity' in Ranabir Samaddar (ed), *Refugee and the State: Practices of Asylum and Care in India, 1947–2000* (SAGE, New Delhi 2003) 443.

[6] Lok Sabha, Un-starred Question No. 277, Answered on 21.02.2006 (for detailed discussion on this, see Section 3.1.1.1 in Chapter 3).

[7] See Asha Hans, 'Sri Lankan Tamil Refugees in India' [1993] 13(3) Refuge 30, 31; see generally P.N. Luthra, 'Problem of Refugees from East Bengal' [1971] 6(50) Economic and Political Weekly 2467, 2470.

[8] See J.N. Saxena, 'Legal Status of Refugees: Indian Position' [1986] 26 Indian Journal of International Law 501, 505.

refugees and asylum seekers.[9] Further to this, Indian laws dealing with foreign nationals play an important role in the life of a refugee in India, since under those laws there is no separate category for refugees who are not economic migrants or illegal immigrants or other foreign nationals who have come to India for any other purpose. Therefore a solution can be reached by way of introducing a definition of refugee as a distinct category in Indian law separate from economic migrants or illegal immigrants or other foreigners; unfortunately this has yet to be done.

The third category of reasons comprises accusations by the Government of India that the 1951 Refugee Convention and the Protocol are ineffective in terms of international burden sharing, the responsibility of states not to create refugees, and the rights and obligations of receiving and source states. In the current world order it must be recognized that the state itself is not always responsible for creating refugees, but rather the military or economic interference of powerful states in those origin states triggers the refugee flow.[10] If India's third category of reasons is to be addressed by the world community, the fundamental questions must include the issue of which countries are responsible for the refugee flows from Afghanistan, Iraq, Syria, former Yugoslavia, Somalia and Rwanda. With regard to former Yugoslavia, Somalia and Rwanda, it has been noted that:

> While the international donor community cannot be held directly responsible for the outbreak of civil war in Yugoslavia, Somalia and Rwanda, the evidence nonetheless confirms that the macro-economic reforms imposed by international creditors in all three countries, played a crucial role in fostering the collapse of state institutions and creating a situation of social and political divisiveness.[11]

The question of the responsibilities of refugees' states of origin in terms of the involvement of non-state actors, the role of international economic organizations and other factors that have contributed to the need

[9] See Myron Weiner, 'Rejected Peoples and Unwanted Migrants in South Asia' [1993] 28(34) Economic & Political Weekly 1737, 1740.

[10] See B.S. Chimni, 'The Geopolitics of Refugee Studies: A View from the South' [1998] 11(4) Journal of Refugee Studies 350, 360.

[11] M. *Chossudovsky, 'Economic Reforms and Social Unrest in Developing Countries'* [1997] *Economic & Political Weekly 1786, 1787.*

to flee, have not been addressed. The refugee-receiving states have therefore adopted the position that repatriation should be the end result of the refugee crisis.[12]

However, recent calls for a democratic theory of refugee protection has been seen to uphold Kantian cosmopolitanism as well as Benhabib's just membership for refugees in society.[13] This new theory questions the practice of differential treatment between nationals and non-nationals and advocates for a global protection regime for refugees.[14] At the same time, there is growing dissatisfaction with the implementation of the 1951 Refugee Convention and Protocol which makes it clear that only states with self-reliance and a commitment to refugee protection can help refugees.

To this effect, there has been an attempt in India to formulate a refugee protection law to be passed as an Act of Parliament to provide equal protection to every refugee group present in India. The drafting of the Model National Law on Refugees (MNLR) was the first attempt to formulate a consistent regime of refugee protection in India.[15] Though drafted in 1997, the government has not yet given it serious consideration. Other attempts have been made recently, including the Asylum Bill, 2015 (hereinafter Asylum Bill), the National Asylum Bill, 2015 (hereinafter National Bill) and the Protection of Refugees and Asylum Seekers Bill, 2015 (hereinafter Refugee Bill) in the Lok Sabha as private members' bills.[16] At the same time, the National Human Rights Commission

---

[12] Chimni (n 10) 362; see also B.S. Chimni, 'The Meaning of Words and the Role of UNHCR in Voluntary Repatriation' [1993] 5 International Journal of Refugee Law 442, 445.

[13] See A. McGrew, 'Democracy Beyond Borders? Globalization and the Reconstruction of Democratic Theory and Politics' in A. McGrew (ed), *The Transformation of Democracy* (Cambridge, 1997) 231, 265; J.P. Hocke, 'Beyond Humanitarianism: The Need for Political Will to Resolve Today's Refugee Problem' in G. Loescher & L. Monahan (eds), *Refugees and International Relations* (Oxford, 1989).

[14] Chimni (n 10) 362.

[15] 'Model National Law on Refugees' [2001] 19 ISIL Yearbook of International Humanitarian and Refugee Law, http://www.worldlii.org/int/journals/ISILYBIHRL/2001/19.html accessed 19 March 2015.

[16] The Asylum Bill, No. 334 of 2015 (India), Introduced in Lok Sabha by Dr. Shashi Tharoor, MP; The National Asylum Bill, No. 341 of 2015 (India), Introduced in Lok Sabha by Feroze Varun Gandhi, MP; The Protection of Refugees and Asylum Seekers Bill, No. 290 of 2015, Introduced in Lok Sabha by Rabindra Kumar Jena, MP.

(NHRC) has supported formulation of a national refugee protection law in line with the MNLR.[17] These important events, along with various judgments of the Supreme Court of India and the High Courts, have highlighted the need for a consistent, non-discriminative, equal protection regime for refugees in India.[18]

Recent administrative measures taken by the Government of India, such as the introduction of the long-term visa for refugees of every nationality and special consideration for the minorities of Pakistan and Bangladesh, can also be seen as a step towards this consistency.[19] However, these administrative measures must be non-discriminative in terms of entitlements and procedures in order to meet international standards of refugee protection and respect for human rights, which can only be attained by enacting a law.

8.2 Suggestions

The following sections more closely scrutinize the four texts drafted to formulate national refugee legislation in India, previously discussed in Chap. 7, with regard to basic practical considerations from an Indian perspective as well as the introduction of new instruments of international standards.

8.2.1 Definition, Persecution and Actors

The MNLR, Asylum Bill and Refugee Bill utilize broad definitions of the term refugee. They all include "sex" and "ethnicity" along with several concepts borrowed from human rights and humanitarian law.[20] The expanded definition of the term "refugee" was common until the 1990s; however, current international standards such as the EU's Qualification Directive include a separate category of "subsidiary protection" regarding the need to protect persons from violations of human rights and humanitarian law.[21] The extended definition of the term refugee is not

[17] For detailed discussion see Section 3.2 in Chapter 3 .

[18] For detailed discussion see Section 2.2 and Section 2.4 in Chapter 2.

[19] For detailed discussion see Section 1.3.3 in Chapter 1.

[20] See Sections 7.2.1, 7.3.1 and 7.5.1 in Chapter 7 for detailed discussions.

[21] See Section 5.3 in Chapter 5.

supported by the Government of India, as the "expansion of the definition of refugees will have an adverse effect on promoting the concept of "durable solutions" and may result in the weakening of protection afforded to genuine refugees."[22] From this point it would be sensible to retain the original definition of refugee, whereas the extended part of the definition could be regarded as "humanitarian protection" separate from refugee status, in line with the Qualification Directive of the European Union. Similarly, none of the bills provided a definition of "persecution" or "perpetrators of persecution" in line with the 1951 Refugee Convention. In this regard, it would also be prudent to include such provisions in the Indian refugee protection law.

8.2.2 Admission or Rejection of Application and Grounds

The skeletal provisions of the MNLR and National Bill, and the detailed provisions in the Asylum Bill and the Refugee Bill with regard to exclusion, cessation and cancellation of refugee status, were drafted considering all practical issues with regard to international and national laws of India, which must be welcomed. However, the international standards currently prevailing in the EU's Asylum Procedures Directive regarding the principles of "first country of asylum" and "safe third country," and the principle of "designated foreign country" in Canada's national refugee law, could be explored by the Indian Government where either those countries are signatories to the 1951 Convention, or they have an established practice of providing asylum or present less risk of persecution.[23] For example, India is currently facing a crisis among the Rohingya refugees of Myanmar. It has been shown that most of the refugees from the Rohingya community have been granted refugee status in Bangladesh and have lived there for a long time such that they can be considered for naturalization as citizens of that country. However, many members of the Rohingya community have chosen to leave Bangladesh and enter India by crossing the international border from the West Bengal side, and subsequently apply for refugee status from UNHCR in New Delhi.

---

[22] See Probodh Saxena, 'Creating Legal Space for Refugees in India: the Milestones Crossed and the Roadmap for the Future' (2007) 19 International Journal of Refugee Law 246, 260.

[23] For further discussion of the concepts of "first country of asylum" and "safe third country," see Section 5.4.2 in Chapter 5.

It is desirable to stop this kind of secondary movement by including the principles of "first country of asylum," "safe third country" and "designated foreign country" in the admissibility clause of the national law for refugees.

8.2.3 *Authorities for Status Determination and Appeal*

The provisions in the MNLR, Asylum Bill and Refugee Bill contain similar strategies for the formation of new authorities for the purpose of refugee status determination and the appeal process.[24] They only differ with regard to the qualifications of appointees and the names of posts. However, in several ways they can be seen as detrimental to the objectives of the proposed legislation.[25]

Firstly, the status determination and appellate authorities will operate from a central point, or more precisely from the capital of India, though there are provisions for the central government to set up offices in other areas of the country. In a vast country like India, it is not sufficient to have one office or several offices in different locations, as non-accessibility by refugees will be a concern along with the generation of new crowds in urban areas. Secondly, ignoring the established set-up of governing of foreign nationals vis-à-vis entry, stay and issue of residence permit and maintenance of data in the country would cause significant administrative as well as security concerns. As per the current administrative set-up, a foreigner, whether a refugee or otherwise, is registered with district-level authorities (i.e. Foreigners Registration Officer) for their legal stay in India, and ignoring this established set-up would be counter-productive. Instead, the proposed legislation for refugees in India should consider including a provision for status determination at the district level, perhaps by a committee constituted and controlled by the District Magistrate or Collector. The preliminary status determination process could be handled by this kind of administrative set-up at the district level, and appeal thereof, if any, would then lie with the statutory Commission. Thus the government should consider a proposal to set up district-level refugee committees for status determination consisting of three to five persons, to include government officials,

[24] See Sections 7.2.3, 7.3.3, 7.5.3 in Chapter 7 for detailed discussions.

[25] See Saxena (n 2) 264.

lawyers, academicians and journalists. Thirdly, there should be state-level commissioners for refugees to hear appeals against the orders of the district-level refugee committees. This kind of state-level office may be constituted by appointing a retired High Court judge as the commissioner for a particular state of India. Finally, a National Commission for Refugees can be put into place for further appeal or other administrative matters.

8.2.4 Procedure for Status Determination

The procedures for determination of refugee status in the MNLR, Asylum Bill and Refugee Bill have been introduced primarily considering the set-up of proposed status determination authorities.[26] As the proposed status determination authorities under all these bills cannot properly serve the objective of refugee legislation for a huge country like India due to the high number of incoming refugees undermining the current administrative set-up for governing foreigners, a decentralized system of preliminary status determination authority as proposed in the previous section will be required in every district in India. At the same time, the requirement for state-level commissioners for refugees with statutory powers and a national commission at the center has also been described in the previous section. At this point the proposed decentralized set-up for status determination procedures needs to be adapted to maintain the fair procedures in place as proposed by the MNLR, Asylum Bill and Refugee Bill. The major change in procedures should be done under the following categories:

1. No return from the port of entry or international un-fenced or fenced border subject to intention to apply for refugee status.
2. No detention for entering India without valid travel document subject to intention to apply for refugee status.
3. As soon as the police or border security forces or immigration authorities identify or intercept a foreigner who wants to apply for refugee status, they should produce the concerned person within 24 h to the district-level refugee committee to start the process of status determination. This 24-h period should not be treated as

[26]See Sections 7.2.2, 7.3.4, 7.5.2 in Chapter 7 for detailed discussions.

detention and the asylum seeker should be given such reception facilities as determined.

4. The district-level refugee committee should preliminarily decide on the place of stay on receiving an asylum seeker from the police or border security forces or immigration authorities, or where an application for refugee status from the concerned person is made directly to the district-level refugee committee. If the asylum seeker wants to stay on his/her own or with relatives or close friends within the jurisdiction of that particular district, he/she should be permitted to do so. In any other case, the district-level refugee committee should arrange for necessary accommodation and other reception facilities for the asylum seeker as determined.
5. The district-level refugee committee should provide all necessary information about the application procedure and all necessary documents of application free of cost.
6. At the time of application, biometric data of the asylum seeker must be taken and preserved. For the purpose of technologically advanced processing, an online server connecting all the district-level, state-level and the national-level commissions should be in place. All applications, decisions, biometric data, appeals and further orders should be preserved on the server.
7. The application for status determination to the district-level refugee committee should be completed within 15 days of arrival in India by the asylum seeker, considering the decentralized set-up of status determination authorities.
8. After receiving the application for status determination, the district-level refugee committee will instruct the Foreigners Registration Officer of that district to issue a temporary residence permit containing all information of the asylum seeker and the rights and obligations acquired after making the application. This temporary residence permit will be valid for a period of no more than 180 days from the date of issue.
9. The district-level refugee committee must complete the status determination process upon hearing and give its decision within 45 days of receiving the application for status determination. The district-level refugee committee firstly considers the application for refugee status, and if found unsuccessful then the application should be considered for "humanitarian protection."

10. If the application is accepted by the district-level refugee committee, they must provide a written and reasoned decision along with the recordings of the full hearing process. Further, they will instruct the Foreigners Registration Officer of that district to issue a residence permit valid for no more than 3 years detailing all information about the refugee and the rights and obligations after receiving refugee status, and recall the temporary residence permit from the refugee. If the asylum seeker is not found to be a refugee but is granted "humanitarian protection," the residence permit should be valid for no more than 1 year. The extension of the residence permit in both of these cases will be dealt with by the district-level refugee committee.
11. In case of a rejected application, the district-level refugee committee will also provide a written and reasoned decision along with the recordings of the full hearing process. The concerned asylum seeker will have the right to appeal this decision to the state-level commissioner for refugees within 15 days of the order by the district-level refugee committee. The state-level commissioner for refugees will decide the appeal within 30 days of filing with a written and reasoned order along with the recordings of the full hearing process. In case of deciding the appeal in favor of the refugee, the state-level commissioner for refugees will order the district-level refugee committee to take measures to issue residence permit.
12. If the appeal is rejected by the state-level commissioner for refugees, the asylum seeker will have the right to make second appeal to the National Commission for Refugees within 15 days of rejection order. The National Commission for Refugees is also entrusted with the duty to give a written and reasoned order to decide the appeal within 30 days of filing. If the appeal is decided in favor of the refugee, the National Commission for Refugees will order the district-level refugee committee to provide a residence permit to the refugee.
13. If the appeal to the National Commission for Refugees is rejected, the asylum seeker will be removed from India. In this case, he/she should not be sent to a place where his/her life or liberty could be in danger. The asylum seeker should be allowed a reasonable amount of time to obtain permission to go to another country.

14. During the process of status determination, the determining authorities should have the power to order the detention of an asylum seeker in the interests of the safety, security and integrity of India.
15. In all these cases, the determining authorities will be required to follow the principles of natural justice.

8.2.5 *Voluntary Repatriation and the Process of Removal*

The provisions related to the process of voluntary repatriation and removal of an asylum seeker from India are well documented in the Asylum Bill. The provisions should be welcomed while enacting the law for its subjective and objective considerations on the effects of such repatriation and removal.

8.2.6 *Mass Influx Situations*

The MNLR, Asylum Bill and Refugee Bill provide detailed provisions for mass influx situations based on India's past experience with mass refugee flows from Tibet, Sri Lanka and Bangladesh. India's experience with such situations has been mixed, as refugees from Bangladesh returned home as soon as the 1971 war was over, but in the case of the Tibetans and the Sri Lankans the situation was different. The Tibetans have been rehabilitated as per the rehabilitation policy of the Government of India, but the Sri Lankans are still living under inconsistent administrative practices. Therefore it is suggested that the provisions for the central government to declare a certain group to be refugees be kept, while the district-level refugee committee would be the actual implementing body for protecting them. Apart from that, residence permits issued to refugees arriving in a mass influx should initially only be valid for 6 months; more specifically, the protection given to these refugees should be considered "humanitarian protection" based on their chances of going back to their country of origin as soon as the situation in the country of origin changes. However, they should also be entitled to all the basic reception conditions such as food, clothing, housing and health care except the right to engage in employment during the first year of their stay.

8.2.7 Rights of Refugees and Asylum Seekers

The MNLR, Asylum Bill and Refugee Bill provide a list of rights available to refugees. The Asylum Bill is more clear about the rights and obligations of refugees and asylum seekers which must be accepted after due consideration by the Parliament. However, the provision about non-refoulement in the Asylum Bill seems vague as it is not clear about undocumented asylum seekers' right of non-refoulement. It would be better to include such a provision in the law, as in India most refugees are undocumented and are from Tibet, Sri Lanka and Myanmar, as identified in the field study. At the same time, there have been a considerable number of cases in the courts about the detention of undocumented asylum seekers, which must be noted while drafting the provision on detention. The practicality of the life of a refugee who is fleeing his/her country of origin or habitual residence due to well-founded fear of persecution or serious violation of human rights may arrive with nothing but his/her life. Therefore express written provisions for non-refoulement and against detention for undocumented entry into Indian territory should be provided.

The right of movement throughout the country has been restricted in the Asylum Bill for mass influx refugees. Utilizing the decentralized status determination authorities may mean that it will no longer be necessary for refugees and asylum seekers to move throughout the country. Apart from that, considering urban planning and poverty, it will be necessary to restrict movement throughout the country. Suitable provisions may entitle refugees and asylum seekers to move freely within the territory of the Indian state where they first entered or applied for status determination. In case of overflow of refugees, the central government can take necessary measures to shift refugees to any state with fewer or no refugees. In practice it has been found that mass influx refugees who arrived from Bangladesh during the 1971 war stayed mainly in West Bengal, Assam, Tripura and Meghalaya, while the Sri Lankan refugees still live mainly in Tamil Nadu. Refugees, then, prefer to stay in a place where people speak a similar language and share a similar socio-religious culture.

The field study found that many of the interviewed refugees lived in dreadful situations due to inadequate support from either the government or UNHCR. Thus it would be better to include suitable provisions to allow self-employment and employment in the private sector immediately upon receiving refugee status. During the process of status determination, benefits in the form of food, clothing, housing and health care should be provided to each asylum seeker. This is to be coordinated by the district-level refugee committee under the supervision of the state-level commissioner for refugees.

At the same time, suitable provisions should be made to provide some integration facilities in the form of educational activities to make asylum seekers and refugees aware of Indian culture, language, law and social norms, which in turn can be utilized to help them understand their obligations to the host nation.

8.2.8 Naturalization and Citizenship Process

The MNLR, Asylum Bill, National Bill and Refugee Bill denote "acquiring citizenship of India" as grounds for cessation of refugee status. Ironically, none of these texts provide further explanation of whether refugees and asylum seekers are entitled to apply for Indian citizenship and by what process. The recent cases in Delhi High Court and Karnataka High Court concerning refugees' right of citizenship of India by birth have been upheld though restricted by the 1987 amendment in the Citizenship Act, 1955. The field study also found that some Tibetans hold both a registration certificate from the Foreigners Registration Office and an Indian voting card or passport, which makes the situation much more complex.

As per the law laid down by the Delhi High Court and Karnataka High Court, Tibetan refugees who were born in India before the effective date of the 1987 amendment of the Citizenship Act, 1955 can receive an Indian passport subject to renouncing the registration certificate as a refugee. However, in many places the actual implementation of this law is in question due to administrative failure. It would be better to include specific provisions allowing refugees to obtain Indian citizenship on the grounds of naturalization under the Citizenship Act, 1955 by renouncing their original nationality and related documents of refugee status. The process of acquiring Indian citizenship through naturalization may not be such an obstacle as getting citizenship at birth by refugee children considering the 1987 amendment in the Citizenship Act, 1955, and at the same time refugees will be integrated into the society at large by their prolonged stay in India, which will help make them better citizens.

8.2.9 Refugees Already in India and Cooperation with UNHCR

All four bills are silent about the process of registering or regularizing the stay of refugees already in India. Suitable provisions should be included to ensure that refugees who are certified by UNHCR or the Government of India have the chance to regularize their status and stay as per the provisions of the new law. At the same time, there must be express provisions for cooperation with UNHCR, mainly in the areas of voluntary repatriation or removal, third country resettlement, relief and rehabilitation and so forth.

8.3 A Road Map for the Future

It has been a concern among legal scholars of India that, considering its past experience with UNHCR, it may not be suitable to become a party to the 1951 Refugee Convention and the Protocol.[27] At the same time, the need to ensure an absence of discrimination between refugees in India has gradually led towards the formulation of a refugee law, which can easily be understood by exploring the role of the National Human Rights Commission, the Supreme Court and the High Courts in extending and ensuring equal and fair treatment for refugees, and the drafting of the four different texts of refugee law over 18 years. This assessment is supported by a field study and by the prevailing and evolving nature of protection of refugees as per international standards. In the previous section, by making an assessment of the four bills and the international standards and national-level practices of legislation, several issues have been highlighted which should be taken into consideration by the Government of India while enacting a national refugee law. There are limitations in all four bills, and perhaps in the suggestions as well, as none of the texts identify the responsibilities of the country of origin of refugees.[28] In the realm of refugee protection it has always been necessary to adapt new approaches to mitigating crises, typically being voluntary repatriation, third country resettlement and local integration. The suggestions provided in the previous section embrace all these approaches while keeping in mind the "conception of legal scholarship

[27] B.S. Chimni, 'The Legal Condition of Refugees in India' [1994] 7 Journal of Refugee Studies 378, 400.

[28] See Chimni (n 10) 363.

which has the potential of articulating a comprehensive and humane response to the contemporary refugee problem through dialogue."[29] The basic structure of the national refugee law of India drawn up in the previous section will be able to confer on India the moral and legal strength to maintain a dialogue for better protection considering history, cultural developments and the Global North–Global South divide. The creation of two categories, "refugee protection" and "humanitarian protection," may contribute to the development of better protection standards in terms of genuine humanitarian protection, with less chance of geopolitical power plays by nations with a colonial history and humanitarian culture.[30] Whatever the strengths and weaknesses of this new approach may be, the Government of India must act in the interests of refugees and table a new draft before the Parliament in order to restart the dialogue on refugee protection.

[29] See Chimni (n 10) 369.

[30] See B.S. Chimni, 'The Birth of a 'Discipline': From Refugee to Forced Migration Studies' [2009] 22(1) Journal of Refugee Studies 11, 17.

Bibliography

Abdullahi A.M., 'The Refugee Crisis in Africa as a Crisis of the Institution of the State' [1994] 6(4) International Journal of Refugee Law 562, 566

Ackers D, 'The Negotiations on the Asylum Procedures Directive' [2005] 7 European Journal of Migration and Law 1-33

Amit R, 'No Refuge: Flawed Status Determination and the Failures of South Africa's Refugee System to Provide Protection' [2011] 23 International Journal of Refugee Law 458-488

Ananthachari T, 'Refugees in India: Legal Framework, Law Enforcement and Security' [2001] 1 ISIL Yearbook of International Humanitarian and Refugee Law 118-143

Anyangnyongo P. & Nyangaya J.A., 'Comprehensive Solutions to Refugee Problems in Africa: Bilateral, Regional and Multilateral Approaches' [1995] 7 International Journal of Refugee Law 164, 166

Arboleda E, 'The Cartagena Declaration of 1984 and its Similarities to the 1969 OAU Convention-A Comparative Perspective' [1995] 7 International Journal of Refugee Law 87, 91

Archibugi D, 'Immanuel Kant, Cosmopolitan Law and Peace' [1995] 1(4) European Journal of International Relations 429-456

Awuxu E O, 'Refugee Movements in Africa and the OAU Convention on Refugees' [1995] 39 Journal of African Law 79, 80

Barnouw V., 'The Sindhis, Mercantile Refugees in India: Problems of Their Assimilation' [1966] 27(1) Phylon40-49

Barzelay & Michael, 'The single case study as intellectually ambitious inquiry' [1993] 3(3) Journal of Public Administration Research and Theory 305–18

S.P. Sarker, *Refugee Law in India*,
DOI 10.1007/978-981-10-4807-4

Baskerville R & Wood-Harper A T, 'A critical perspective on action research as a method for information systems research' [1996] 11(3) Journal of Information Technology 235-246

Bates E, Bond J and Wiseman D, 'Troubling Signs: Mapping Access to Justice in Canada's Refugee System Reform' [2016] 47(1) Ottawa Law Review 17

Beek I.V., 'Prima Facie Asylum Determination in South Africa', in Jeff Handmaker, Lee Anne de la Hunt & Jonathan Klaaren (eds.), *Perspectives on Refugee Protection in South Africa* (Pretoria: Lawyers for Human Rights 2001) 17-59

Beitz C R, 'Rawls's Law of Peoples' [2002] 110(4) Ethics 669-696

Benhabib S, 'Another Universalism: On the Unity and Diversity of Human Rights' [2007] 81(2) Proceedings and Addresses of The American Philosophical Association 7-32

Benhabib S, 'Borders, Boundaries, and Citizenship' [2005] 38(4) Political Science& Politics 673, 674

Benhabib S, 'Carl Schmitt's Critique of Kant: Sovereignty and International Law' [2012] 40(6) Political Theory 688-713

Benhabib S, 'Citizens, Residents, and Aliens in a Changing World: Political Membership in the Global Era' [1999] 66(3) Social Research 709-744

Benhabib S, 'Claiming Rights across Borders: International Human Rights and Democratic Sovereignty', [2009] 103(4) American Political Science Review 691, 692

Benhabib S, 'The Law of Peoples, Distributive Justice, and Migrations' [1761-1787] 72(5) Fordham LRev 1761-1787

Bertrand P, 'An Operational Approach to International Refugee Protection' 26 Cornell International Law Journal 495-504

Bhattacharjee S, 'India Needs a Refugee Law' [2008] 43(9) EPW 71-75

Bodin J, *On Sovereignty Four Chapters from the Six Books of the Commonwealth* (Julian H. Franklin ed& trans, Cambridge University Press 1992) 1

Boeles P and Terlouw A, 'Minimum Guarantees for Asylum Procedures' [1997] 9 International Journal of Refugee Law 472-491

Bohman J, 'Living without Freedom: Cosmopolitanism at Home and the Rule of Law' [2009] 37(4) Political Theory 539-561

Bryman A, *Social Research Methods* (Oxford University Press 2001) 05

Bryman A, Stephen M &Campo C, 'The Importance of Context: Qualitative Research and the Study of Leadership' [1996] 7(3) Leadership Quarterly 353-370

Cantor D.J, & Barrichello S.E, 'The Inter-American Human Rights System: A New Model for Integrating Refugee and Complementary Protection?' [2013] 17(5-6) The International Journal of Human Rights 690

Cavallar G, 'Cosmopolitanism in Kant's Philosophy' [2012] 5(2) Ethics and Global Politics 95-118

Chandrahasan N, 'Access to Justice and Aliens: Some Insights into Refugee Groups in India' [1998] 16 Windsor Yearbook for Access to Justice 135-145

Chatterji J, 'Dispersal and the Failure of Rehabilitation: Refugee Camp-dwellers and Squatters in West Bengal' [2007] 41(5) Modern Asian Studies 995-1032

Chaudhary O, 'Turning Back: An Assessment of Non-Refoulement under Indian Law' [2004] 39(29) Economic &Political Weekly 3257-3264

Chimni B. S., 'Reforming the International Refugee Regime: The Dialogic Model' [2001] 14(2) Journal of Refugee Studies 151-168

Chimni B. S., 'Status of Refugees in India: Strategic Ambiguity', in Ranabir Samaddar (ed) *Refugee and the State: Practices of Asylum and Care in India, 1947-2000* (SAGE New Delhi 2003) 443-471

Chimni B. S., 'The Birth of a 'Discipline': From Refugee to Forced Migration Studies' [2009] 22(1) Journal of Refugee Studies 11-29

Chimni B. S., 'The Geopolitics of Refugee Studies: A View from the South' [1998] 11(4) Journal of Refugee Studies 350-374

Chimni B. S., 'The Legal Condition of Refugees in India' [1994] 7 Journal of Refugee Studies 378-401

Chimni B. S., 'The Meaning of Words and the Role of UNHCR in Voluntary Repatriation' [1993] 5 International Journal of Refugee Law 442-460

Chimni B.S. (ed.), *International Refugee Law: A Reader* (Sage Publications, New Delhi 2000)

Chimni B.S., 'Legal Condition of Refugees in India', in B.S. Chimni (eds), *International Refugee Law: A Reader* (New Delhi 2000)

Chossudovsky V, 'Economic Reforms and Social Unrest in Developing Countries'[1997]Economic & Political Weekly

Citizenship and Immigration Canada (CIC), *Guidance on Interpreting the Definition of a Convention Refugee*, Government of Canada, <http://www.cic.gc.ca/english/resources/tools/refugees/resettlement/eligibility/definitions.asp> accessed 3 August 2016

Citizenship and Immigration Canada (CIC), *Resettlement from Outside Canada*, Government of Canada, <http://www.cic.gc.ca/english/refugees/outside/> accessed 3 August 2016

Collacott M, *Canada's Immigration Policy: The Need for Major Reform* (The Fraser Institute, Vancouver 2002) 6-10

Costello C, 'The Asylum Procedures Directive and the Proliferation of Safe Country Practices: Deterrence, Deflection and the Dismantling of International Protection?' [2005] 7 European Journal of Migration and Law 35-69

Dallmayr F, 'Cosmopolitanism: Moral and Political' [2003] 31(3) Political Theory 421-442

Dasgupta A, 'Repatriation of Sri Lankan Refugees: Unfinished Tasks' [2003] 38(24) Economic &Political Weekly 2365-2367

Dauvergne C, 'Evaluating Canada's New Immigration and Refugee Protection Act in its Global Context' [2003] 41(3) Alberta Law Review 742

Denscombe M, *The Good Research Guide* (Mc-Graw Hill International USA 2007) 173

Donkoh B, 'A Half-Century of International Refugee Protection: Who's Responsible, What's Ahead?' [2000] Berkeley Journal of International Law 260-267

Doyle M.W, 'One World, Many Peoples: International Justice' in John Rawls, 'The Law of Peoples' [2006] 4(1) Perspectives on Politics 109-120

Eaton J, 'The Internal Protection Alternative Under European Union Law: Examining The Recast Qualification Directive' [2012] 24 International Journal of Refugee Law 765-792

Edwards A, 'Refugee Status Determination in Africa' [2006] 14 African Journal of International and Comparative Law 204, 205

Elahi K.M, 'Refugees in Dandakaranya' [1981] 15 (1/2) The International Migration Review 219-225

FairweatherR. G. L., 'Canada's New Refugee Determination System' [1989] 27 Canadian Yearbook of International Law 295-308

Fiddian-Qasmiyeh E, Loescher G, Long K, and Sigona N (eds), *The Oxford Handbook of Refugee and Forced Migration Studies* (Oxford University Press, Oxford 2014) 679

Fischel De Andrade J.H, 'Refugee protection in Brazil (1921–2014): An Analytical Narrative of Changing Policies', in David James Cantor et al (ed) *A Liberal Tide? Immigration and Asylum Law and Policy in Latin America* (London 2015) 153-183

Fischel De Andrade J.H, 'Regional Policy Approaches and Harmonization: A Latin American Perspective' [1998] 10(3) International Journal of Refugee Law 389-409

Fischel de Andrade J.H & Marcolini A, 'Brazil's Refugee Act: model refugee law for Latin America?' [2002] 12 Forced Migration Review37

Fortin A, 'The Meaning of Protection in the Refugee Definition' [2000] 12 International Journal of Refugee Law 548-576

Garvey J, 'Toward a Reformulation of International Refugee Law' [1985] 26 Harvard International Law Journal 483

Ghosh G, "GOD IS A REFUGEE': Nationality, Morality and History in the 1947 Partition of India' [1998] 42(1) The International Journal of Social and Cultural Practice 33-62

Gibney M.J., 'Liberal Democratic States and Responsibilities to Refugees' [1999] 93(1) The American Political Science Review 169-181

Goldenziel J.I., 'Regulating Human Rights: International Organizations, Flexible Standards, and International Refugee Law' [2013-2014] 14 Chicago Journal of International Law 453, 464

Goodwin-Gill G S, 'Non-Refoulement and the New Asylum- Seekers' [1986] 26 Virginia Journal of International Law 897

Goodwin-Gill G S, 'The Politics of Refugee Protection', in Helene Lambert (ed), *International Refugee Law* (Ashgate Publishing Limited 2010) 145-160

GotliebA. E., 'Canada and the Refugee Question in International Law' [1975] 13 Canadian Yearbook of International Law 7

Gould J.B, Colleen Sheppard, and Johannes Wheeldon, 'A Refugee from Justice? Disparate Treatment in the Federal Court of Canada' [2010] 32 Law and Policy 454 - 486

Grahl-Madsen, *The Status of Refugees in International Law* [1966] 193

Grant A & Rehaag S, 'Unappealing: An Assessment of the Limits on Appeal Rights in Canada's New Refugee Determination System' [2016] 49 University of British Columbia Law Review 212-214

Guebre-Christos G, 'State Building and Humanitarian Intervention: New Dimensions in Refugee Protection' [2001] 24 In Defense of the Alien 33-39

Hailbronner K, 'The Right to Asylum and Future of Asylum Procedures in the European Community' [1990] 2 International Journal of Refugee Law 341-360

Handmaker J, 'Advocating Accountability: The Reforming of a Refugee Rights Discourse in South Africa' [2007] 25 Netherlands Quarterly of Human Rights 53, 68

Handmaker J, 'No Easy Walk: Advancing Refugee Protection in South Africa' [2001] 48(3) Indiana University Press 91-92

Handmaker J., 'Who Determines Policy? Promoting The Right of Asylum in South Africa' [1999] 11(2) International Journal of Refugee Law 291

Hans A, 'Sri Lankan Tamil Refugees in India' [1993] 13(3) Refugee 30-33

Harris H, 'The Greek Origins of the Idea of Cosmopolitanism' [1927] 38(1) International Journal of Ethics 1, 7

Hart T. & Rogerson C. M., 'The Geography of International Refugee Movements in Southern Africa' [1982] 64(2) South Africa Geographical Journal 125, 135

Hathaway J.C & Cusick A.K, 'Refugee Rights are Non Negotiable' [2000] 14 Georgetown Immigration Law Journal 481, 593

Hathaway J.C, 'A Reconsideration of the Underlying Premise of Refugee Law' [1991] 31 Harvard International Law Journal129

Hathaway J.C, 'Selective Concern: An Overview of Refuge Law in Canada' [1987-88] 33McGill Law Journal 682

Hathaway J.C., 'Reconceiving Refuge Law as Human Rights Protection' [1991] 4(2) Journal of Refugee Studies, 113, 123

Hayden P, 'From the Law of Peoples to Perpetual Peace' [2000] 17(2) International Journal of World Peace 47-61

Hdvell tot Westerflier W.J.E.M.V, 'Africa and Refugees: The OAU Refugee Convention in Theory and Practice' [1989] 7 Netherlands Quarterly of Human Rights 172, 174

Helton A C, 'What is Refugee Protection?' [1990] 2 International Journal of Refugee Law 119

Hinsley F. H., *Sovereignty* (Cambridge University Press, 1986) 121

Hocke J. P., 'Beyond Humanitarianism: The Need for Political Will to Resolve Today's Refugee Problem', in G. Loescher & L. Monahan (eds) *Refugees and International Relations* (Oxford, 1989)

Hutchman S, 'An historical examination of Kant's Cosmopolitanism' [2000] 1 Glendon Journal of International Studies 50-56

Ibeanu O, 'Apartheid, Destabilization and Displacement: The Dynamics of the Refugee Crisis in Southern Africa' [1990] 3(1) Journal of Refugees Studies 47, 51

Jalais A, 'Dwelling on Morichjhanpi: When Tigers Became 'Citizens', Refugees 'Tiger-Food'' [2005] 40(17) Economic &Political Weekly 1757-1762

Johnsson A B, 'Two Decades of the 1969 OAU Convention Governing the Specific Aspects of the Refugee Problem in Africa' [1989] 1 International Journal of Refugee Law 557

Jonas O, 'Reflections on the Refugee Protection Regime in Africa: Challenges and Prospects' [2012] 14 University of Botswana Law Journal 71, 76

Jubilut L.L &Menicucci de Oliveira SelmiApolinario S, 'Refugee Status Determination in Brazil: A Tripartite Enterprise' [2008] 25(2) Refugee 30

Jubilut L.L ,'Refugee Law and Protection in Brazil: A Model in South America' [2006] 19(1) Journal of Refugee Studies 22

Kalra V., 'Citizen Nymgal' *Indian Express* (27 January 2011)

Katju M, 'India's Perception of Refugee Law' [2001] 1 ISIL Yearbook of International Humanitarian and Refugee Law 251-253

Kelley J, 'Refugee Protection: Whose Responsibility is it Anyway?' [1990] 2 International Journal of Refugee Law 277-282

Kelley N, 'International Refugee Protection Challenges and Opportunities' [2007] 19 International Journal of Refugee Law 401-439

Kennedy D, 'International Refugee Protection' [1986] 8 Human Rights Quarterly 1-69

Kerber K, 'The Temporary Protection Directive' [2002] 4 European Journal of Migration and Law 193-214

Klaaren J & Sprigman C, 'Refugee Status Determination Procedures in South African Law', in Jeff Handmaker, Lee Anne de la Hunt & Jonathan Klaaren, *Advancing Refugee Protection in South Africa* (Berghahn Books, New York 2007) 61-88

Kleingeld P, 'Kant's Cosmopolitan Law: World Citizenship for a Global Order' [1998] 2 Kantian Review 72-90

Klotz A, *Migration and National Identity in South Africa 1860-2010* (Cambridge University Press, New York 2013) 202-215

Lambert H, 'The EU Asylum Qualification Directive, Its Impact on the Jurisprudence of the United Kingdom and International Law' [2006] 55 International and Comparative Law Quarterly 161-192

Landgren K, 'The Future of Refugee Protection: Four Challenges' [1998] 11(4) Journal of Refugee Studies 416-432

Li P, *Destination Canada: Immigration Debates and Issues* (Oxford University Press, Toronto 2003) 48

Loescher G. & Scanlan J., *Calculated Kindness* (The Free Press, New York 1986) 59

Loescher G., *Beyond Charity: International Cooperation and Global Refugee Crisis* (Oxford University Press, New York 1993) 59-60

Luthra P. N., 'Problem of Refugees from East Bengal' [1971] 6(50) Economic and Political Weekly 2467-2472

Mallick R, 'Refugee Resettlement in Forest Reserves: West Bengal Policy Reversal and the Marichjhapi Massacre' [1999] 58(1) The Journal of Asian Studies 104-125

Maluwa T, 'The Refugee Problem and the Quest for Peace and Security in Southern Africa' [1995] 7 International Journal of Refugee Law 653, 670

Marie de Voe D, 'The Refugee Problem and Tibetan Refugees' [1981] 6(3) The Tibet Journal22-42

Marrus M. R., *The Unwanted: European Refugees in the Twentieth Century* (Oxford University Press, New York 1985) 317-324

Mazur R.E, 'The Political Economy of Refugee Creation in Southern Africa: Micro and Macro Issues in Sociological Perspective' 2(4) Journal of Refugees Studies 441, 461

Mazur R.E., 'Linking Popular Initiative and Aid Agencies: The Case of Refugees' [1987] 18(4) Development and Change 437-461

Mazur R.E., 'Refugees in Africa: The Role of Sociological Analysis and Praxis' [1988] 36(2) Current Sociology 43,49

McAdam J, 'The European Union Qualification Directive: The Creation of a Subsidiary Protection Regime' [2005] 17 International Journal of Refugee Law 461-516

McGrew A., 'Democracy Beyond Borders? Globalization and the Reconstruction of Democratic Theory and Politics', in A. McGrew (ed) *The Transformation of Democracy* (Cambridge, 1997 231-265)

McNamara D, *Foreword*, Commentary on the Refugee Convention 1951, Division of International Protection of the United Nations High Commissioner for Refugees, 1997

Michael F, 'Survival of a Culture: Tibetan Refugees in India' [1985] 25(7) Asian Survey 737-744

Mireku O, 'South African Refugee Protection System: An Analysis of Refugee Status, Rights and Duties' [2002] 35(3) Law and Politics in Africa, Asia and Latin America 399, 410

Nagel T., 'The Problem of Global Justice' [2005] 33(2) Philosophy &Political Affairs 113-147

Nariman F.S, 'Refugee Protection' [2002] 2 ISIL Yearbook of International Humanitarian and Refugee Law 07-17

Nogueira M. B & Marques C.C, 'Brazil: Ten Years of Refugee Protection' [2008] 30 Forced Migration Review 58

Norbu D, 'Refugees from Tibet: Structural Causes of Successful Settlements' 26(2) The Tibet Journal 3-25

Nyniah M.K, 'Reflections on the Institution of Asylum, Refugee Criteria, and Irregular Movements in Southern Africa' [1995] 7(2) International Journal of Refugee Law 291-316

Oberoi P, 'Regional Initiatives on Refugee Protection in South Asia' [1999] 11 International Journal of Refugee Law 197

Ogg K, 'A Sometimes Dangerous Convergence: Refugee Law, Human Rights Law, and the Meaning of 'Effective Protection' [2013] 12 Macquarie Law Journal 109-130

Olivier W.H, 'The New Asylum Law in South Africa' [2002] 4 Journal of South African Law 650, 658

Oloka-Onyango J, 'Human Rights, The OAU Convention and the Refugee Crisisin Africa: Forty Years After Geneva' [1991] 3 International Journal of Refugee Law 453

Pakrasi K.B, *The Uprooted: A Sociological Study of the Refugees of West Bengal, India* (S. Ghatack, Calcutta 1971)

Panezi M, 'The 2005 Asylum Procedures Directive: Developing the European Asylum Law' [2006-2007] 13 Columbia Journal of European Law 501-512

Parrish M.J, 'Redefining the Refugee: The Universal Declaration of Human Rights as a Basis for Refugee Protection' [2000-2001] 22 Cardozo Law Review 223-267

Peers S, 'Legislative Update 2011, EU Immigration and Asylum Law: The Recast Qualification Directive' (2012) 14 European Journal of Migration and Law 204

Philpott D, 'Sovereignty', (Edward N. Zalta ed, Summer 2014) *The Stanford Encyclopedia of Philosophy*, <http://plato.stanford.edu/archives/sum2014/entries/sovereignty/>

Piotrowizc R & Eck C.V, 'Subsidiary Protection and Primary Rights' [2004] 53 International and Comparative Law Quarterly 107-138

Pogge T.W, 'Cosmopolitanism and Sovereignty' [1992] 103(1) Ethics 48-75

Pogge T.W, 'Review: Rawls on International Justice' [2001] 51(203) The Philosophical Quarterly 246-253

Pojman L.P, 'Kant's Perpetual Peace and Cosmopolitanism' [2005] 36(1) Journal of Social Philosophy 62-71

Polkinghorne D E, 'Narrative Configuration in Qualitative Analysis' [1995] 8(1) Qualitative Studies in Education 5–22

Prasad C, 'Migration and the Question of Citizenship: People of Chittagong Hill Tract in Arunachal Pradesh' [2006] 67(3) The Indian Journal of Political Science 471-490

Prasad C, 'Students' Movements in Arunachal Pradesh and the Chakma-Hajong Refugee Problem' [2007] 42(15) Economic & Political Weekly 1373-1379

Presidency Conclusions, Tampere European Council, 15-16 October, 1999 <http://www.europarl.europa.eu/summits/tam_en.htm#a> accessed 2 December 2015

Rankin M.B., 'Extending the Limits or Narrowing the Scope? Deconstructing the OAU Refugee Definition Thirty Years On' (2005) 21 South African Journal on Human Rights 406, 410

Rawls J, 'The Law of Peoples' [1993] 20(1) Critical Inquiry 36-68

Rawls J, *A Theory of Justice* (Harvard University Press, Cambridge 1971)

Reason P, 'Choice and Quality in Action Research Practice' [2006] 15 Journal of Management Inquiry 187-203

Reneman M, (2009) 1 Amsterdam Law Forum 65-98

Richmond A., 'Sociological Theories of International Migration: The Case of Refugees' [1988] 36(2) Current Sociology 7, 21

Rogers N, 'Minimum Standards for Reception' [2002] 4 European Journal of Migration and Law 215-230

Rutinwa B, 'The End of Asylum? The Changing Nature of Refugee Policies in Africa', in Helene Lambert (ed.), *International Refugee Law* (Ashgate Publishing Limited 2010) 35-61

Sagar A & Ahmed F, 'The Model Law for Refugees: An Important Step Forward?' [2005] 17 Student Bar Rev. 73-91

Sagar A &Ahmed F, 'The Model Law for Refugees: An Important Step Forward?' [2005] 17 Student Bar Rev. 74-91

Samaddar R, 'Institutional Requirement on Protection and Care of the Victims of Forced Migration in South Asia' [2002] 2 ISIL Yearbook of International Humanitarian and Refugee Law 74-87

Samaddar R, 'Introduction' in *Refugees and the State*, Ranabir Samaddar (ed) (Sage Publications, New Delhi 2003)

Sanderson M, 'The Role of International Law in Defining the Protection of Refugees in India' [2015] 33 Wisconsin International Law Journal 46-113

Sarker S.P., 'How Humanitarian is this?' *The Statesman* (08 October 2015)

Saxena J. N., 'Legal Status of Refugees: Indian Position' [1986] 26 Indian Journal of International Law 501-515

Saxena P, 'Creating Legal Space for Refugees in India: the Milestones Crossed and the Roadmap for the Future' [2007] 19 International Journal of Refugee Law 246, 247

Sen S, 'Paradoxes of the International Regime of Care: The Role of the UNHCR in India' in Ranabir Samaddar (ed) *Refugee and the State: Practices of Asylum and Care in India, 1947-2000* (SAGE New Delhi 2003) 396-442

Shaw B J, 'Doctrine of Right, Rawls, Kant's and Global Distributive Justice' [2005] 67(1) The Journal of Politics 220-249

Skinner Q, *Liberty Before Liberalism* (Cambridge University Press 2012)

Solomon K, *Refugees in the Cold War: Toward a New International Refugee Regime in the Early Post-War Era* (Lund University Press, Lund 1991) 53

Steinbock D.J, 'Interpreting the Refugee Definition' [1998] 19 Immigration and Nationality Law Review 137-220

Steinbock D.J,'The Refugee Definition as Law: Issues of Interpretation', in Nicholson and Twomey (eds.), *Refugee Rights and Realities: Evolving International Concepts and Regimes* (Cambridge University Press, Cambridge 1999) 20

Stoffman D, *Who Gets In? What s Wrong with Canada's immigration System and How to Fix It* (Macfarlane Walter and Ross, Toronto 2002) 3

Suryanarayan V., 'Need for National Refugee Law' [2001] ISIL Yearbook of International Humanitarian and Refugee Law254-262

Sztucki J, 'The Conclusions on the International Protection of Refugees Adopted by the Executive Committee of the UNHCR Programme' [1989] 1 International Journal of Refugee Law298

Tarwater J.R, 'Analysis and Case Studies of the 'Ceased Circumstances' Cessation Clause of the 1951 Refugee Convention' [2001] 15 Georgetown Immigration Law Journal 563-624

Thouez C. V., 'New Directions in Refugee Protection' [1998] 22 Fletcher Forum of World Affairs 89-105

Tinker C & Sartoretto L M, 'New Trends in Migratory and Refugee Law in Brazil: The Expanded Refugee Definition' [2015] 3(3) & 3(4) Panorama of Brazilian Law 145

Travers V, *Qualitative Research Through Case Studies* (SAGE, London 2001)

Tshosa O. B., 'National Refugee Laws in the Light of International Standards: Some Reflections on the Refugee (Recognition and Control) Act, 1967 of Botswana' [2007] 5 University of Botswana Law Journal 49-76

UNHCR Sub-regional Operations Profile - South Asia (2015) <http://www.unhcr.org/pages/49e4876d6.html> accessed 19 November 2015

United Nations General Assembly, Resolution No: A/RES/36/148, 16 December 1981 <http://www.un.org/documents/ga/res/36/a36r148.htm> accessed 12 December 2016

Varghese R, 'Country Paper- India', *Presented at the Seventh Informal Regional Consultation on Refugees and Migratory Movements in South Asia* (15-16 December 2002 New Delhi)

Vijayakumar V., 'Judicial Response to Refugee Protection in India' [2000] 12 International Journal of Refugee Law 235-243

Walzer M, *Spheres of Justice: A Defense of Pluralism and Equality* (Basic Books, New York 2005)

Weiner M, 'Rejected Peoples and Unwanted Migrants in South Asia' [1993] 28(34) Economic & Political Weekly

Westhues A et al, 'The Creation of Knowledge: Linking Research Paradigms to Practice' [1999] 16(2) Canadian Social Work Rev. Vol. 129-154

Wilkins B. T., 'Principles for the Law of Peoples' [2007] 11(2) The Journal of Ethics 161-175

Index

S.P. Sarker, *Refugee Law in India*,
DOI 10.1007/978-981-10-4807-4

Kolibri 360 GmbH
Ferdinand-Jühlke-Straße 7
99095 Erfurt, Deutschland
produktsicherheit@kolibri360.de